JEWISH
RELIGIOUS POLEMIC

of
early and later centuries,
a study of
documents here rendered in English

by
OLIVER SHAW RANKIN
D.D., D.Litt.

KTAV PUBLISHING HOUSE, INC.
1970

REPRINTED BY SPECIAL ARRANGEMENT WITH
THE EDINBURGH UNIVERSITY PRESS
FIRST PUBLISHED 1956

SBN 87068-007-2

Library of Congress Catalog Card Number: 68-25578

Manufactured in the United States of America

CONTENTS

FOREWORD

WHEN Professor Rankin died it was found that the book on Jewish Religious Polemic which he was known to have been writing was in completed form and virtually ready for publication. The Edinburgh University Press very willingly undertook to publish it in the shortest possible time. Thanks to the meticulous care which had evidently been given to the preparation of the type-script the editorial work has proved to be light. The volume which is now presented to the public maintains to the full the high standard of scholarship which was characteristic of everything which Professor Rankin wrote and indeed is certain to enhance his reputation as an authority on Judaism. In his chosen field of research he has at the moment so far as I am aware, no successor among Christian scholars in this country and readers of this book will be sadly aware how much more the learned author might have given us had he been granted the years of retirement to which he was looking forward. As it is, he has afforded us a fascinating glimpse into the obscure region of knowledge in which he himself moved as a master. He has, moreover, given an example of fair-mindedness and charity which will make this book acceptable to Christian and Jewish readers alike and will do something to promote that mutual understanding between two great faiths which was a concern very near his heart.

NORMAN W. PORTEOUS

PREFACE

IT is the purpose of this book to let the translation of certain Hebrew documents which contain, in greater and lesser degree, a defence of the Jewish faith, reveal how this defence took shape at various times from the early centuries of our era up to the seventeenth century. An example of apologetic or polemic writing is presented in each of the literary categories of narrative, poetry, letters and record of debate. The aim of the author and translator has been threefold: to acquaint those who are interested in the literature of Judaism with the content of important texts which have not hitherto for the most part been available in English; to examine the thought of these texts impartially and with sympathy from the point of view of the history of religion; and, since up to the present the *adversus Judaeos* aspect of Judaeo-Christian discussion has been predominant, to restore the balance of equity by bringing to light writings which, each in its own way, represent a contribution of value on the part of Judaism in its reactions to pagan and Christian attacks.

It has been said with truth that it is difficult to recapture the atmosphere of a time with which we have lost touch or to have sympathy with disputants whose arguments are based on premises which we no longer accept (cf. Danby *The Jew and Christianity*, Sheldon Press, 1927, p. v). In the sphere of religious discussion, arguments and averments often lose much of their force and influence in course of time. And questions that have been asked and answers that have been given, in reference to doctrine, undergo change at least in form, even where a fixed statement of that doctrine has come into existence, as age succeeds age. Besides this, a religious polemic based upon an interpretation of the Bible of the kind which prevailed before the rise of the critical historical school of interpretation in the middle of the nineteenth century is at once distinguished as belonging to a stage of thought which has now been overcome. But the student of the culture of any particular epoch will

vii

desire to investigate what was the thought of the age which he
is engaged in studying, and what were the limitations and conditions that accompanied it. The history of religious polemic
in all its aspects, apologetic, discussive, disputative or even
merely quarrelsome and vituperative, reveals at least what in
the development of thought lay deepest and warmest in the
hearts of men, and, while what it reveals is not uncommonly a
story of futility, tragedy, persecution, baseness, pride and conceit, there may also emerge much that evokes admiration,
entertainment and possibly—as in the case of the Rittangel
correspondence—amusement. Nor can it be said that all the
discussing and arguing between the adherents of the different
faiths has led to nothing but hatred and strife. The mills that
are driven by the zest and the spirit and, at times, by the fury
of polemic move very slowly, but they do produce at length a
sense of what teachings are lasting and valuable, what issues
are central and cannot be removed, what fundamental differences between one creed and another still await solution and
what answers can no longer be put forward as satisfactory explanations but stand in need of improvement. The conflict of
ideas is one that is prescribed by life itself, since life and thought
are bound together, and constitutes that warfare in which, as
the author of Ecclesiastes says, 'there is no discharge'—either
for Gentile or Jew.

It affords me much pleasure to express my thanks to my
friend and former student, the Rev. J. M. Wilkie, B.D., Lecturer
in Old Testament in the University of Cambridge, for reading
through the manuscript of this work and undertaking most
willingly the tasks of correction and revision. Also I acknowledge with gratefulness the kindness of the Rev. J. B. Primrose,
M.A., Librarian of New College, Edinburgh, in securing for me
and suggesting to me literature relevant to the subject here
submitted, and his interest in its theme.

O. S. RANKIN

1953

PART I

POLEMIC IN NARRATIVE

CHAPTER I

THE HAGGADIC MIDRASHIM
THE CHRONICLE OF MOSES

THE word Midrash (plural Midrashim) is derived from the Hebrew *darash* meaning to search, investigate or study. Midrashim therefore are compositions which serve in greater or lesser degrees as expositions of, or commentaries upon, the text of scripture, according to current conceptions of the nature of exegesis. Midrashim are of various kinds. They may be liturgical as is the Passover Haggadah; or chiefly exegetical and homiletic, such as the Midrash Rabbah on the Pentateuch and the 'Five Rolls'; or kabbalistic, as are the Zohar and the Bahir; or kabbalistic-philosophic, as is the Book of Formation (Sepher Jeçirah); or juristic—see below on Halakah; or historical. To the last category belong the canonical books of the Chronicles, the Megillath Ta'anith, the Seder Olam and the Dibre ha-yamin shel Moshe, that is, the Chronicle of Moses.

The historical midrashim aim at edification and have been described as being free creations of the speculative imagination which combine with reasoned deductions from what is told in scripture (cf. Schürer, Vol. 2, p. 407 f).[1] They do not confine themselves to drawing from the text what the language and logic of the passages to be explained allow, but they read into the text and enlarge upon the written word, overlaying it with additional matter. The oldest historical midrash is the biblical 'Books of the Chronicles' which expands the account of Hebrew history known to us from the Books of Samuel and Kings by narratives about David and other Jewish kings and of the services these rendered in the development of the priestly cultus. The author of Chronicles, from the point of view of the age in which he lived (*c.* 400-300 B.C.), and of the importance which the cult held in his own eyes, brings the older sources of history up to date by re-interpreting them and adding to them. That

[1] Schürer, *Geschichte des Jüdischen Volkes*, etc., 4th ed., 1909.

he brought his new material from other historical sources than were available to the composers of Samuel and Kings seems improbable (see Schürer Vol. 2, p. 402). For the succeeding midrashim adopt the same method with increasing boldness, though with other ends in view. In the Chronicle of Moses we observe, under the form of a commentary, the same working over of a biblical narrative, namely, the story of Moses as told in the Book of Exodus, and the expansion of what is there related through a narrative of incidents real or imaginary in the history of Israel and of other peoples.

After what has been said of the historical midrashim, it is not surprising that M. Friedmann concludes of such writings that they have not even an historical core, but convey only thoughts that are of an ethical quality.[1] But that the nature of these writings is of so unsubstantial and nebulous a kind cannot be maintained. Their compilers doubtless had an aim in composing them. It is best to regard them as mirrors of Jewish life which reflect the response of Judaism to the needs, religious or otherwise, of Jewry in some particular period or to the criticism of the world to which Jewry was exposed. In such a light the Chronicle of Moses would seem most readily to reveal what the purpose of its writer in composing it was. Its background, under the cover of a description of the oppression of Israel in the time of Moses, would appear to be the hostility of the world to a Jewry of a later day. There is no trace in the book of an anti-Christian polemic. The polemic or apologetic that may be detected in the book is not addressed to non-Jews, nor is it pursued by the method of argumentative debate, but, nevertheless, it is made explicit enough in the narrative that adorns the biblical history and was well calculated to be appreciated by the Jewish hearer or reader. That the Chronicle of Moses reflects conditions of a certain period of history it is the task of this study to show. But we must first of all seek to gain an impression of the part which the midrashic literature played in Judaism and of the value which has there been assigned to that portion of it to which our Chronicle belongs.

Though, as we have seen, midrashim are of various kinds, they can be divided into two distinct classes, namely, the *halakic*

---

[1] Cf. H. L. Strack, *Jesus, die Häretiker und die Christen nach den ältesten Jüdischen Angaben* (Schriften des Institutum Judaicum in Berlin), 1910, p. 40, note 2.

and the *haggadic*. Both are founded upon scripture. The first are juristic, concerned with *halakah* (lit. custom or rule), that is, with the accepted legal decisions which regulate religious practice, with the extent to which these decisions apply and with the consequences of their application. This halakic or consuetudinary law, which is codified in the Mishnah and constitutes the larger part of the midrashim that are called Mechilta, Siphra and Siphre,[1] was determined by the majority of the Rabbis,[2] and was at first only oral, existing alongside the written law. The deduction of the halakah from scripture was moreover a fairly rigorous discipline, being governed by rule and method and tradition, and was subject to the test of practice and living. On the other hand, those midrashim which are called haggadic (from *higgid*, to tell or narrate) occupied themselves with the elaboration of the historical and religious-ethical portions of scripture, did not suffer from the restraint of tradition and gave free scope to speculation. Both the historical midrashim of which we have spoken, the biblical Chronicles and the Chronicle of Moses, are of this haggadic quality.

Each of the above-named classes of midrash appears to have existed orally or in writing before becoming current literature and to have been delivered in the form of lectures and addresses in the synagogue or the school (beth ha-midrash) on festivals or other high days. That the learned appreciated the halakic address while the ordinary man was attracted by the haggadic is apparent from the following story: 'Rabbi Abbahu and Rabbi Hiyya ben Abba came to the same town at the same time. Rabbi Hiyya delivered a scholarly discourse on the Law, while Rabbi Abbahu delivered a midrashic sermon. Thereupon all the people left Rabbi Hiyya and came to Rabbi Abbahu. Rabbi Hiyya was greatly discouraged, but his colleague said to him: "I will tell thee a parable. Two men once entered the same town, the one offering for sale precious stones and pearls, the other tinsel. To whom do you think the people thronged? Was it not to him who sold the tinsel, seeing that that was what they could afford to buy?" ' (Sotah 40[a]). In contrast with the halakic midrashim, haggadic writings had little or no authority

---

[1] Midrash Mechilta comments on a part of Exodus; Siphra on Leviticus; Siphre (or Siphri) on Numbers and Deuteronomy.
[2] Schürer, op. cit., Vol. 2, p. 292 f.

at all in matters of religious dispute. The course of controversy
between Jews and Christians shows that this fact was occasionally overlooked. In the debate between Moses ben Nachman
and the monk Paulus Christiani, a convert from Judaism, in the
thirteenth century (see Part IV below) Paulus supported his
arguments with citations from the haggadic literature, with
which he was well acquainted. Nachman's reply to him was
that these midrashim 'are not authoritative, even if they do
represent the deliberate opinion of individual teachers'.[1] Since
the main characteristic of Jewish religion is that it is not credal
or dogmatic[2] but preceptory and halakic, it is obvious that
haggadah is disqualified from being applied to questions that
only halakah can decide, and that in matters of faith and belief,
that have nothing to do with halakah, haggadah (das Product
der freien Einsicht des Einzelnen, Zunz, p. 61)[3] has the authority only of the individual writer's opinion.

But while the esteem in which halakah was held, as emanating from the authority of governing councils, the schools and
the teachers of the law, was immeasurably greater than that
extended to the haggadah it must not be considered that haggadic midrashim are worthless tinsel. The haggadic midrash must
be judged in the same way as any other apocryphal book is
judged, namely, on its own merits, and some of these books have
a very high merit indeed. Within and behind the conventional
legend-mongering there may be elements of religious-historical
value. The mind of the individual, though it has not the
authority of the conclave and the council, has often more inspiration than a council has and may, in a period when there
are few witnesses to the history of thought, be able to give a
testimony that is of importance as a record of the spirit of the
times in which he wrote. The more sustained the sufferings of
the Jews were, says Zunz, the more attracted were noble natures
by the midrashic treatment of the traditional text (p. 63).
Through the narratives which the haggadists composed, to
which the names of the men of antiquity were made to contribute, truths were preached, problems were solved, hope and
comfort were conveyed (p. 125). If this be so, these narrative

---

[1] See Part IV ad loc. and L. Williams, *Adversus Judaeos*, p. 247.
[2] On this subject ('Das Judenthum habe überhaupt keine Dogmen', Moses
Mendelssohn) see Schürer, op. cit., Vol. 2, p. 410, for discussion and bibliography.
[3] Zunz, *Die gottesdienstlichen Vorträge der Juden*, 1892.

midrashim might be expected to have apologetic value, since truths are not contended for, nor are problems solved, nor are hope and comfort provided *in vacuo*: but faith is normally strengthened in resistance to, or with reference to existing conditions and circumstances. Those who preferred the haggadic addresses to the halakic lectures may well have had their interest in the former awakened by some novel turn of exegesis given to a biblical text, or by the stories that, especially in the historical midrashim, were added as embellishments to the biblical narrative; but it is probable that they were attracted, and this for the most part, by those elements in the address which were of a sermonic, topical, didactic, apologetic or even political type.

Does our Chronicle give any indication of the period of history in which is was composed? At first sight all that presents itself is that this midrash, while adding new material to the story of Moses as told by the Book of Exodus, keeps in contact with that story so far as it describes the persecution of the Israelites in Egypt up to the time of the ten plagues and the passage of the Red Sea. Without doubt we are entitled to discern as the purpose of the author the aim of encouraging the Jewish people in hard times by reminding them of those who in the days of old endured hardships with fortitude and with God's help. But persecutions have occurred frequently in the history of Judaism and the close contact of this midrash with the biblical narrative tends to frustrate any attempt to determine the time and circumstances in which it was written. According to Zunz (p. 148) certain haggadic midrashim of a national character belong 'in their present form' to the period A.D. 840-1040. Among this group of writings and within this period he places the Chronicle ('The Life') of Moses and the great midrash which is called the Book of Jashar. At the same time Zunz (p. 356) asserts that the greatest activity in the collecting of haggadic materials fell within the three centuries 680-980, 'when practically all our stock of earlier and later haggadah was gathered together and increased'. This statement would seem to imply that the Chronicle of Moses, prior to receiving its present shape, might in some form have been as early as the seventh century. This however would still represent a comparatively late date. The reason for assuming a late date for the Chronicle of Moses has rested practically entirely upon the fact that it is written in a pure Hebrew that is very close to the language and style of the Bible (Zunz, p. 153, 'an imitation of the biblical style'). This same judgment has been passed, on the same grounds, namely, the purity of their Hebrew, upon the Book of Josippon and the Book of Jashar, the former midrash recording events from the time of Ezra to the destruction of the second temple and the latter giving a narrative which starts at the creation and extends to the time of the Judges.

Against the literary canon which ascribes a late date to works that are written in a pure Hebrew of biblical style, objection has been raised in more recent times. Dr M. Gaster, the translator of the Hebrew midrash 'The Chronicles of Jerahmeel', says in his introduction (1899, p. xvii) to that work: 'For what reason a book written in a pure style should be considered as modern and not archaic has not been made clear by anyone and it does not seem to have struck any critics to demand a reason.' He further points out that, while a Hebrew of pure simple biblical form is not by itself a proof of antiquity, it is incomprehensible why 'for no visible reason' a writer of a later period should so successfully have avoided using the literary language of his own time and resorted to an earlier style. Therefore Gaster concludes that 'internal evidence alone must finally decide the true character and date of each composition'. The only criticism which might weaken Gaster's case against those who assign a late date to writings employing a biblical style is that, were a certain late period indubitably established as being one in which a revival of Hebrew had been cultivated and in which a biblical *prose* had been imitated, and had, further, a work similar in type to Jashar and the Chronicle of Moses been proven to belong to this period, then there would be some evidence in favour of these writings being of this period also. But short of such proof there remains only the task of investigating what the internal evidence may indicate concerning these documents.

The 'Chronicles of Jerahmeel' which has much relevance to our study of questions relating to the Chronicle of Moses since it itself contains a version of this Chronicle, is a collection of apocryphal and pseudo-epigraphical books. Drawing upon the midrash Josippon and having similarity, in content and sources,

to the midrash Jashar, it deals, as do these midrashim, with a
long period of history and gives a narrative of world-events
from the time of Creation down to the days of Judas Maccabaeus. Dr Gaster's criticism of this large *corpus* of legend is that
it is a collection of tales of extreme antiquity which, with few
exceptions, were written in the 'first centuries before or after
the Common Era', and thereafter were preserved by a copyist
in the sixth or seventh century. Later in the tenth or eleventh
century they were again copied by a compiler who made some
enlargements and who in turn was followed by an equally
conscientious continuator in the thirteenth century (see p. cxv,
op. cit.). In Gaster's opinion all the texts in the Chronicles of
Jerahmeel are 'many centuries older than the date at which the
compiler [viz. Eleasar in the fourteenth century] connected
them into one volume' (p. xx) and, in particular, the more important portion of the Chronicle of Moses 'goes back to the time
of Josephus and is even older' (p. xxviii). It is here that another
stage in the history of the criticism of the Chronicle of Moses
should perhaps be indicated. Against the bestowal of an early
date upon the Chronicle of Moses it can now no longer be
urged that the sentence which appears near the end of that
Chronicle in the Jerahmeel version, and at the end in the version in the Paris edition (translated below), to the effect that
the rest of the words of Moses are written in the Book of Jashar,
implies that the Chronicle is later in date than Jashar and that
consequently the version of the Chronicle of Moses which is
found in Jashar (ch. 67-81) is a later interpolation. For, as
Gaster shows (p. lxxxviii), the title 'Book of Jashar' (lit. book of
the upright one) as this appears in the Chronicle does not signify
the *midrash* Jashar but the pentateuch or simply the scriptures
in general. The latter sense is given to *Jashar* in a very old
Massoretic treatise *Diqduqei Hateamim* (Leipzig 1879, published
by Baer and Strack) and in the Jerahmeel version of the Chronicle the words 'Book of Jashar' are actually explained by the
addition of the sentence: 'which is the law of God.' The use of
the term 'Book of Jashar' in this sense, Gaster remarks, proves
'the extreme antiquity' of the text of the Chronicle of Moses.

Coming now to the examination of the contents of our
Chronicle we find that there are a number of stories of a pseudo-
historical nature, typical midrashic elements which go back to

B

the first century of our era, appearing in the writings of Josephus who was born *c.* A.D. 38 and lived into the second century. These elements are comparatively numerous. But besides these, and interwoven with them, there are apologetic elements which could be considered to be much later than the legend narratives were it not that they reflect the conditions and thought of the same period, namely, that of the early Roman Empire and in a measure even of the Greek period which preceded. Quite apart from the question of the date of our Chronicle in its present forms or in a possible earlier form, the fact still remains that these elements to which we have pointed have to be assessed and to be related to their particular *Sitz im Leben*, that is, to the particular historical conditions which give them the most relevance and significance. That there is nothing in the Chronicle of Moses which gives any glimpse of the existence of the Christian faith and culture is perhaps only an argument from silence in favour of an early date of this writing, but it at least supplements the other evidence which supports that view.

The elements of legendary character

The narratives which, allowing for slight variations, are common to Josephus and the Chronicle are, as told by Josephus (Ant. 2, ch. 9, §§ 2, 7; ch. 10, § 1-2; ch. 16, § 5) the following. A scribe foretells that a child about to be born would bring low the dominion of Egypt. This is the reason why Pharaoh decreed that the male children of the Hebrews were to be slain at birth. Pharaoh's daughter loved the child [Moses] who had been found in an ark on the river where his parents had placed him. She admired the boy on account of his size and beauty. The child refused to take suck from the breasts of any of the Egyptian women who were brought to nurse him. Hence a Hebrew woman—the child's mother—was hired as nurse. As the boy grows older, Pharaoh one day as a mark of favour puts his diadem on the child's head, but Moses throws the diadem down and tramples on it. The sacred scribe sees in this action an evil omen betokening misfortune and proclaims it as a fulfilment of his former prediction. Moses when grown to manhood makes his character and ability known and gains fame by making an expedition against the Ethiopians who had invaded and plundered Egypt. He becomes general of the Egyptian forces. Josephus here tells the story about the serpents and the ibises which we read of in the Chronicle of Moses and of Moses' 'wonderful stratagem to preserve the army safe and without hurt'. The city of the Ethiopians which is besieged by Moses is described as strongly defended by nature 'after the manner of an island' with strong walls and ramparts and almost impregnable. The account of Josephus is here very close to that of the Chronicle. Moses marries the daughter of the Ethiopian king on the condition that she helps him to possess himself of the city. In relating the story of Moses Josephus gives us some information about the source from which he drew it, for he states: 'As for myself I have delivered every part of this history as I found it in the sacred books' (Ant. 2.16 § 5). The sacred books are not in the main the scriptural narratives, for Josephus' narrative differs widely from these, but must be midrashic works (cf. 8.6 § 2, 'our books') which were current in Josephus' day.

Other midrashic references, occurring in the literature of the early centuries, have also their parallels in the Chronicle of Moses. In the New Testament the second epistle to Timothy (3.8)—the date of which is given by Appel in his *Einleitung in das Neue Testament* as 'at latest' A.D. 100—seems to share with the Chronicle the account of how 'Jannes and Jambres withstood Moses'. Pharaoh's dream about the weighing scales, which is told by the Chronicle and by the Palestinian Targum on Exodus (ch. 1, see Etheridge, *The Targums*, etc., Vol. 1, p. 444), probably had been current a long time before finding lodgment in a document of so official a nature as was a Targum. The Talmud tractate Sotah 13ᵃ mentions the great light that filled the house when Moses was born—an incident which is reported in the Chronicle—but the saga about Joseph's coffin is more fully developed in this tractate than it is in the Chronicle. This may be due to the earlier date of the latter work.

The elements of an apologetic or polemic nature which appear in the Chronicle and in early Jewish sources

(a) The providence of God presides over God's people, protecting them and disciplining them in all events of history. This is the general theme of the Chronicle. This also may be said of the scriptural narrative in Exodus in the account there given of events preceding and leading up to the deliverance of the Hebrews from Egypt. Indeed it is upon Exodus that the Chronicle is a midrash or commentary. But in the Chronicle the idea of a presiding and guiding providence of God is much more explicit. The interpositions of the deity in aid of the Hebrews and Moses are much more marked. The story of how the mothers in Israel, when the slaughter of the male children had been decreed, left their offspring in the open fields at the time when their babes were born, and of the wonderful way God cared for the infants, is in some respects the masterpiece of the Chronicler's stock of stories. Angels, Gabriel, Michael and others, are always at hand, in times of stress and difficulty, to guide events, to deceive the adversaries of the Hebrews, to avert calamity and to direct circumstances into results favourable to Moses in his childhood and manhood. The author of the Chronicle does not have any perception that miracles of a *deus ex machina* kind rather detract from than promote a true conception of providence. What he wrote evidently corresponded to the simple tastes of those whom he addressed.

The topic of a divine providence is met with as an apologetic element at an early date in the first centuries, namely, in Philo (*c.* 25 B.C.-after A.D. 40). Philo's treatise 'Against Flaccus', bearing the sub-title 'Concerning Providence', supports the belief in providence by the same method as does our midrash, by an interpretation of biographical and historical events, not by reasoning in abstract theological terms. Philo demonstrates his doctrine of Providence by a description of the career of Flaccus, the prefect of Alexandria, the persecutor of the Jews in that city, by showing how he fell from grace, lost the favour of Caligula and fell a victim to that Emperor's wrath; how he was first banished and then eventually put to death. The treatise concludes thus: 'Such was the end of Flaccus who suffered thus, being the most manifest evidence that the nation of the Jews is not left destitute of the providential assistance of God.'[1]

(*b*) The doctrine of retribution. Divine retribution overtakes those who persecute the people of God. Jethro, the Midianite, the Chronicle relates, advises Pharaoh not to listen to

[1] Cf. *The Works of Philo Judaeus*, Vol. IV, p. 99, in translation of C. D. Yonge. See also Hans Leisegang (in *Journal of Bib. Lit.*, 1938, Vol. LVII, p. 377), 'Philons Schrift über die Gesandtschaft der Alexandrinischen Juden an den Kaiser Gaius Caligula.'

those who counsel him to persecute the Jews 'since who has ever put forth his hand against them and has been unpunished?' According to the Chronicler each of the ten plagues which God brought upon Egypt corresponds to some particular injury or insult which the Israelites received. For example, in the plague of lice, the lice were made to cover the whole ground, because the Israelites in their servitude had been forced by the Egyptians to sweep their rulers' houses, their courts and their streets. Throughout the description of the plagues this nice balance and correspondence between the injury inflicted and the retribution meted out is carefully preserved. In its fuller form this aspect of the doctrine of retribution is first observed in the Wisdom of Solomon (ch. 11-19; c. 30 B.C.-A.D.10). In this book it is taught that the punishments which God exacts are extraordinarily appropriate and apposite—'by measure and number and weight thou, O God, didst order all things' (11.20). The river Nile was turned into clotted blood in vengeance for the slaughter of the Israelite babes (11.5 f) because 'by what things a man sins by these is he punished' (11.16). A little later than the writer of the second portion of the Wisdom of Solomon, Philo in his writings exhibits a similar subtlety in his treatment of the subject of retribution. In the case of the ten plagues God, he teaches (Vita Mosis 1.17), brought earth, water, air and fire—the four elements out of which the universe is made—into a state of hostility against the Egyptians who had violated all natural feeling in their treatment of the Jews. But Philo's teaching about the correspondence of a man's sin with his sin's punishment appears most clearly and crudely in the above-named treatise *Contra Flaccum*. Flaccus, in his banishment on his lonely island, is depicted as bewailing his fate and, in soliloquy under the starry heavens, reflecting upon his inhuman conduct toward the Jews—'I consented when they were stripped of their possessions, giving immunity to those who were plundering them; and on that account I have myself been deprived of all my paternal and maternal inheritance' (op. cit., § xx). When Flaccus had been arrested in Alexandria he was banqueting with friends. Philo remarks on this: 'It was fitting that Justice should begin to visit him at a feast, because he had deprived the houses of innumerable innocent men of all festivity.' When finally in his place of exile, resisting the soldiers sent to take his life, he dies of many wounds, his crime and its penalty are now equally balanced—'Justice righteously inflicting on his own body wounds equal in number to the murders of the Jews whom he had unlawfully put to death' (§ xxi).

(*c*) Moses as military leader. Moses is described in the Chronicle as a man of great wisdom, in particular of great military ability, superior in strategy to Balaam the sorcerer who, in the Ethiopian campaign, aided the forces resisting Moses. This picture of Moses, in this Hebrew midrash, is drawn, we must suppose, with the aim of supplying Jews living in the midst of antagonism and criticism with an answer to their detractors, since such an answer had its value in early Hebrew polemic. Foreign critics of Jewry had availed themselves of the argument that history shewed that the Hebrew race suffered from a singular dearth of men of eminence. We may observe this from Josephus' discussion of this point in his second book 'Against Apion', where he replies to Apion's charge that 'we Jews have not had any wonderful men amongst us, nor any inventor of arts, nor any eminent in wisdom' (§ 13 ad loc.). Josephus says that any person who had read his 'Antiquities' must know that the Jews had men as deserving of commendation as any other nation could boast of having. He then shows that 'Moses was Israel's best governor and counsellor' (§ 16), that his greatest achievement was the deliverance of his people from Egypt and that in the difficulties of the march from that country 'he became an excellent general of an army' as well as legislator. As far back as *c.* 300 B.C. Hecataeus of Abdera had depicted Moses as a military chief. 'The Lawgiver', says Hecataeus, 'also took great interest in military affairs and obliged the younger men to practise exercises of strength and courage and the endurance of hardship in general. He also undertook campaigns into the territories of neighbouring nations.'[1] Thus the characterisation of Moses as military leader was already old in the days of Josephus, although in those days it still served a polemic purpose. Josephus even seeks new realms to conquer when he attempts to answer the reproach that the Jews had 'produced no inventors in crafts or literature' (cf. *Cont. Ap.* II, ch. 20 or § 182 in the Loeb Series). It is not surprising that but

[1] This passage cited in Ewald's *History of Israel*, Vol. 2, p. 91, appeared according to Photius in the lost fortieth book of Diodorus Siculus.

a little later, namely, in the middle of the second century, the full claim was made by Aristobulus 'that the Greek philosophers, Pythagoras, Socrates and Plato had drawn their wisdom from the writings of Moses' (*Cambridge Ancient History*, Vol. IX, p. 434). Josephus himself had made some approach to this position (*Cont. Ap.* I, § 22). But for the simpler people for whom our midrash was composed, the representation of Moses is that of the hero as warrior, an ideal which will always occupy in the popular imagination the summit of eminence.

(*d*) The enemies of the Jews allege that the Jews overreach and deceive their neighbours, injuring the peoples with whom they come into contact. This charge, supported by scriptural stories about Jacob and Esau, Jacob and Laban, Jacob's sons and the Shechemites, Isaac and the Gerarites, our Chronicle puts into the mouth of Balaam, the arch-adversary of Israel. The author of the Chronicle does nothing to rebut this adverse criticism. He evidently regards it simply as a commonplace of anti-Semitism. In so far as it is an accusation of insociability on the part of Israel it appears already in the Hecataeus passage to which (see above) Photius refers. Hecataeus there states that Moses 'introduced misanthropic habits and a hatred of strangers'. Later, in the first century B.C., Apollonius Molo blamed the Jews 'because they would not have fellowship with those who choose to observe a different way of living' (cf. *Cont. Ap.* II, § 37). Charges to this effect continue to be made in the following centuries. See Théodore Reinach's *Textes d'auteurs grecs et romains relatifs au Judaisme* (pp. 64, 183, 293, 297). The novelty in the Chronicle's formulation of this charge is that it makes Balaam quote scripture in support of it.

(*e*) A condemnation of Gentile morals. Pharaoh is represented by the Chronicle as scoffing at the threat that all the firstborn of Egypt would be put to death, and as asserting that even if all the firstborn were to die, this would mean the loss of only a negligible portion of the population. Here the Chronicler allows himself what he doubtless thinks to be a justifiable exaggeration, and states that the threat would involve the fate of the whole nation, since so general was the unchastity of the Egyptians that practically all the members of any particular family were born out of wedlock and thus 'all were bastards, every single one of them being a firstborn of his father'. The language and thought of the Chronicle on the morals of the Egyptians have a striking parallel in a passage in Philo's treatise 'On the Decalogue'. Speaking of Moses as law-giver and of the evils which prevail in cities and of the impieties which are there rife, Philo says: 'For such people [namely, image-worshippers] the sacred scripture aptly compares to children begotten of a harlot. For just as such children are registered as having for their fathers all the men whom their mother had had as lovers, since no one knows the man who is their actual father, so the people who live in cities do not know the truly existing God and deify an innumerable host of things falsely so-called.'[1] That which Philo says of a harlot's brood of children and of each child being registered as a child of a different father has immediate reference to polytheistic religion. But Goodenough (op. cit.) perceives that, in the passage cited, Philo is referring to the Romans in such a way that his intention would be quite plain to the Alexandrians of his day and that 'under cover of a criticism of their [the Romans'] religious vagaries he is even bold enough to call the Romans a harlot's litter of bastards!' In other words, Philo is attacking Roman morals. Goodenough regards the above-given passage from Philo's treatise as being one among others in Philo's writings which shows how the Jews of Alexandria hated and despised their Roman masters.

There can be little doubt that our Chronicler also, while embellishing the biblical story of Moses' time, had actually, as had Philo, the conditions of his own time before his eyes, and directed the attention of his hearers or readers to the morals of the governing people under whom they lived. In the comparison of a harlot's litter Philo and the Chronicler would seem to be employing a current witticism appreciated by their fellow Jews because of its sharp polemic edge. It still enjoyed vitality in the eleventh century, for the commentator Rashi offers it as a serious explanation of the text (Exod. 12.30) 'there was not a house where there was not one dead.'[2]

(f) 'You are haters of God, in so much as you do not think

---

[1] Cf. E. R. Goodenough, *The Politics of Philo Judaeus*, New Haven, 1938, p. 39 f. See also C. D. Yonge, *Philo's Works*, Vol. III, p. 137 f.

[2] Rashi ad loc. 'Another explanation is: the Egyptian women were unfaithful to their husbands and bore children from young men, unmarried, and thus they [the Egyptian men] had many firstborn sons, sometimes there were five to one woman, each being the firstborn to his own father.'

that I am a God, I who am already confessed to be a God by
every other nation, but who am refused that appellation by you.'[1]

Immediately before his disquisition on the ten plagues, the
Chronicler describes the last interview which Moses and Aaron
had with Pharaoh. In the name of God the Hebrew leaders
request permission to take their people a three days' journey
toward the desert that they might sacrifice there. Pharaoh
challenges the authority and power of the Hebrews' God. 'In
all the books of Egypt', he tells them, 'there is nothing mentioned about this deity.' Moses and Aaron thereupon inform
the king that the God of the Hebrews is the God who is the
Maker of the heavens and the earth, before whom all creation
trembles. They add that this God will strip the king of his
power and deprive him of his life, causing him to return as dust
to the ground. Pharaoh then, provoked to wrath, declares:
'There is no deity in any of the lands can do as I do. Mine is
my Nile and I made myself' (cf. Ezek. 29.3). In hot displeasure
the king drives the petitioners from him and orders the lot of
the Hebrews to be made heavier.

The biblical record in Exodus says nothing of a claim made
by the Pharaoh to divinity, but with considerable skill our midrash draws upon an oracle against Egypt in the Book of Ezekiel,
where Pharaoh is likened to 'the great dragon that lies in the
midst of his rivers, which has said, My river (or my Nile) is my
own and I have made myself.' The rendering of A.V. and
R.V., namely 'made it for myself', avoids giving the Hebrew
text the literal sense which is essential to the Chronicler's intention. The latter's intention is to contrast the claim to divine
kingship, customary in Egypt and adopted by the Roman
Emperors, with the belief in the divinity of the one God, the
Creator of all things. In the period of the early Roman Empire
the situation in which the opposition between the State and
Judaism reached its most acute stage was when the Emperor
Gaius Caligula (37-41), taking with a greater seriousness than
hitherto attained by his predecessors the ascription of Godhead,
announced himself to be Jupiter Epiphanes (cf. Eusebius, *Eccl.
Hist.* Bk. 2, ch. 6). The centre of the conflict which was now
forced upon the Jews by the assumption of divine honours on

[1] Gaius Caesar Caligula to the Jewish delegates—Philo's *Embassy to
Gaius*, § 44.

the part of Caligula was at first at Alexandria. Here the Greek and Egyptian parts of the population, in the name of religion and patriotism, sought to compel the Jews to place images and statues of the Emperor in their synagogues. When this was refused, pogroms and looting broke out. At length, in the year 40, a Jewish embassy was sent to Rome under the leadership of Philo, who must have been a man of about sixty years of age at the time, to endeavour to persuade the Emperor to exempt the Jews from any obligations of the Emperor-cult. The story of the events at Alexandria which led up to this embassy and of what occurred when the Jewish delegates met Caligula is told in Philo's treatises, the 'Against Flaccus' and 'The Legation to Gaius'.

Josephus' lively account of the mission to Rome seems to have preserved the popular tradition of this event. He tells us that at first Gaius was highly esteemed by his subjects, but 'in process of time he went beyond the bounds of human nature in his conceit of himself and by reason of the vastness of his dominions made himself a God and took upon himself to act in all things to the reproach of the Deity itself' (Ant. xviii, 7.3). When the Jewish delegation secured an audience of the Emperor, an ambassador of the Greek party accused the Jews of neglecting to accord to the Caesar the honours which were his due. Philo attempted to answer this charge; 'but Gaius prohibited him and bade him begone', being 'in such a rage that it openly appeared that he was about to do them some mischief' (xviii, 8.1). As token of the mental state of Caligula, Josephus recounts one of the Emperor's 'pranks', namely the building of a bridge across the sea between two promontories, connecting thereby two coastal townships, because 'he esteemed it to be a most tedious thing to row over in a small ship and thought withal that it became him to make that bridge, as he was lord of the sea and might oblige it to give marks of obedience as well as the earth.' The Pharaoh of Ezekiel's oracle who claimed the Nile was indeed a fitting counterpart to Caligula as lord and master of the sea.

The account given in the Chronicle of Moses of the interview with Pharaoh, his claim to divinity, his rage as he drives the petitioners from his presence, the prediction that God would deprive him of his power and of his life—Caligula was murdered in the course of the ensuing year—all this seems to suggest that the author has here described a history more recent than Moses, a history living in the consciousness of the people whom he is addressing, and that he is furnishing the polemical weapons which he conceives as essential for the equipment of his Jewish contemporaries. When the midrash was written it is probable that the question of the imperial divinity-claims was not one which could yet be regarded as altogether beyond possibility of returning and of bringing anew to Jews persecution and suffering. Goodenough (op. cit., pp. 120, 140) goes so far as to state that Christianity, when it took over quite readily all the ancient theories of kingship except that of the king's divinity, profited from the legacy left by the forgotten Jews of the diaspora who had defended their Jewish heritage against Hellenistic and Roman royalty.

(g) Midrashim as vehicles of polemic. Galen (A.D. 129-199), physician, philosopher and grammarian, born in Pergamum and from his thirty-third year a resident in Rome, made certain references to Jews and Christians. These references, recently examined by R. Walzer—*Galen on Jews and Christians*, Oxford University Press, 1949—are of much interest, since they come from a pagan writer of a singularly independent and unbiased mind. One of Galen's sayings, contained in an Arabic quotation from one of his lost medical works, the six books on Hippocrates' *Anatomy*, is that those who practise medicine without scientific knowledge are comparable to 'Moses who framed laws for the tribe of the Jews, since it is his method in his books to write without offering proofs, saying "God commanded, God spake".' In a second passage, which occurs in the work *De differentiis pulsuum*, we have the statement that 'one should not at the very beginning, as if one had come into the school of Moses and Christ, hear talk of undemonstrated laws', and finally in a passage from Galen's lost summary of Plato's *Republic* and preserved in Arabic quotations, this sentence is found: 'Most people are unable to follow any demonstrative argument consecutively: hence they need parables and benefit from them ... just as now we see the people called Christians drawing their faith from parables [and miracles].' The purport of these passages, in brief, is that Galen complains that so far as he has had conversation with Jews and Christians on their beliefs, or has had any knowledge of their books, these sects do not rely on demonstration or logic in proof of their teaching. They emphasize the divine command and faith in God's word. Galen praises, and contrasts with the Jewish and Christian methods of teaching, the effort to obtain exact knowledge which is the product of logically trained reasoning. Cf. Walzer, p. 40. We may notice that Galen is not speaking of disputes between Jews and Christians—these disputes took a long time to develop to the critical level represented by the *Chizzuk Emunah* (the Confirming of Faith) by Isaac Troki (1594)—but is speaking of contacts between these and pagans. His complaint does not seem to be altogether justified, for Josephus in his work 'Against Apion', so far at least as the questions answered are concerned, employs reasonably adequate arguments. But in general the impression which Galen conveys of the Jewish and Christian method in defence of their faiths must be accepted as the impression which pagans received. The description which the pagan physician gives, in the second century of our era, of the character of the argumentation which was common to Judaism and Christianity corresponds closely with the literary and religious character of the haggadic midrashim. These belong to that level of exposition and instruction which does not proceed by the method of dialectic, though the beginnings of this are not absent, but by narratives, parables and tales of God's wonderful and providential acts. That these narrative midrashim could prove to be most effective and powerful instruments of apologetic may be gathered from what is said in a homiletic midrash of the end of the third or beginning of the fourth century, the so-called Pesikta de rab Kahana (Piska XII), which states: 'when the money was at hand one desired to hear the word of the Mishnah and the word of the Talmud. Now, however, when the money is not to be got and, moreover, when we are sick in consequence of the (treatment by the) government, one pines for the word of the Bible and for the word of the Haggadah.'[1] Days of poverty or days of pressure on the part of the State drove men to scripture and haggadah for comfort, for confirmation of their faith and for mental support. The Chronicle of Moses seems to be a good example of the nature of such

[1] Translation by Schiller-Szinessy in his valuable article on Midrash in *Ency. Brit.*, 9th ed., Vol. XVI, p. 285.

support as was appreciated by the Jews in their reaction to the
pagan world.

The translation of the Chronicle of Moses which follows has
been made as literal as possible. It is a translation of the Hebrew
text of the *Dibre ha-yamim shel Moshe* (Chronicle of Moses) found
in Gilbert Gaulmyn's *De Vita et Morte Mosis*, Paris 1629, a copy
of which is in the Library of New College, Edinburgh. The
Latin *interpretatio* which Gaulmyn appends is rather of the nature
of a summary than of a translation. The *Dibre ha-yamim shel
Moshe* was also printed in Constantinople in 1516. This is the
text, 'critically revised', which Adolph Jellinek offers (see Gaster
op. cit., p. lxxxviii) in the collection of Hebrew midrashim which
is entitled *Beth ha-Midrash* (Leipzig, 1853; reprinted, Jerusalem,
1938: See Part II, p. v, f). Other printed editions appeared in
Venice (1544) and Amsterdam (1735). The differences between
the texts of Jellinek and Gaulmyn are only in respect of variant
readings and these, though numerous, are not important. Gaulmyn's is the better text[1] but that given by Jellinek has proved
useful in rectifying certain slips—see the notes to the translation
—which appear in the Paris edition.

While the narrative of the Chronicle of Moses which appears
in the Chronicles of Jerahmeel (chs. xlii-xlviii), the Book of
Jashar and the Constantinople-Paris editions is based upon the
biblical story of Moses, and, for the most part, on a common
stock of midrashic material, the Jerahmeel version (abbrev.
Jer. Ch. of M.) is larger by quite a third than the Gaulmyn text;
and the Jashar version is larger, by about the same amount, than
the Jer. Ch. of M. The existence of two such larger versions
might well be expected to have given birth to the suggestion
that the text presented by the Constantinople-Paris editions is
a short recension (see Jellenek, Part II, p. viii) of a larger and
original Chronicle of Moses, and that the larger account in the
Jerahmeel work or in the Book of Jashar may represent the
original Chronicle. But this conclusion is not warranted, for in
the Jer. Ch. of M. and in Jashar certain elements found in
Gaulmyn are wanting. To give two examples: the 'Come up

---

[1] The first two emendations which Jellinek (Part II, p. ix, note 7) makes to his
text—apparently only on his own conjecture and authority—accord with the
text of Gaulmyn.

O Ox' incident in the legend about Joseph's coffin is missing; also the treatment given to the story of the ten plagues is quite different from that which the subject receives in Gaulmyn. Both the Jer. Ch. of M. and the Jashar version of the Chronicle of Moses, when reporting of the plague caused by the wild beasts invading the houses of the Egyptians, have preserved a remarkable corruption of the text. This corruption is due to the confusion of the word for channels (*sillonim*) with a word interpretated as signifying a sea-monster. In consequence, the narrative, which as it is is imaginary enough, reaches the level of the preposterous. In contrast with this, the text of the Constantinople and Paris editions contains what is obviously the original and uncorrupted reading. But this would hardly have happened had this text been a recension of a text so deeply corrupted in the passage indicated as are both Jer. Ch. of M. and the Jashar version.

The Gaulmyn text is certainly not the result of an abbreviating of the Jer. Ch. of M. In comparing the two texts the Jer. Ch. of M. reveals rather the tendency to expand sections where references are made to biblical characters and their doings. This tendency may be explained through the author's zeal to make the list of biblical examples cited in illustration of any point more exact and complete (cf. Gaster's translation, pp. 111, 117). Possibly on this account the impression is made that the natural sequence of the narrative of Moses' life seems to be postponed or interrupted. The section in Jer. Ch. of M. which appears in the Chronicle of Jerahmeel as Chapter XLVI, §§ 1-6, is an ill-assorted and repetitive piece of writing, badly connected with that which follows. The compiler of the Jer. Ch. of M.— and this is true also of the author of the Jashar version—is in the first place a collector of stories, an epigone at whose hands the narratives have lost much of the apologetic aim and outlook which they possess in the Gaulmyn text. Both the Jerahmeel and the Jashar versions of the Chronicle of Moses seem to belong to days when the apologetic interest was no longer urgent and both of them have lost the original character of a midrash which Zunz defined by the term *Vortrag*, namely, lecture or address, and which the smaller texts of Gaulmyn and Jellinek preserve.

When the prejudice against the ascription of an early date to the Chronicle of Moses, on account of its being written in a pure

Hebrew and because of its mention of the 'Book of Jashar', has been removed and when the internal evidence of the midrashic and apologetic elements has been weighed, there appears to be no reason why the Chronicle, as represented by the Constantinople and Paris versions, should be placed later than the second century A.D. In this century anti-semitic feeling was rising among the populations of the Greek cities (cf. *Cambridge Ancient History*, Vol. IX, p. 433) and the Jews needed to be assured of the great truths of their religion, to be strengthened in faith in their destiny, to become proud of their history and of their great leader Moses. And already in the preceding century there lay to hand a history of Jewish contact with the non-Jewish world and an apologetic, both of these reflected in the writings of Philo and Josephus, upon which a midrash could draw. The Chronicle of Moses is best understood in the light of this age and its composition should not be too far removed from it.

THE CHRONICLE OF MOSES

being a translation of Gilbert Gaulmyn's edition
of the Dibre ha-yamim shel Moshe

published at Paris 1629 apud Tussanum du Bray,
via Jacobaea sub Spicis maturis

CHAPTER II

THE CHRONICLE OF MOSES, OUR TEACHER

A HUNDRED and thirty years after the children of Israel had gone down to Egypt, and after sixty years had passed since the death of Joseph, Pharaoh dreamed a dream. And, behold in his dream an aged man was standing before him with weighing-scales in his hand. The aged man made all the inhabitants of Egypt, men, women and children mount up into one of the balances, and in the other balance he set a lamb[1] —and the lamb outweighed all the Egyptians. Pharaoh was much astounded at this and was turning over in his mind this great miracle when he awoke and, behold, it was a dream. Then Pharaoh gathered together all the wise men of Egypt and all his magicians and told them his dream and all the people were in a state of much alarm because of it.

Presently there came one of the princes into the King's presence. 'This dream', he said, 'betokens great misfortunes for Egypt and a calamity.' 'What may that be?' asked the King. The prince replied: 'There will be born among the children of Israel a male child who will destroy all Egypt. And now my Lord, O King, I give you the good advice that you command that every male child that is born in Israel be slain and perhaps this dream may not become true.' What the prince advised seemed good to Pharaoh and to his ministers. So the King of Egypt summoned the Hebrew midwives and said to them (cf. Exod. 1,16-22 R.V.): 'When you do the office of a midwife to the Hebrew women . . . if it be a son, then you shall kill him; but if it be a daughter, then she shall live.' But the midwives feared God and did not as the King of Egypt commanded them, but saved the men children alive. And the King of Egypt called

---

[1] Heb. טלה, Gaulmyn tr. *puer*, i.e. *boy*. But in the story of the weighing-scales as told by the Targum Jonathan on Exod. 2, it was a טליא בר אימרתא, 'a lamb, the young of a sheep' (cf. Etheridge, *The Targum on the Pentateuch*, Vol. I, p. 444).

for the midwives and said to them 'Why have you done this thing and have saved the men children alive?' And the midwives said to Pharaoh 'Because the Hebrew women are not as the Egyptian women; for they are lively.' 'They are lively,[1] like the wild animals, and they have no need of midwives' was their answer. Then Pharaoh charged all his people, saying 'Every son that is born you shall cast into the river.'

When the Israelites heard of the order which Pharaoh had given that the male children be cast into the river [Nile],[2] then some of them kept apart from their wives. But some of them kept together with their wives to beget children and (when male children were born to them) their mothers left their offspring out in the open fields. And God, who had promised to their forefathers to make their seed plentiful as the dust of the earth, sent His angels to the babes to wash them and to anoint them[3] and to wrap them in swaddling clothes. The angels were also commanded to place at hand for them two different sorts of stones, namely, the manna[4] of the milk-sucker and the manna of the honey-eater. In His pity also God let the hair of each child grow long, right down to its knees, that the babe might be covered and feel happy and comfortable. And since the Blessed One had compassion and sought to make them increase upon the face of the whole earth, He ordered the Realm of His Earth to receive them and to protect them until they should grow up. After which time the earth should open her mouth and spawn them forth that they might 'flourish as the grass of the earth' (Ps. 72.16) and that they might return each one of them to his father and family and be united with them. But while yet they were making[5] in the earth's crust tabernacles (*Sukkoth*) and were hiding themselves there, the Egyptians used to plough[6] above them but were not able to hurt them. As it is written (Ps. 109.3)

---

[1] *lively* (*hayeh* in v. 19) is explained by the Midrashic writer by reference to the word hayyah = wild animal.

[2] The word translated *river* is an Egyptian loan-word meaning the stream of the Nile.

[3] Gaster: 'rub with salt.'

[4] Gaulmyn's Heb. text, here followed, is: מָן יוֹנֵק חָלָב וּמָן אוֹכֵל דְּבַשׁ. Jellinek's text reads: 'stones from one of which he should suck milk and from the other honey.'

[5] Or *celebrating* (the festival of) tabernacles (booths), as it were, in advance of the statute ordaining it.

[6] As in Jell. Gaulmyn's text, though blurred, appears to read פוֹרְשִׁין i.e., used to pass above them. See Jastrow's Talmud Dictionary.

The ploughmen ploughed my back
And long they drew their furrows.

There was then living in the land of Egypt a Levite named Amram, a son of Kohath, a son of Levi, a son of Israel. This man married his father's sister Jochebed, who conceived and gave birth to a daughter whom she called Miriam, because at that time the Egyptians, the children of Ham, had begun to make the lives of the Israelites bitter (Heb. *mar*). And she conceived again and gave birth to a son. His name she called Aaron because at the time of her conceiving (*heraion*) Pharaoh began to shed upon the earth the blood of the male children and to cast others of them into the Nile. But God extended His mercy to them and of those who were thrown into the river not one died. Their support was the Holy One Blessed be He. And those who were cast upon the fields, the ministering angels provided them with nourishment, delivering them and restoring them, when they were grown-up youths, to their fathers.

Now when the command of the king and his decree that the sons of the Hebrews be cast into the Nile became known, and many of the people of Israel who were dwelling in the land of Egypt were keeping apart from their wives, Amram likewise had separated from his wife. And it came to pass at that time, after three years had gone by, that the spirit of God came upon Miriam and she prophesied in the midst of the household saying: 'A son shall be born to my father and mother yet once again, one who will save Israel from the hand of Egypt.' When Amram heard the damsel's words he took to himself his wife from whom he had parted three years since, at the time of the king's decree. And it came about that after six months she conceived and bore a son. And at his birth the whole house was filled with a great light like the light of the sun and the moon at their rising. The woman saw that he was a goodly child, pleasing to look upon, and she hid him for three months in her bed-chamber.

In those days the Egyptians devised a cunning plan how they might quite do away with the Jews. Egyptian women, carrying on their shoulders[1] their young whelps, babes yet unable to

---

[1] See picture in Calwer's *Bibellexikon* (Stuttgart 1924; article *Gesindel*) of Egyptian women carrying their babies in open baskets slung on their shoulders.

speak, went to the land of Goschen where the Israelites were. Now whenever an Israelite woman had given birth to a male child, she would hide him from the Egyptians that they might know nothing of the time of her bearing nor destroy that which was born. But when the Egyptian women with their children came to Goschen and entered into the homes of the Israelite women, it so happened that an Egyptian child would prattle after the manner of his own language, and the Hebrew child, hidden away in the bed-chamber, answered after the style of his language. Then the Egyptian women told their husbands, and Pharaoh used to send an overseer to take the infant sons of the Israelites away. And so it was that three months after Jochebed had given birth to her son, this became known to the household of Pharaoh. And the woman made haste before the officers should come.

Taking an ark of bulrushes, the child's mother put the child in it and laid it in the reeds by the Nile's bank, while his sister stood afar off. And God sent a great and glowing[1] warmth throughout the land of Egypt, so that everyone, scorched by the powerful rays of the sun, was ill at ease through the excessive heat. It was on account of this that the daughter of Pharaoh came down to the river to bathe. Her maidens were walking along by the river's side and also all the women of Egypt as their custom was. And Pharaoh's daughter saw the ark as it floated on the water and sent her handmaid to fetch it; and she opened the ark and saw the child. Egyptian women who had been for a walk by the river's bank came and offered to nurse the boy but he was not content at their nursing. (This was God's doing, Who had willed that the child be restored to his mother's breasts.) Then said the boy's sister to the daughter of Pharaoh: 'Shall I go and call a nurse of the Hebrew women?' Pharaoh's daughter said to her 'Go'. So she went and called the child's mother. Then said Pharaoh's daughter: 'Take the child and suckle him for me and I will give you as wages two pieces of silver a day.'

When two full years had passed, the child's mother brought him to Pharaoh's daughter and he became her son. And she called his name *Moses*, because, she said, I drew him (*meshithihu*)

---

[1] 'Glowing' here translates *sharab*; cf. Isa. 35.7, 49.10, and Delitzsch in Rev. 7.16 (Heb. N.T.).

out of the water. His father called him *Haber* because for his
sake he had become united (*nithhaber*) with his wife. His mother
called him *Jekuthiel* because she had nursed him (*henikathu*) at
her breasts. His sister called him *Jared* because she had gone
down (*jareda*) after him to the river to see what would happen
to him. Aaron called him *Abizanuah* because, he said, my father
(*abi*) forsook (*zanah*) my mother and for his sake brought her
home again. Kohat, his grandfather, called him *Abi-gedor* because, for the child's sake, God had closed up (*gadar*) a breach
in Israel; for the Egyptians from this time onwards ceased
throwing children into the Nile. His nurse called him *Abi-Soko*,
for she declared, God will hide him in His pavilion (*sukko*, cf.
Ps. 27.5) from the strife of the Egyptians. But Israel called him
Shemayah ben Nathaniel, because in his days God would listen
(*yishma*) to their moaning.

In the third year after Moses' birth, Pharaoh was sitting at
table at a meal—the queen at his right hand, Bithiah (cf.
1 Chron. 4.18), Pharaoh's daughter, at his left and his princes
and ministers directly opposite him—when the boy Moses, who
sat beside Bithiah, reached out his hand, took the crown from
the king's head and set it upon his own head. At this the king
and princes were moved to consternation and each looked, in
amazement, at his neighbour. Then Balaam, the magician,
who was one of the king's chamberlains[1] and counsellors, said:
'May my lord the king remember the dream that he did dream
and which I, his servant, did interpret to him. Does my lord
not know that this young child is one of the Hebrew children,
that the spirit of God is in him, that he has done this wittingly
and that this is he who will destroy Egypt? Now, therefore, let
the king with all haste command that the head of this child be
removed.' The king and his friends thought that Balaam's
advice was good. But God sent the angel Gabriel who came in
the likeness of one of the king's favourite princes and said: 'My
lord, O king it would not be proper to put anyone to death who
is guiltless of blood, for the boy lacks knowledge. But now
command that a precious stone and a glowing charcoal be
brought and put in front of him. If he should stretch out his
hand and take the precious stone, then that will be proof that

---

[1] Lit. *eunuch*, but as Balaam is the father of Jannes and Jambres (see below), the
word may mean no more than officer of the household.

he possesses knowledge that is worthy of death; and judgment
has been passed upon him by himself. But if he should stretch
forth his hand and take the charcoal, then that will be proof
that he is without knowledge and free from guilt.' Therewith
all the king's wise men agreed and thought the plan excellent.
So the stone and the charcoal were brought and the boy
stretched out his hand to lift up the stone; but the angel pushed
his hand and diverted it. Then the boy lifted up the charcoal
and brought it to his mouth and it touched his lips and the
tip of his tongue, and that was how he became heavy in speech
and slow of tongue; but by this action he was saved.

After this the king took counsel with his counsellors as to what
should be done with the people of Israel since they were growing
greater every day. And his wife spoke with him saying: 'Does
not the whole land belong to my lord, the king? Let him do
then according to what seems fit.' But Balaam's reply to the
king was this: 'From the earliest times the history of this race
has been marked by deceit. Jacob their ancestor cheated his
brother Esau and took away his birthright. Through guile he
came into his father's presence and received the blessing intended for his brother. Whereupon he fled to Laban. Laban
gave him his two daughters in marriage, yet Jacob plundered
his flock and all the persons of his household. Isaac too, the
father of Esau and Jacob, when he was a sojourner in Gerar
caused the men of that place to stumble when he said of his wife
that she was his sister. Thereby both man and wife made profit
of the people of Gerar, with all whose goods Isaac betook himself off. In like manner also did the sons of Jacob treat Shechem
and Hamor of whom it was demanded that they be circumcised.
When the men of Shechem had become so, and on the third day
were suffering sorely because of it, the sons of Jacob arose, put
them to the edge of the sword, and plundered and robbed them
of all their wealth. So now—if my lord will take my advice—
he will not put them to the sword. But he will lay upon them
many hard afflictions that they may come to an end of themselves.'

To Pharaoh and his servants the plan of Balaam seemed to
be a good one. Then Jethro, the Midianite, addressed the king
as follows: 'But, my lord, who has ever put forth his hand
against Israel and has been unpunished? Has my lord never

heard what happened to Pharaoh because he took Sarah, Abraham's wife?—or what happened [to Abimelech] in the case of Isaac?—or what befell the four kings on account of Abraham's brother's son, or what happened to Laban? None has stretched forth his hand against this people and has gone unpunished.' At this the king was very angry with Jethro, the Midianite, and ordered him to betake himself home at once.

Now after this when God had delivered him from the hand of the Egyptians so that they did not slay him, Moses stayed in Pharaoh's palace, clad in royal apparel. A precious stone adorned his head and all the king's princes supported him. But when fifteen years had passed and Moses had grown up in Pharaoh's household, the lad yearned[1] to see his father and his mother.

And Moses looked on their burdens: and he saw an Egyptian smiting a Hebrew, one of his brethren (Exod. 2.11): When the man who was being struck saw Moses he ran to him for help, for Moses was now grown up and held in honour in the palace of Pharaoh. And the man said to Moses: 'My lord, this Egyptian came to my house at night-time, bound me fast and went into my wife before my very eyes and now he is seeking to take my life.' When Moses heard this, he turned this way and that way and, there being no one within sight, he smote the Egyptian and rescued the Hebrew from him who had struck him. Then Moses returned to the palace and the Hebrew to his home. On coming home the Hebrew thought to divorce his wife, since it was not right to have her as his wife after she had been defiled. So the woman went and told her brothers and these sought to slay the man, but he escaped.

And Moses went out the second day unto his brethren and he looked upon their burdens *and behold two men of the Hebrews strove together and he said to him that did the wrong, Wherefore do you smite your fellow? And he said, who made you a prince and a judge over us? Do you think to kill me as you killed the Egyptian?* (Exod. 2.13-14). Now when Pharaoh heard of this report of the killing of the Egyptian, he sought to slay Moses, and so he handed him over to the executioners to slay. But the sword could not prevail over him, for God performed a miracle in his behalf whereby Moses' neck became as a pillar of marble. And it was in regard

[1] Jell., *resolved* (ho'il).

to this miracle that when Moses' son Eliezer was born, Moses said: 'The God of my father was my help (*ezer*) and delivered me from the sword of Pharaoh' (Exod. 18.4). It was in regard to this too that the Holy One spoke to Moses when Moses had declined his mission and said: 'Send I pray Thee by the hand of him whom Thou wilt send.' The Holy One answered: 'Who has made man's mouth or who was it taught you to speak when you were being judged before Pharaoh on account of the Egyptian? Or who is it makes dumb? Who made Pharaoh that he did not persevere in his command to kill you? Or who made him deaf and his attendants deaf that they did not hear his command to slay you? Who made them blind so that they did not see you when you fled from the fortress and escaped?' But what God did was that He sent Michael, the chief of the heavenly host, in the guise of the captain of the executioners. The angel took the captain's sword from him and put him to death,[1] for the captain's likeness had been changed into the likeness of Moses,[2] and took Moses by the hand and brought him out of Egypt, and left him beyond the border of Egypt, a distance of three days' journey.

But Aaron still remained in the midst of Egypt and prophesied and spoke with the children of Israel saying: 'Let each of you cast away the things that are detestable for him to look upon and do not defile yourselves with the idols of Egypt.' This was said in accord with the scriptures which say (cf. Ezek. 20.8): 'But the children of Israel rebelled against me and would not hearken unto me.' And the Lord thought to destroy them, had it not been that He remembered His covenant with Abraham, Isaac and Jacob: but He strengthened the hand of Pharaoh against the Israelites to afflict them ever more sorely and He caused them to be oppressed until the season when He sent forth His word[3] and visited them.

Now when Balaam saw that his advice had not been taken and that the plan of exterminating the children of Israel in

---

[1] According to Jell.

[2] Our text joins together two different accounts of the miracle. Cf. Midrash Debarim Rabbah, Part II, ch. III.41: 'Rabbi Janai said: the executioner had already come to behead him . . . but the sword blunted itself on his [Moses'] neck, because this was changed to marble. Rabbi Abiathar said: Not only did the sword become blunt on his neck but it was deflected against the executioner himself. Bar Kapra said: An angel came down in the form of Moses and so enabled Moses to escape and people thought that the angel was Moses.'   [3] Cf. Ps. 107.20, 147.18.

accordance with the evil intention he had conceived had not
been given effect, he set out from Egypt and betook him, together with his two sons Anis and Samris[1] to king Nikanus[2] who
was king of Edom.[3] And in those days there was warfare between Kush and the people of the East, the latter losing many
prisoners and becoming subject to Kush. It was on his departure to engage in the war of the Kushites with the people of
the East that Nikanus had left Balaam (the soothsayer, the son
of Laban the Aramaean) and both his sons, Anis and Sanbis,[1]
in charge of the city [of Kush] and they dwelt there. The
lowest of the people were with Balaam and with the common
people he took counsel that he might raise sedition against king
Nikanus and prevent him from entering the city. And the
common people listened to Balaam, bound themselves by oath
to him and made him king over them; and he appointed his
own sons as chiefs of the armies at the head of the people.
Furthermore the people heightened the walls on two sides of
the city and on the third side they dug innumerable trenches
round about and directed therein the waters of the river which
encircled the whole land of Kush. On the city's fourth side they
assembled, by means of their magic arts, many serpents so that
no one could go out from nor come into the city. Thus it
happened that when Nikanus and all the military chiefs returned from the war and lifted up their eyes and saw the exceedingly high wall of the city, they looked at each other in
astonishment and said: 'The inhabitants of the city have seen
that we tarried at the war and they have heightened the city
wall and fortified it to prevent the kings of Canaan from advancing against them.'

---

[1] *Anis and Samris—Sanbis,* possibly a corrupt form, also appears (cf. below).
Jellinek gives the names as *Janis and Mamris;* The Chronicles of Jerachmeel (Gaster) offer *Janis and Jambris*—are the *Jannes and Jambres* of 2 Tim. 3.8, the Egyptian
magicians against whom Moses prevailed. Their names do not appear in the Old
Testament, but are known to St. Paul through the Jewish Midrashic tradition (cf.
Targum Pseudo-Jonathan) which related that they were the sons of Balaam, had
persuaded Pharaoh to slay the children of the Israelites and had led the Israelites
to fashion the golden calf. Cf. Exod. 7.11, 22 and 8.7. For Balaam as son of Laban,
cf. Talmud B. Sanh. 105ᵃ.
[2] Other forms of the name are Kikanus (in the 'Book of Jashar', a midrash
probably originating in southern Italy in the twelfth century. See Halper, *Post-
Biblical Heb. Literature,* p. 101) and Kinkanos (Gaster).
[3] Both Gaul. and Jell. read *Edom* but in the context of the story as here given,
as well as in 'Book of Jashar' and Gaster, Nikanos is king of Kush. The city which
Nikanos leaves in charge of Balaam (see below) is also called Kush.

When near the city the army of Nikanus saw that the gates were shut; they called to the gate-keepers to open to them, but the gate-keepers, in accord with the command of Balaam, the soothsayer, refused to open and did not let them enter. Battle was therefore joined at the entrance of the gate and there fell of the army of Nikanus one hundred and thirty men. Next day the fighting was on the other side of the river, but thirty cavalrymen riding along by way of the wadi sank in the water-pits and perished. Then the king ordered that rafts be built that by this means a crossing should be made. This was done; but, when they came to the places where the pits were, the waters of the river were in a whirl and on that day two hundred more men were drowned. On the third day attack was made on the side of the city where were the serpents and basilisks, but it was impossible to drive these back upon the city and the serpents killed seventy-seven men. So the army of Nikanus gave up fighting against Kush but beleaguered it for nine years, allowing none to depart or enter.

It was at the time of the siege of Kush that Moses fled from Egypt and came to the camp of Nikanus, king of Kush. When he came to the army of Nikanus which was laying siege, Moses was thirty years of age. During the nine years in which Nikanus besieged Kush, Moses was continually with the besiegers and found grace in their sight, the king and all the officers and the whole army feeling friendly towards him because he kept increasing in their esteem. The king was exceedingly well inclined towards him and appointed him to be chief of the army.

For many days, until king Nikanus sickened and died, they remained there at the siege. Then the king's officers thought to themselves: What shall we do? If we retreat from the city then the enemy will pursue after us and cut off the very remembrance of us. But it is better for us now to die in the siege than to return to our land as a people returns that has been put to shame. Thereupon they consulted together about appointing Moses as king over them, inasmuch as among the people there was none his like. This they did. And they gave him as wife the queen who had been the wife of Nikanus, but Moses remembered the covenant of the Lord his God and did not approach unto her, but placed a sword between himself and her and did not sin with her.

Three days after Moses had been made king, his officers said to him: 'Give us advice and say what we shall do, since for nine years we have not seen our wives and children and we are desirous of seeing them.' To this Moses replied: 'If you listen to what I say you will prosper and return to your homes in peace.' And they said to him: 'All that you command us we shall do.' So he gave them orders as follows: 'Go to the mountain and fetch, every man of you, fledglings of the stork.' This they did with speed. Then Moses said to them: 'Train them to hunt game in the same fashion as do the young hawks.' When they had accomplished this, Moses instructed them: 'Let each man mount his horse, put on armour, take his weapons of war and follow me to the side of the city where the serpents are; and, when the serpents come out, let loose the young storks upon them that the storks may devour them and we take the city.' After this had happened thus, Moses and his men drew near to the city and put it to the edge of the sword. And when Balaam the son of Beor, saw that the city was captured he took augury and omens and flew through the air, he and his sons, and fled to Egypt to Pharaoh and dwelt with him.

So every man returned to his own home. And when the people saw that the king had saved them and that by his good counsel the city had been subdued, they loved him exceedingly. But Moses feared his own God and departed not from the ordinances of his fathers, Abraham, Isaac and Jacob, to the right hand or to the left.

For forty years Moses was king of Kush, when on a day when he was sitting on his throne, and the queen sitting beside him, the queen said to the princes: 'Behold, the king whom you appointed to reign over you these forty years gone by has not approached me as a husband.[1] So now set over you as king the son of your lord Nikanus for his is the kingdom by right and you should not make a foreigner king over you.' Then said all the chiefs of the army to Moses: 'Exceeding good have you been in our sight, but all the people of the provinces advise that there be set over them as king the son of their lord. So now take wealth and go from us to your place in peace.'

[1] Philo (*Vita Mosis* I.28) says that Moses participated in no sexual pleasure 'save for the lawful begetting of children'. The Rabbis, unlike Philo, considered that sexual relationships which did not seek procreation were nevertheless a marital obligation. See S. Belkin, *Moses and the Oral Law*, p. 219.

Moses therefore went to the land of Midian; *and he sat down by a well. Now the priest of Midian had seven daughters: and they came and drew water . . . And the shepherds came and drove them away: but Moses stood up and helped them . . . And when they came to Reuel their father, he said, How is it that ye are come so soon to-day? And they said, An Egyptian delivered us out of the hand of the shepherds . . . and he [Reuel] said unto his daughters . . . call him that he may eat bread. And Moses was content to dwell with the man* (R.V. Exod. 2.15-21). Reuel said to him: 'Where are you from? What is your country and of what people are you?' To which Moses answered 'I am Moses' and told him all that had happened to him in Egypt.[1] Then thought Jethro [called also Reuel]: 'This is the man who put forth his hand to the crown. Now I shall take him and deliver him into the hand of Pharaoh.' So Jethro gave command that Moses be fed with the bread of affliction and the water of distress.[2] But Moses found favour in the eyes of Zipporah, Jethro's daughter; and since she had pity on him and kept providing him from day to day and from time to time with bread and nourishment,[3] he remained there [in prison] seven years. At the end of this time Zipporah spoke to her father and said: 'The prisoner whom you bound and cast into the dungeon these many days and years ago, should you not make enquiry about him? For every day he cries out against you to his God and the guilt of sin will come upon you.' To this Jethro replied: 'Who has ever heard that a man who has not taken meat or drink these many years should yet be alive!' They then went into the prison house and found Moses standing and praying to his God: and they brought him out from thence.

In those days Jethro commanded that proclamation be made throughout all that country that to anyone who should come and uproot a certain rod that had been planted in his garden, he would give his daughter Zipporah to wife. There then came kings and princes, nobles and warriors but they were unable to uproot the rod. Now, after Moses had been let go from the prison, he was walking in the garden and there he saw fixed in

---

[1] Text='all the origins in Egypt', i.e. all his early life there.

[2] Cf. 1 Kings 22.27. According to Oxford Hebrew Dictionary the phrase means 'water (which is) distress because drunk in imprisonment. In our text the phrase means absence of bread and water, i.e. starvation, a condition in which affliction and distress are the only food.

[3] This story of Zipporah is also told in Targum Jonathan on Exod. 2.

the Earth, the rod, which was of sapphire and had engraven upon it the Ineffable Name.[1] Whereupon the Earth[2] uprooted it and dislodged it immediately from the spot and it became in his grasp as a staff and he returned home with it. And when Jethro saw the rod in Moses' hand he was very much ástonished and gave him Zipporah his daughter to wife.

And Zipporah gave birth to a son who was called Gershom. Moses was seventy-seven years of age when he came out of prison. And Zipporah walked in the way of the righteous mothers,[3] Sarah, Rebekah, Rachel and Leah and in the way of the Lord, as Moses, her husband, laid charge upon her.

Now Moses was keeping the flock of Jethro (Exod. 3.1) and the Lord thought to record the oath which he had sworn to Abraham, to Isaac and to Jacob. So He (lit. The Name) appeared to Moses in the bush and sent him to Pharaoh to perform signs and wonders. *And Moses returned to his father in law and said to him, Let me go, I pray, and return to my brethren who are in Egypt* (Exod. 4.18) . . . *and Moses took his wife* (v. 20) . . . *And it came to pass on the way at the lodging place that the Lord met him and sought to kill him* (v. 24) because he had not been mindful to circumcise his son. Moses fell before the angel of the Lord; when Zipporah took one of the sharpest of flint-stones, circumcised her son therewith and saved her husband and son from the angel's power.

And the Lord said to Aaron, Go into the wilderness to meet Moses. And he went and met him in the mountain of God, and kissed him (Exod. 4.27). And Aaron lifted up his eyes and saw Moses' wife and sons and said: 'Who are these whom you have there with

---

[1] We learn from Pirqe Aboth V.6 that this rod was one of the ten things that, at Creation, were created between the sixth and seventh days. The legend has it that before the rod was given to Moses to do signs and wonders in Egypt it had belonged to Adam. See Hertz, *Sayings of the Fathers*, p. 80; Targum Jonathan on Exod. 2 and Chron. of Jerachmeel (Gaster, p. 121). The Ineffable Name inscribed on the rod, which gives it its wonderful power is the tetragram, the divine name of four letters, pronounced *Jahweh*. See Bacher, *Die älteste Terminologie der jüdischen Schriftauslegung*, p. 159 f.

[2] Jellinek's text reads: 'And Moses set his hand on the rod and uprooted it, etc.' In the Targum Jonathan on Exod. 2, the rod is fixed in Jethro's bedchamber and Moses stretches out his hand and takes it. But in Gaulmyn the subject of 'uprooted' is feminine and must refer to *Earth*. If this text be correct, the thought is that no human agency, not even that of Moses in his own strength, gives him the sapphire rod.

[3] Cf. Targum on Num. 23: 'I see this people who are conducted through the merit of their righteous fathers, Abraham, Isaac and Jacob who are like mountains and of their four mothers, Sarah, Rebekah, Rachel and Leah.'

you?' Moses answered: 'The children whom God graciously gave me in the land of Midian.' Now this was very displeasing to Aaron and his reply to Moses was: 'On account of those who are our nearest relations we are in sorry plight and have you come to add to their number?' So Moses told his wife to return to her father's house and she did so.

After this Moses and Aaron entered Egypt and came to Pharaoh's palace. At the palace gate there were two lions, and no man was ever able to come near or enter the royal gate, for fear that the lions would tear in pieces whomever they saw, until those in charge of them should come and take them away. But when the lions' keepers heard that Moses and Aaron were coming, they unleashed the lions and left them at the entrance of the gate. This was done on the advice of Balaam the sooth-sayer and of the magicians of Egypt. When, however, Moses and Aaron came to the entrance of the gate Moses stretched his rod over the lions, which went forth to meet him with joy and followed after him and sported before him as dogs do about their masters when they return from the field. Observing this, Pharaoh and his officers held Moses and Aaron in great awe and thus addressed them: 'What wonder is this you are work-ing? and what do you wish?' They replied: 'The Lord God of the Hebrews has met with us (cf. Exod. 3.18) and says, Let my people go that they may serve me.' Thereon Pharaoh said to them: 'Return to me to-morrow that I may give you answer.' Accordingly the prophets departed and went their way.

After this Pharaoh summoned the wise men, the magicians, the omen-givers and the soothsayers, among whom was Balaam, and told them the purport of what the prophets Moses and Aaron had said to him. Balaam then explained to them how Moses and Aaron had approached the palace gate without the lions mauling them. These men, he said, had appeared before the lions which did them no hurt but sported with them as though the men had reared them and had been as joyous as dogs are in the company of their masters, because in fact Moses and Aaron had reared up the animals when these were young. 'These men', exclaimed Balaam, 'are not equal to us at all, but let the king send now and call them that we may be put to the proof together before him.' So the king sent and called them and they and the elders of Israel, when they came into the king's presence, spoke to him the same words as formerly. But Pharaoh, holding the divine sceptre in his hand, replied to them: 'Who is he who would believe you?'

Moses and Aaron went . . . and so did as the Lord had commanded: and Aaron cast down his rod before Pharaoh and before his servants, and it became a serpent. Then Pharaoh also called for the wise men and the sorcerers: and they also, the magicians of Egypt, did in like manner with their enchantments. For they cast down every man his rod and they became serpents (R.V. Exod. 7.10 f). But Aaron's serpent arose[1] and swallowed the serpents of the magicians. Then Balaam and his magicians demurred saying: 'This is no miracle, wonder or anything extraordinary on the part of your serpent that it has swallowed our serpents, for it is a law prevailing throughout the whole world that one animal swallows another; but if you would have us know that the spirit of God is with you, cast your rod on the earth, and if your rod, while it is yet wood, swallow a rod of ours while it is yet wood, then we shall know that the spirit of God is with you.' Accordingly each man cast his rod —the rods became serpents and after they had become wood again Aaron's rod swallowed them.

Then Pharaoh commanded that all the books of Egypt be brought and searched through to find the name of the Holy One, Blessed be He, but nothing could be found therein because the books were books of error. Pharaoh therefore said to Moses and Aaron: 'I have searched through all my books and have not found the name of your God.' To this Moses and Aaron replied: 'The Lord God of the Hebrews is named upon us.'[2] Then Pharaoh said: 'Who is the Lord that I should hearken to his voice?' 'He it is', replied Moses, 'who has commanded us that we should go a three days journey that we may sacrifice to the Lord our God, for, from the day that Israel went down to Egypt, we have not sacrificed to Him. And if you do not let us go He will send against you many sore misfortunes.'

---

[1] That Aaron's serpent *arose* does not appear in the biblical narrative, but Philo (*Moses* I, line 93 f; see Colsen, Loeb Class. Lib.) says of this serpent that it 'shewed superiority by rising high, widening its chest and opening its mouth when with the suction of its breath it swept the others in with irresistible force'.

[2] *named upon us.* Heb. *niqra alenu,* translated in Exod. 3.18 'has met with us' (R.V. see above). But Targum Jonathan on Exod. 5 renders: 'The name of the God of the Jews *is invoked by* (or *upon*) *us.*' See Etheridge, *Targum on the Pentateuch,* Vol. I ad loc. The Targum Onkelos gives the sense of the phrase as (God has) 'revealed Himself to us' in Exod. 5.3.

Pharaoh now asked of Moses and Aaron: 'What is the power and strength of this God?' They said to him: 'He has made heaven and earth, light and darkness, sea and dry land: and the whole world trembles before Him. And your power He will take away from you and will cause you to return as dust to the ground.' Then Pharaoh became wroth with them and said: 'There is no deity of any of the lands can do as I do. Mine is my Nile and I created myself' (Ezek. 29.3 according to M.T.). And in hot anger the king drove them forth and ordered (in regard to the children of Israel) that their yoke should be made heavy. The Lord then brought against the Egyptians ten great plagues which are to be accounted as equal to two hundred and fifty strokes.

The First Plague which the Holy One brought upon them was (the plague of) blood. And why did He bring this upon them? Because the Egyptians used to prevent the daughters[1] of Israel from performing (the rite of) ablution.[2] Wherefore he brought upon them (the plague of the change of water into) blood.

The Second Plague[3] which God brought upon them was that of frogs. For frogs fell into their kneading-troughs and appeared in their decorated rooms[4] and in their farmsteads[5] and leaped and croaked in their entrails.[6] And because of all these things the plague of frogs was severe. And therefore God brought frogs, because the Egyptians used to say to the Hebrews: 'Go and catch fish for us.' For this reason the frogs came.

The Third Plague which God brought was a plague of lice[7] which, for a cubit's height, covered the earth: and when the Egyptians put on fresh clothing, this was at once filled with lice. This was because the Egyptians used to say to the Israelites: 'Go and sweep our houses and our courts and our streets.' Therefore (the dust) was turned into lice.

[1] Jell. reads 'Children of Israel'.   [2] *ritual ablutions*: cf. Lev. 15.18 f.

[3] The plagues are numbered thus in Gaulmyn's text in large letters.

[4] I.e. in the Egyptians' *best rooms*. See in Gressmann's *Texte und Bilder*, Figs. 69, 70, etc., for examples of Egyptian frieze-work and wall-painting. The Heb. phrase appears in Ezek. 8.12, translated as 'Chambers of (his) imagery'. The versions render 'secret chambers' in Ezek. 8 and the Targum to Ezek. renders 'in his bed-chamber'. Perhaps this is all that is intended in our text.

[5] Jastrow's Talmud Dictionary gives this word as = *surrounding of an oven*, brick-work. Cf. Exod. 8.9.

[6] See Rashi's Commentary on Exod. 7.29: 'The frogs made their way right into their bodies and croaked.' Cf. Pentateuch with Rashi's Commentary, ed. Silbermann, London, Shapiro Valentine, 1930.

[7] The Heb. word is sometimes translated 'gnats'.

D

The Fourth Plague. God brought upon them a mixed multitude of lions, wolves, bears and leopards and these were about to enter into the houses of the Egyptians and the Egyptians shut the doors of the houses. But the Holy One sent a creature of the ground which made channels[1] and then entered through the apertures thus made and opened the doors. So the bears and leopards and lions and wolves found entry and devoured the Egyptians and their infants in their beds. But for what reason did God bring upon them the mixed multitude? Because the Egyptians used to say to the Israelites: 'Go and tend our cattle.' So He brought upon them the mixed multitude and the pestilence that all their cattle might die. And this (namely the pestilence) was the Fifth Plague.

The Sixth Plague which God brought upon them was the plague of boils, on man and on beast. Why did He bring boils upon them? Because the Egyptians used to say to the Israelites: 'Prepare baths for us that we may refresh ourselves.' And therefore He brought against them boils to heat their flesh, while they themselves would irritate their bodies by much scratching.

The Seventh Plague which God brought upon them was the hail. For what reason did He bring hail upon them? Because the Egyptians used to say to the Israelites: 'Go, plough and sow our fields for us.' So He brought hail upon them which broke what was sprouting and what had been sown.

The Eighth Plague. God brought upon them locusts, in such manner that, while their teeth were as the teeth of locusts, their jaws were the jaws of lions. For what cause did the Holy One bring upon them the locust? Because the Egyptians used to say to Israel: 'Go and plant trees for us and guard their fruit.' Therefore God brought upon them the locust which ate what was left over by the hail.

The Ninth Plague. God brought upon them the darkness of Gehenna. Who was sitting was unable to stand and who was standing was unable to sit because of the intensity of the darkness. And what was the reason why God brought darkness upon them? Because there were sinners in Israel and the Holy One sought to put them to death during the three days of thick

---

[1] *Sillonim* (=ducts, channels) is read also by Jellinek. Gaster (Jer., ch. of M), p. 126 reads *silonith*=sea-monster.

obscurity, so that the Egyptians might not look upon their downfall and rejoice over them.

The Tenth Plague. This was the smiting of the firstborn. The wise say that before the Holy One brought this plague upon the Egyptians, Moses went to Pharaoh and said to him: 'Take heed, for the firstborn of Egypt shall die in the night.' Then Pharaoh began to deride Moses, saying: 'How many first-born are there in Egypt? There are not three hundred.' But the fools were not aware that all of them were firstborn since they (the Egyptians) were steeped in unchastity and were all bastards, every single one of them being a firstborn of his father.[1]

Moses likewise went to the firstborn themselves and said to them: 'Thus saith the Lord, In the middle of the night I shall go forth throughout Egypt and every firstborn in the land of Egypt shall die.' Then they went at once, every one of them, to their fathers, saying: 'Take note that all the plagues which Moses spoke of, every one of them, have come to pass and now we are told that every firstborn in the land of Egypt shall die.' Their fathers replied: 'Go to Pharaoh, for he is a firstborn.' Without delay they went to him and said: 'Let this people go, for, if you do not let them go, this very night all the firstborn of Egypt shall die.' 'Who told you', Pharaoh asked them, 'to come and speak with me on this matter?' 'Our fathers told us', they said. Then said the king to them: 'Get you hence and slay each man of you his own father. I tell you that either my will or the will of Israel must yield[2] and you, you say to me that I should let them go!' What the firstborn of Egypt then did was that, at the king's command, each of them took up his sword and they slew their fathers—which is recorded in scripture (Ps. 136.10) thus: '(Give thanks) to Him who smote Egypt through their firstborn.'

After this, at midnight, the Holy One smote, among the Egyptians, every firstborn of man and beast and even the like-ness of them which had been engraven (upon the walls of their

---

[1] Cf. Rashi on Exod. 12.30: 'there was not a house where there was not one dead.' See p. 16, note 2, above.

[2] Text lit. has 'will of the enemies of Israel'. *Enemies of Israel* is a technical ex-pression for *Israel*, occurring when the people of Israel is spoken of as threatened with evil, punishments, etc. Cf. Ber. 32ª, where 'the feet of Israel would totter' is rendered lit. by 'the feet of the enemies of Israel would totter'. A certain magical power resides in the written or spoken word and the terminus technicus, *enemies of Israel*, deflects the threatened evil away from Israel to those who hate them. Gaulmyn's translation: *aut mihi, aut Israel inimicis, moriendum* takes נֶפֶשׁ as = self and תֵּצֵא as signifying the departure of the soul or life, as in Gen. 35.18.

houses) He destroyed. And the Egyptians handed over to the Israelites silver and gold, horses and garments—according to the promise of the Holy One to Abraham our father when He said to him (Gen. 15.14): 'And also that nation whom they [thy seed] shall serve will I judge: and afterward shall they come out with great substance', and of which it is later written (Ps. 105.37): 'And He brought them forth with silver and gold: and there was not one feeble person among His tribes.'

On their departure from Egypt the Israelites were mindful of the oath which Joseph had made them take when he said: 'God will surely visit you: and you shall bring up my bones away hence with you' (Exod. 13.19). And Moses wrote the Ineffable Name and cast it into the Nile and he wrote 'Ascend O Ox, Ascend O Ox'.[1] Immediately the coffin of Joseph floated and the Israelites took it and all the coffins (of the forefathers) of the rest of the tribes, each several tribe bearing its forefather and they brought them to the desert.

And with the Israelites there went out from Egypt many people; and a numerous company of camp-followers[2] went up with them and abode in the desert. This company complained saying: 'Did not Moses say: "We will go three days journey into the desert?" And now let us start together betimes to-morrow—if the Israelites return to Egypt then it is well, but if they do not we shall make war on them.' So on the morrow they told Moses that he was celebrating a festival and that they along with the Israelites had observed the festival. 'Now that the three days are already over', they said, 'we are turning back.' Moses' reply was: 'The Lord has said to us: "The Egyptians

---

[1] *The Tzeenah u-Reenah* (a commentary on the Pentateuch by Rabbi Jacob of Frankfurt, 1693; the portion on Genesis being translated from the Yiddish by Hershon under the title *A Rabbinical Commentary on Genesis*) tells us: 'When Israel came out of Egypt, the coffin of Joseph was in the river Nile, for the Egyptians said "Let the river be blessed for his sake". Moses took a silver plate and engraved on it: "Come up Ox, Come up Ox" which means: "Come up Joseph who is named Ox" (cf. Deut. 33.17). And Moses exclaimed: "Israel is going out of Egypt and the Shekinah is waiting for thee! Tarry not but come out of the river! If thou wilt not come out, Israel will then be free from thy oath." On this the coffin swam out of the river. Because Moses personally busied himself with the bones of Joseph, he was accounted worthy that God himself should bury him' (Deut. 34.6). See also Targum Onkelos on Gen. 50; Targum Jerus. and Sotah 13ᵃ. Cf. the Book of Jashar (ch. 59.27; 62.23) in the translation of Noah and Gould, New York (144 Nassau Street) 1840.

[2] The Hebrew word bears the significance of *rabble* or *riff-raff*, but *company of camp-followers* accords with the fact that those in question rendered service to the Israelites who were their 'masters'.

whom you have seen to-day, you shall see them no more for ever" ' (Exod. 14.13). Moreover Moses said to them: 'You are dealing treacherously with your masters.' Warfare then at once broke out between Israel and them and Israel arose and slew among them with great slaughter and they that survived of them went to Pharaoh and told him that the people of Israel had fled.

And the people of Israel went down toward the sea and the Egyptians overtook them encamping by the sea; and the children of Israel came into the midst of the sea upon the dry ground (cf. Exod. 14.22) and Pharaoh and his forces went after them and sank in the sea. And there was not left a single man of them except Pharaoh king of Egypt, who made confession to the living God and believed in Him, saying: 'The Lord is righteous and I and my people are wicked' (Exod. 9.27). Then the Holy One commanded Michael and Gabriel, the captains of the heavenly host, to bring Pharaoh thence and to lead him to the great city of Niniveh and Pharaoh reigned over Niniveh for four hundred years.

The children of Israel now went toward the desert and Amalek, the son of Eliphaz, the son of Esau, came against them to fight with them. Amalek's people were one hundred thousand and eighty-seven[1] myriad men, all of them soothsayers, necromancers and wizards, but the Lord delivered them all into the hand of Moses his servant and into the hand of Joshua the son of Nun, the Ephrathite, and they put them to the edge of the sword.

Then came the Canaanite, the king of Arad, and he fought against Israel and the Lord put him as also Sihon and Og wholly into the power of the children of Israel, who, in the third month, came to mount Sinai where God gave them His holy law and spoke with them from heaven. And Israel made a sanctuary and a tent and an ark; and an altar for the whole burnt-offering and for the sweet incense. Aaron and his sons made offering and atonement for the iniquities of Israel. And Israel journeyed in the desert for forty years—'your clothes waxed not old upon you, nor your shoes upon your feet' until the forty years were ended (cf. Deut. 29.5).

And in the fortieth year in the first month, on the tenth day

---

[1] So according to Jellinek.

of the month, Miriam died; and in the twelfth month on the seventeenth day of it Moses, our teacher, upon whom be blessing died, a hundred and twenty years old. He was buried in the valley opposite Beth Peor. And the Lord raised up Joshua as governor over Israel. Joshua brought Israel across Jordan and took the land of the thirty-one kings and divided it among Israel. The rest of the words of Moses and all that he did are they not written in the book of Jashar![1]

The end of the Book of the Chronicle of Moses, our teacher—upon him be blessing

[1] According to Gaster, 'Chronicle of Jerahmeel', the 'Book of Jashar' here signifies the Pentateuch.

PART II

POLEMIC IN POETRY

CHAPTER III

INTRODUCTION TO THE 'MEMOIR OF THE BOOK OF NIZZACHON OF RABBI LIPMANN'

(ZIKRON SEPHER NIZZACHON DE RABBI LIPMANN)

THE word 'Nizzachon' has very generally been held to mean 'victory'. Wagenseil in his Latin preface to the work called the 'Old Nizzachon' (see below), while taking this word in the sense of '*victoria*', comments on its common use among Jews in describing writings that have been written against the Christian religion. Zunz (cf. Kaufman, cited below, p. 61) interprets the word as signifying *Sieg*. But as Steinschneider shows in his *Jewish Literature from the eighth to the eighteenth century* (p. 317, note 25), the term 'Nizzachon' means practically the same as the commoner word *Wikkuach*, that is, debate, discussion or dispute. For example, Jehuda Ibn Tibbon (*c.* 1190), in his Hebrew translation of the *Kusari of Jehuda ha-Levy*, uses the phrase *b'derek ha-nizzachon* (Sec. V, § 1) in the sense of 'in a dialectic manner' (cf. Cassel, *Das Buch Kusari*, ad loc.). Karpeles (*Geschichte der jüdischen Literatur*, Vol. 2, p. 166) translates 'Nizzachon' as *Wettstreit*, i.e. contest. The English terms 'refutation' or 'confutation' seem to recommend themselves as adequate renderings; they preserve the idea of a process of reasoned debate and at the same time retain the notion of gaining a victory or triumph which is present in the Hebrew verb of which 'Nizzachon' is a substantive.

Two Jewish polemical works bear the title of 'Nizzachon'—the so-called 'Old Nizzachon' which was composed in the twelfth century and a 'Nizzachon' by Rabbi Lipmann who lived at the beginning of the fifteenth century. A third writing is in poetic form and is entitled 'A memoir (Zikron) of the book of Nizzachon of [by] Rabbi Lipmann'. The old Nizzachon and the memoir are both contained in the collection of Jewish polemic works commented upon and published by John Christopher

Wagenseil (1633-1705) in his *Tela Ignea Satanae* (Altdorfi Noricorum, anno 1681).

As a study of the Zikron, or memoir, depends to some extent upon a knowledge of the other two works, something must first be said about these. The Old Nizzachon is a book of considerable scope—260 columns in Wagenseil—which deals with the numerous Old Testament passages which the Christianity of the twelfth century sought to expound as proving Christian doctrines or as prophesying events which occurred in the life of Jesus. Towards the close of the work special attention is given to the contents of the Gospels themselves. The author, whether he possessed any speculative ability or not, does not avail himself of it. He was doubtless very conscious of the fact that his criticism of the Christian exegesis had to be practical and popular. He is skilful and competent. The Nizzachon of Lipmann, a polemic against Christians and Karaites, which Wagenseil (p. 106) calls a *librum prolixum*, is a still larger work covering more or less the same ground as the Old Nizzachon, while showing an individual spirit. It was composed according to Kaufman between 1401 and 1405, exhibits, as does its predecessor, a knowledge of the New Testament writings and is on the whole modest in tone and skilful in argument. The Hebrew text of Lipmann's Nizzachon was published by Theodore Hackspan in his book *Liber Nizzachon Rabbi Lipmanni* (Nuremberg 1644). A perusal of both the 'Nizzachons' gives the impression that Lipmann was well acquainted with the earlier writing.

The title of the poem 'Zikron Sepher Nizzachon de Rabbi Lipmann'—'memoir of the book of Nizzachon of Rabbi Lipmann'—has, for the most part, up till recently been understood as implying that Lipmann himself was the author of the memoir as well as of the Nizzachon. Wagenseil's Latin version of the title—'Carmen memoriale libri Nizzachon a R. Lipmanno compositi'—shows perfectly accurately that what Lipmann composed was the Nizzachon, but Wagenseil also assumes that Lipmann was the author of the poem as well and that he here set down the *potiora argumenta* which he had culled from his prose Nizzachon in order that his readers might have the points he had made against the Christians *tanto magis in promtu* (op. cit., p. 106). This current view continued to be held even though the title of the poem says nothing to endorse it, and although the scholar Abraham Geiger (1810-1874), a student of Jewish polemic writings, had declared (cf. *Bresslauers Deutcher Volkskalender*, iii.48) Lipmann's authorship of the poem to be doubtful.

Two recent studies of the Zikron, namely those of Judah Kaufman and Israel Davidson, prove that Lipmann's authorship of this poem is hardly any more tenable. Kaufman in his Hebrew work *Rabbi Yom Tov Lipmann Mülhausen, the Apologete, Cabbalist and Philosophic writer, etc.* (publication of the Dropsie College, Philadelphia, 1927, p. 82 f) made the discovery that the name Meshullam—certainly the signature of the author of the poem—appears as an acrostic in the first four stanzas of the memoir. In the following stanzas however the acrostic becomes indecipherable. But Davidson, paying attention to the structure of the poem and to its scheme of rhyming, reveals, in his article on 'The author of the Poem Zikron Sepher Nizzachon' (in the *Jewish Quarterly Review*, Vol. XVIII, No. 3, 1928, p. 257 f), that the full acrostic as completed in the succeeding stanzas runs: 'Meshullam ben Uri of Modena.' The poem as printed in Wagenseil had, through no regard having been paid to the structure of the piece, suffered to the extent that the latter part of the acrostic had been obscured. Davidson presents the poem as one of eleven stanzas, each stanza consisting of thirteen lines and having six different sets of rhymes. He provides the Hebrew text with vowel points and suggests various textual emendations, some of which have been adopted in the translation which follows.

The name Meshullam in the acrostic of the memoir suggested to Kaufman that this Meshullam, the author of the memoir, was one of Lipmann's younger followers, who in honour of his master, had put the essence of his master's book into poetic form. Kaufman at the same time (p. 83, note 126) put forward an alternative hypothesis, identifying the Meshullam of the Zikron with a poet whom Zunz (*Literaturgeschichte der synagogalen Poesie*, p. 507) names as 'Meshullam Sofer of Perugia' and whose probable date he gives as the first half of the fourteenth century. The poet's verses, Kaufman observes, have a certain content of polemic. But as 'Meshullam Sofer' is earlier in date than Lipmann, Kaufman conjectured that what the Zikron gives is not an abstract of Lipmann's Nizzachon but is founded on the Old Nizzachon, which was written in the twelfth century.

In the light of the fuller name 'Meshullam ben Uri of Modena' discovered by Davidson, the idea that the author of the Zikron might be the Meshullam Sofer of Perugia may now be dismissed. The Meshullam ben Uri of Modena is quite an unknown person. He might quite well be a younger contemporary of Lipmann. His verses yield his signature and their title states them to be a memoir of Lipmann's *Book of Refutation*. But though the alternative hypothesis of Kaufman cannot be maintained, since it is impossible to equate the Meshullam of Modena with the Meshullam Sofer of Perugia, it is of interest to observe that Kaufman thought that the Zikron might be based not upon the Nizzachon of Lipmann but on the Old Nizzachon. The failure of his hypothesis on the question of the identification of persons leaves the literary question quite untouched. The fact that Davidson emends the text of the Zikron through references to readings from the Old Nizzachon would seem to have revelance to the question of literary dependence. It is possible that the Zikron may be in the main a memoir of Lipmann's Nizzachon, but yet be influenced by the Old Nizzachon. The relationship of the three documents can only be determined by subjecting them to a comparison. The references given in the following comparison are to the stanzas of the Zikron (abbr. Z; Z (I) = Zikron, Stanza I); to the pages in Hackspan's edition of Lipmann's Nizzachon (abbr. L.N.); and to the pages in Wagenseil's edition of the Old Nizzachon (abbr. O.N.).

Excluding mention of similar traits which are to be expected in documents dealing with the explanation of the same biblical passages, there are a number of likenesses between the Zikron and Lipmann's Nizzachon which point to literary dependence.

(*a*) Both Z (I) and L.N. p. 8 cite the passages Deut. 10.27 and Gen. 39.20 as providing an example of a word which, in the Hebrew idiom, adopts a plural form while retaining the significance it has in the singular number.

(*b*) The chronological notions of O.N., L.N. and Z are vague. According to O.N. pp. 85-86, Jesus was born 'more than 300 years after the death of Ahaz'. By L.N. (p. 124), Jesus' date is described as 'more than 400 years after the time of Ahaz'. Z (VIII) reckons that the period between Nebuchadnezzar and Jesus is 400 years. Z is not referring, as Davidson's note (op. cit. ad loc.) might seem to suggest, to the period between Nebuchadnezzar and the Maccabean kings. The reckoning of 400 years between Nebuchadnezzar and Jesus in Z appears to be not the result of any close calculation, but simply an echo of the calculation in L.N. which reckoned 'more than 400 years' for the period between Ahaz and Jesus.

(c) In following the same line of argument, both L.N., p. 28, and Z (VIII) mention the *blinding* of King Zedekiah by Nebuchadnezzar as a dramatic act which emphasizes the coming to an end of the Davidic line of kings.

(d) In Z (IV, line 13) and in L.N., p. 10, what in substance is the same question is asked in reference to the account (1 Sam. 28.15) of the calling up of Samuel from the dead. L.N. asks: 'Why was Samuel angry that he had been brought out of Gehenna?' The question as formulated in Z is given more point than is obvious in the context of L.N.

(e) Both Z (X) and L.N., p. 149, when dealing with the subject of usury—concerning which, on the grounds of words in Psalm 15, Christians made accusations against Jews—emphasize that the law on the subject (Deut. 23.20) is not contradicted by David in Psalm 15, but that David confirms Moses. To the Christian opponent who would try to exploit the meaning of the words of Psalm 15 in argument against the Jews, L.N. says: 'Who is the fool who would interpret the prophecy of David as contradicting the prophecy of Moses?' The law on usury is also mentioned by O.N. (pp. 138-139) in connection with Psalm 15, but O.N. is interested in another phase of Christian polemic on the subject, namely the argument that as Esau was a brother of Jacob, the Edomites should, if the Mosaic law were held, not be asked to pay interest on loans from Jews.

The number of similarities between Z and L.N. which we have given could doubtless be increased on the making of a stricter comparison. There are also certain passages in O.N. which so clarify the argument in Z that it would seem that Z in some degree is dependant upon these passages. These are:

(a) O.N., p. 25, where the contents of Z (IV, lines 1-6; V, 4-6) are found in the following statement: 'The Christians affirm that Jacob descended to Gehenna. Because the first man sinned it was decreed that all the world should descend to Gehenna whether they were good or bad.' O.N. then proceeds to say that it is clear from the words of Jesus ('I came not to call the right-

eous, but sinners') that 'Jacob and the other righteous men [of
the O.T. dispensation] did not descend to Gehenna nor had any
need of the advent of Jesus nor of redemption by Jesus.' Later
(p. 103), O.N. again reverts to comment on the enormity of the
idea that all men, before the advent of Jesus, descended to Gehenna to await redemption by Jesus, whether their souls were
good or evil, Israelites or Ishmaelites, Philistines, Moabites, etc.
etc. In the eyes of the authors of O.N. and Z, the Church doctrine in regard to the righteous men of the O.T. is particularly
distasteful in that it makes no distinction between the sons of
Jacob and 'the seed of evil-doers' Z (V, line 5), but regards
all persons alike as in need of redemption through Jesus'
sacrifice.

(b) O.N., p. 30—Davidson (op. cit., p. 263) asserts that the
whole passage in Z (VIII) which treats of the verse Gen. 49.10
('The sceptre shall not depart from Judah until Shilo come')
'becomes clear when we compare it with the passage in the Old
Nizzachon on this verse.' In Z (VIII) and O.N. (p. 30) the
view expressed is that the Christian identification of Shiloh with
Jesus does not make sense of history. The words in O.N. which
shed the light of a commentary on Z (VIII) are these: 'After
Zedekiah who lived when the first temple stood there was no
king of Judah. Indeed throughout the period of the second
temple there was no king in Israel, but prefects only who were
under the kings of the Medes, Persians and Romans—and there
was thus a great interval from the days of Zedekiah king of
Judah until the time when Jesus was born. How then can anyone say: "The kingdom of Judah shall not depart until Jesus
come"? And further, what relevance has Shilo to the name of
Jesus?'

(c) O.N. pp. 136-137—O.N. here directs attention to an
interpretation given by Christians to words in Dan. 9.26, viz.
'an anointed one will be cut off' (R.V. the anointed one . . .).
Christians, O.N. says, understand these words to refer to a Jewish king and to mean that, with the cutting off of this king, the
succession of Jewish kings would cease, and the act of unction or
anointing would come to an end. The Christians therefore, on
the ground of this Daniel passage, said to the Jews: 'Your unction will be cut off.' To this O.N. replies that the Christians
must admit that Daniel was a Jew, and if he had been address-

ing Jews in the passage mentioned would have said 'our anointed one', or 'our unction' will be cut off. Besides, since, before Daniel's time, Jewish kings had ceased to be, the 'anointed one' in 9.26 cannot be a Jewish king. The account in O.N. of the discussion between Jew and Christian on the subject of the consecration, by anointing, of kings and on the meaning of Dan. 9.26 illumines completely the polemic background of the last stanza of the Zikron, setting its argument in a clear perspective, and settling a question that has arisen from its textual criticism. An excerpt from O.N. which justifies this claim runs thus: 'Why was it that Daniel did not utter this prophecy about Israel, but about other peoples? Because already, before the prophecy was spoken, there was no longer a king in Israel. And thus what Daniel says is that when the Most Holy One, that is, God Blessed be He, comes to judge the earth, then your [viz. Gentile] unction (*meshichuthkem*) will cease—for there will not be any king in the world nor any anointed one, but God will be King over all the earth and the Lord of Hosts will be exalted alone in that day. But according to your view [namely that Daniel refers to the *Jewish* unction as ceasing], since Daniel was himself a Jew, why did he say "your unction will cease" when the proper thing for him to say, in that case, would have been "our unction"?'

According to O.N. the prophet Daniel in 9.26 is speaking of the End-time and, as this is so, and as the anointing of Jewish kings had ceased long before the prophecy was made, the words, about 'an anointed one who will be cut off' must refer to the Gentile, in effect to the Christian, rule or dominion which will altogether disappear when the Lord Himself will come to judge the earth. It is within this complex of thought that the retort which the Jew is asked to make to the Christian in Z (XI, line 6) finds its place: 'It is your own Chrism (anointing) which will be cut off.' Both Kaufman and Davidson (see Z (XI, line 6 below)) thought that the original text of Z (XI, line 6) was not *your Chrism* but *your Christ* and Kaufman remarks that L.N. gives no guidance as to the thought of Z at this point. But the passage that has been cited from O.N. proves that the text of Z in its present form preserves the language and substance of the old Jewish and Christian polemic. The term which O.N. uses for *anointing* or *unction* is the Hebrew *meshichuth* (Wagenseil: *unctio*), while Z uses the Greek term *chrisma*, which was familiar to the Christians.

As a result of the comparison of Z with L.N. and O.N., it would seem that for the most part Z bases upon Lipmann's *Nizzachon* and that it is also acquainted with the *Old Nizzachon*. But besides being influenced by these documents, Z exhibits a measure of independence. For example, in dealing with the charge that the Jews profaned the Sabbath by the practice of usury—or that (cf. below) the practice of usury *ipso facto* profaned the Sabbath, cf. Z (X, line 5 and note)—the author of the Zikron does not appear to be relying on L.N. or O.N. and in his answer makes use of his Talmudic knowledge. The dry and effective humour at the end of Z (IV, line 13) appears to be quite spontaneous, though the author is dealing with older material (see above). Refuting the Christian exposition of the Shiloh passage (Gen. 49.10), the writer depends, in his explanation of the word Shiloh Z (VIII, line 12), upon the Targum Pseudo-Jonathan and not on L.N. or O.N. Further, the author of the Zikron, see Z (IX, line 12), regards all the names (Wonderful, Counsellor, etc.) mentioned in Isa. 9.6 as names given to the child Hezekiah, while L.N., p. 125, and O.N., p. 87, read the text in such a manner that the names Wonderful, Counsellor, Mighty God, Everlasting Father refer to God, and the last mentioned, the 'Prince of Peace', alone is given to Hezekiah.

In the 'Nizzachons' we must suppose that there is a high degree of originality corresponding to the learning and competence of both the writers. On the other hand, there can be little doubt that the substance of these works consists in an account of the current interpretations given to old Testament texts by Christians and in the traditional replies given by Jews to these interpretations. While the 'Nizzachons' are records of the controversy between the two faiths from the twelfth to the fifteenth century, they reflect the controversies of still earlier centuries. The Zikron, a memoir or memorandum of Lipmann's Nizzachon, represents Meshullam ben Uri's desire to give to the ordinary Jew a short manual of replies which could be most suitably made to the Christian propagandist. That these replies might more readily come to the tongue and remain in the memory they were put into rhyme. The Zikron preserves in its eleven stanzas as much of the substance of the debate between

Judaism and Christianity, on the basis of the Old Testament scriptures, as can be presented at not too great length, and it affords a valuable illustration of the sort of exegesis which was employed in the interest of these two religions in the middle ages and later.

MEMOIR OF THE BOOK OF NIZZACHON OF RABBI LIPMANN

being a translation of the poem
entitled
ZIKRON SEPHER NIZZACHON DE RABBI LIPMANN

from the Hebrew text contained in J. C. Wagenseil's
Tela Ignea Satanae (Altdorf, 1681)

CHAPTER IV

MEMOIR OF THE BOOK OF NIZZACHON OF RABBI LIPMANN

I

1. What shall I answer to Epicurus
2. Who comes to undo and to break down
3. The law of the guardians of the faithful?
4. For against the unity of God he speaks vauntingly
5. (Citing Gen. 1.1): 'In the beginning God (Heb. Elohim) created . . .'
6. But our reply to the Minim (i.e. heretics) is that
7. They are giving the word Elohim (= God) a plural sense
8. While the verb *bara* (= created—3rd person *singular*) proves (that) the unity of the deity (is implied).
9. Since the verb is not written in the plural form (*bar'u*)
10. The name of God is exalted in its singleness.
11. Moreover the idiom of the language of Scripture
12. Is to express the terms for ownership and lordship in the plural form.
13. Thus, Joseph's *master* (Gen. 39.20) has (in the Hebrew) the form Joseph's *masters*; *owner* is written as *owners* (Exod. 22.14); *Lord* of Lords as *Lords* of Lords (Deut. 10.17).

1. A reference to the 'Sayings of the Fathers', II.14: 'Be diligent to learn wherewith thou mayest answer Epicurus.' Epicurus, the Athenian philosopher (300 B.C.) represents (Sanh. 38b) the non-Israelite free-thinker—here the Christian opponent of Judaism.
5. *-im* in Hebrew is a plural ending, e.g. *cherubim, seraphim.*
6. Minim=heretics, in particular Jewish-Christians—here Christians as such.
8. Elohim (plural in form) has its accompanying verb in the singular. This point is common to Midrash Rabbah on Gen. I, § 1, to *O.N.*, p. 5 and to *z*. Cf. also Midrash Rabbah on Gen. VIII, § 9.

II

1. Further, those who would mislead us find support for their heresy

2. In the passage 'Let us make man in our image' (Gen. 1.26)
3. Their refutation is found written near by (viz. v. 27)
4. In the words 'And God created man . . .'
5. A lowly creature of flesh and blood!
6.   And what need was there to consult together upon it?
7. With whom took He counsel (cf. Isa. 40.14) when he established the lands,
8. The world and its fulness, and His heavens also?
9. (Yet) the counsel of his angels He upholds,
10. Making peace in His celestial realms.
11. Likewise He deliberates with Earth and Heaven
12. The givers of grain and fruit, of dew and water,
13. Of scarcity and of plenty, upon the earth for good (cf. Hos. 2.21 f).

1. *Those who would mislead*, or our *accusers. Find support*, etc. The Heb. verb is *faḳar*, to be free, sceptical, irreverent, to find support for a heretical opinion.
3. Cf. Sanh. 38b: 'Wherever in a biblical passage the heretics seem to find support for their scepticism, their refutation is always near by', i.e. in a text near by.
7. *lands*—the word so translated appears to be from the Aramaic *arak*=earth (cf. Jer. 10.11 *arka*) but probably it is a textual error, perhaps for *raḳia'*=firmament.
11. Cf. Midrash Rabbah to Gen. VIII, § 3: 'Rabbah Joshua ben Levi said: He took counsel with the works of heaven and earth', ibid. § 8 'He took counsel with the ministering angels.'
12. *Grain*, i.e. reading *sheber*, with Davidson.

III

1. 'Why do the nations rage?' (Ps. 2.1)
2. They bring the time for judgment nigh.
3. They declare that the Father took counsel with His son
4. At the creation of the world; but how were Father and son then separate
5. When, according to their (i.e. our opponents') own words, the Father and son were united
6. Up to the time of the second temple in its finished state?
7.   After being separated from the Father,
8. And 'his flesh upon him suffering pain' (Job 14.22)
9. He cursed the day of his birth.
10. Alas for the son and alas for the Father!
11.   And before he had become flesh
12. Who was it appointed him a Counsellor and a Prince (cf. Isa. 9.6)

13. 'To set (him) with the dogs' of his flock? (cf. Job 30.1)

6. in its finished state—lit. 'at its building'. Cf. Succ. 51ᵇ: 'Whoever has
not seen the temple in its finished state (bᵉbinyano)' where the reference is, as above,
to the temple of Herod. The date of the incarnation was when Herod's temple was
standing. Cf. John 2.19 f. Wagenseil's *ad destructionem usque templi secundi* misunderstands the text. See Jastrow's Talmud Dictionary on Binyan.

13. A gibe, somewhat unclear, which seems to mean that if Jesus suffered over-
whelming misfortune, after He had become flesh, how could He have been
appointed, prior to incarnation, to become a Counsellor and Prince, or to occupy
even such a position as the rulers of the Church afterwards held. Solomon Gabirol
(1021-1058), in his poem 'on leaving Saragossa', also, in a mood of disdain, falls
back upon the language of Job 30.1 and exclaims: 'This is a people whose fathers
are rejected by me from being the dogs of my flock.'

IV

1. On the words 'Of the tree of the knowledge of good and
   evil' (Gen. 2.17)
2. The Minim base conclusions that lead to evil,
3. Teaching that all mankind descended to the Underworld,
4. There to await, until the day of Jesus' death
5. By stoning and hanging,
6. His remission of their penalties and curse.
7.   'Why is his chariot so long in coming' (Judges 5.28)
8. To deliver them that put their trust in him?
9. And why are the steps of his course so slow
10. When he has (already) paid for his brethren the redemp-
    tion price?
11.   A proof they bring is from the Book of Samuel—a mys-
    tery to be explained
12. The prophet's plaint: 'Why hast thou disquieted me to
    bring me up?' (1 Sam. 28.15)
13. And why he felt no joy at that release!

1-6. concern those who died before the coming and death of Christ.

3. *The Underworld*, i.e. Sheol or Hades.

5. *stoning and hanging*: cf. Sanh. 43a: 'On the day before the festival of Passover,
they hanged Jesus. Forty days previously the herald had proclaimed: he will be
led away for stoning because he has practised magic and tempted Israel to apos-
tasy: who has anything to say in his defence let him come and plead it. As nothing
was brought in his defence, he was hanged on the day before Passover.' Cf. Mishna
Sanh. VI.4: 'All that have been stoned must be hanged. So R. Eliezer. But the
sages say: None is hanged save the blasphemer and the idolator.' The question of
stoning (the penalty for blasphemy, Deut. 25.3, Lev. 24.16) also arises in the trial
of Jesus as narrated in the Gospel of Nicodemus.

6. *Curse*: 'All mankind by their fall lost communion with God, are under his
wrath and curse and so made liable to all miseries in this life, to death itself and to
the pains of hell for ever' (*Westminster Shorter Catechism*).

7-9. seem to refer to the Christian hope of a second coming of Christ on the part
of His *brethren* (*them that trust in him*).

11-13. refer to the story of the Witch of Endor and the raising of Samuel from
the dead.

V

1. Understand, you senseless ones, who live among a people void of counsel,
2. Who grope as a blind man in the streets!
3. How can your teachings be believed?
4. The fathers, the kings and the pastors of our people,
5. How can they be assigned to the seed of evil-doers,
6. Or our forefathers to the burning stakes?
7.   He who has been hanged and buried
8. And His form altered by death,
9. Can He save anything at all
10. Who was not delivered in the day of His own death?
11. When He cried out: 'Why hast thou forsaken me?'
12. Who also declared: 'Am I not a son of man?'
13. 'And have nowhere to lay my head' (cf. Matt. 8.20).

6. The Heb. (burning stakes) possibly means regions (dwellings) of fire. But cf. Isa. 30.33: 'The pile (heap, pyre) thereof is fire.'

VI

1. Many base their unsound teachings, so that the earth trembles,
2. Upon the verse (Gen. 6.6): 'It repented the Lord that He had made man . . .
3. And it grieved Him at His heart.'
4. We all are subject to the will of Heaven (in all things)
5. Except in the matter of our fear of God.
6. By this, the Lord discerns the man that loves Him.
7.   Over the heart of man God grieved
8. And said: 'I will destroy man . . . ' (Gen. 6.7)
9. 'Shall the axe boast itself against him that heweth therewith?' (Isa. 10.15)
10. Do not rejoice when they (whom God destroys) perish.
11. Nor because of worthless men
12. Wilt thou, O Lord, subvert the words of the righteous.
13. Let us still say that '(holiness) becometh Thy house' (Ps. 93.5).

4-5. Cf. 'Sayings of the Fathers', III.15: 'Everything is foreseen, yet freedom of choice is given.' Berakoth 33b: 'Rabbi Hanina said: All is in the hands of Heaven except the fear of God, for it is written (Deut. 10.12) "What does the Lord require of thee but to fear the Lord thy God".'

7. Reading with Davidson the Perfect Hithpael of the verb.

VII

1. David has said that 'Mercy shall be built up for ever'.
   (Ps. 89.2)
2. Blessed be 'God, Most High, the Possessor . . . ' (Gen. 14.22)
3. Who desired a place for His dwelling (cf. Ps. 132.13 f)
4. And will look how his [David's] brethren fare. (cf. 1 Sam.
   17.18)
5. 'There is a time to mourn and a time to dance' (Eccles.
   3.4)
6. (And) in the hour of gladness, we shall be glad
7. (For) 'He who declares the end from the beginning' (Isa.
   46.10)
8. Has answered and said: I shall not destroy (thee) (Deut.
   4.31)
9. —And why should we cut off a Gentile adversary
10. Whom God is ready to destroy?—
11. The alien who is hostile to the people whom I have
    formed
12. Serves as in former times, 'that I may shew
13. These my signs in the midst of them' (Exod. 10.1).

1. Heb. is lit. 'he has said', i.e. David in the Psalms has said. Cf. line 4.
8. (thee)—namely, Israel.
9. Davidson emends this line; but *ṣar goy* (Gentile adversary), the reading of the text, is very appropriate.
10. Possibly the line should be translated: '(A Gentile adversary) who is ready to destroy.'
11. *hostile to the people*, etc., gives effect to the preposition *bᵉ* in *bᵉ'am*.

VIII

1. The heretic answers, in taking up his well worn plea:
2. '(The sceptre—Hebrew: Shebet—shall not depart from
   Judah) . . . until Shiloh come.' (Gen. 49.10)—
3. In answering his blasphemy
4. Refute his arguments and prove yourself a foeman to be
   feared.
5. Say to him: what sceptre or what nation do you summon
6. To the kingdom of the line of David when that kingdom
   ceased?
7. For, prior to your master's birth and death upon the
   gallows,

8. Throughout four hundred years, there was a lack (of Jewish kings)
9. After Nebuchadnezzar had sent the Jewish people into exile
10. And had made (their ruler) Zedekiah blind.
11.   But 'answer a fool according to his folly' (Prov. 26.5)
12   And explain that *Shebet* (sceptre) means a Prince, and *Shiloh* signifies Shilyatho 'one who shall descend from him.'
13. This one will be the son of David when the Redemption comes.

1. *in taking up*, etc. Lit. *and takes up his parable*.
4. Lit. *blunt his teeth that you may be feared*.
5. Text is corrupt. Reading is according to Davidson's emendation.
7. Lit. *prior to the birth and hanging*.
8. *lack* or withholding (of kings). The place for the appearance of Shiloh would have been at the point of time when the sceptre, as symbol of power, had departed from Judah in 586 B.C.
12. *Sceptre means a Prince*, i.e. a prince shall not depart from Judah, until Shiloh, etc. The poem here follows the LXX (*archon*=prince) and Targum of Onkelos, which renders: 'He who exercises dominion shall not pass away from the house of Judah.' *Shiloh signifies Shilyatho. Shilyatho*='his afterbirth' (see Driver, *Internat. Crit. Commentary on Deut. 28.57*). In this passage in Deut. R.V. translates the word as 'young one': 'And toward her young one that cometh out from between her feet.' The Targum of Pseudo-Jonathan on Gen. 49.10 preserves both the view that *Shiloh* signifies the Messiah and that its meaning is as indicated in Deut. Thus this Targum renders: 'Till the time that the King, the Messiah, shall come, the youngest of his sons.' *Shilyatho* in our text is best translated as 'he who shall descend from him (i.e. from a prince of Judah or from Judah himself)', the thought being that he is the last (youngest) descendant of the princely line. The author of the poem bases his exegesis of Gen. 49.10 on Onkelos and Pseudo-Jonathan. The main views of the interpretation of *Shiloh* may be tabulated in brief as follows: (*a*) *Shiloh* as above (Ps.-Jonathan)=*Shilyatho*, meaning newly born son (cf. late Heb. *Shalil*=embryo). (*b*) The name of the shrine or place (*Shiloh*) where the ark was kept (*Delitzsch*)—'Until he [Judah] comes to Shilo', i.e. when the tribes in the time of Joshua entered Canaan. (Cf. Spurrell's notes on Gen., p. 377.) (*c*) Name of the Messiah. Cf. Sanh. 98b. (*d*)=*Shaluach*, i.e. he who is sent (*qui mittendus est*—Jerome). (*e*) A misreading of *Shelo* (an abbreviation of *asher-lo*)=*whose is it*; to whom it (viz. the kingdom) belongs or for whom it is reserved. Cf. Ezek. 21.32—(R.V., v. 27) a passage which possibly had Gen. 49.10 in view—'until he come whose right it is'. The LXX interprets Gen. 49.10 as 'The ruler will not fail from Judah and the Governor from his loins until that which is reserved for him comes.' Cf. Origen (*Cont. Cels.*, Bk. I, ch. 53) and Justin Martyr (*Dial. with Trypho*, Ante-Nic. Lib., p. 251). (*f*) Shiloh is a corruption of some other word, e.g. of *moshelo*=his ruler (Gressmann) or of *Shalev*=the peaceful, tranquil one (Gunkel). (*g*)=Shelah, the son of Judah (Gen. 38.5)—'till Shelah comes' (Ehrlich and Schroeder in *Zeitschrift* d. A. T. Weiss —Z.A.W. xxix, 186). (*h*)=Accadian *Shelu*, the root meaning of which is 'to be sharp', 'to be shining', to be a prince or ruler (So Nötscher in Z.A.W., 1929, p. 323). Hence in Gen. 49.10 'until his ruler comes'. Other official names in Hebrew are of Accadian origin, e.g. *sagan* and *pehah* (governor), *Saris* (eunuch, military officer). Of these various explanations, (*e*) in spite of the uncertainty of the subject—to whom *it* belongs, etc.—(*f*) and (*h*) appear to be the most acceptable.
Davidson emends Wagenseil's text (*Shilyatho*) by reading *Shalwatho* (=his Peace; his Tranquility) on account of a passage in the polemical work called the 'Old Nizzachon', which explains *Shiloh* thus.

IX

1. Many of our opponents urge (in proof of their claims) the words: 'Behold the 'Almah (i.e. young woman: A.V., R.V., a virgin) shall conceive. . . . ' (Isa. 7.14)
2. The answer to this is to their shame and reproach;
3. (For the prophet says): 'And I went unto the prophetess (and she conceived)'. (Isa. 8.3)
4. (The son was born therefore) through the contact of flesh with flesh as the rest of children are.
5. (Further God said): 'I will take unto me faithful witnesses to record (Uriah the priest and Zechariah)' (Isa. 8.2)—
6. (Thus the prophet) appeared before Uriah and Zechariah.
7.   (In scripture) the ground is called accursed; (Gen. 3.17)
8. Accursed is woman, and whoso is hanged; (Deut. 21.23)
9. And any that touches a dead body is unclean. (Num. 19.11)
10. But (our adversaries say) that God had pleasure in all these things.
11. They also propound falsehood and error (in interpreting Isa. 9.6)
12. Since it was concerning King Hezekiah that the prophecy was spoken:
13. 'For unto us a child is born . . . and his name shall be called Wonderful, Counsellor, mighty God' and Terrible (cf. R.V.).

1. Robertson Smith (*Prophets of Israel*, p. 272) defines *'Almah* as meaning no more than 'a young woman of age to be a mother' whether she be married or not. The author of the poem regards the 'Almah as Isaiah's wife 'the prophetess' (Isa. 8.6) following the view of Rashi and Ibn Ezra. Moffatt translates Isa. 7.14 as: 'There is a young woman with child who shall bear a son'. The commentators Abravanel (1473-1508) and Kimchi (1155-1235) thought the *Almah* was one of the women of the harem of King Ahaz.
3. Isa. 8.3 deals with the birth of Maher-shalal-hash-baz whom the poem seems to take to be the Immanuel of 7.14.
8f. Cf. Erub. 100b. 'Eve was cursed with ten curses.' The thought is that the incarnation, as a descending to an earth that is under a curse, the virgin-birth, the crucifixion and death of Jesus convey a conception that is derogatory to the idea of divinity.
12. Sanh. 99a. 'R. Hillel said: The Israelites have no longer a Messiah since they have already enjoyed him in the days of Hezekiah.'
13. *and Terrible* here departs from the Massoretic text. Davidson thinks this title reflects the content of the verse Isa. 9.5.

X

1. (Our adversary) makes common cause with scorners (cf. Hos. 7.5)

2. When he reproves us on the ground that they who lend
   on interest
3. Shall 'be moved' and shall not dwell on the mountains of
   holiness. (Cf. Ps. 15)
4. And he goes still further in publishing his calumnies
5. When he says that the practice of usury profanes the Sabbath.
6.   'He who speaks falsehood shall not be established' (Ps.
   101.7)
7. For the words of David (in Ps. 15.5) only occur
8. To remind us of the pronouncement of My legislator. (Cf.
   Heb. of Ps. 147.19)
9. As Malachi has warned us in that passage where God says:
10. 'Remember ye the law of Moses My servant' (4.4).
11. (The law on usury is): 'Unto a foreigner thou mayest lend
    upon usury' but not to an acknowledged brother (Cf.
    Deut. 23.20)
12. What is forbidden (on the Sabbath) is: 'The finding of thine
    own pleasure' and 'the speaking about business'. (Cf.
    Isa. 58.13)
13. To think about business is permitted: to rest (from trans-
    acting it) is that which is ordained.

   2. The Christians accuse the Jews of incurring the threat uttered in Ps. 15
against lending on interest. The reply to this is that the Psalm is only a general
reminder of what the Mosaic law on usury is, and that the law as defined in Deut.
23.20 is kept by Jews.
   5. Lit. *that the interest profanes*. This seems to mean that thinking upon or arran-
ging profitable loans was done on the Sabbath. But Wagenseil in his Latin note
on this line thinks that the Christians argued that the money, which had been lent,
made interest on the Sabbath as on the other days, and so profaned the Sabbath,
because the money did not rest on that day (*nec ulla quies sit pecuniae*). Wagenseil
condemns this argument because it would regard the use of the fruit of trees as
illegal because the trees had grown and matured on the Sabbath as on ordinary
days.
   12. *the speaking about business*. R.V. 'nor speaking thine own words.'
   13. The Talmud tractate Sabbath 150a quotes a teacher as saying: 'Speaking
(about business) is forbidden, thinking (planning) is permitted.' This opinion is
questioned a little further on—'Can R. Johanan have said that only speaking is
forbidden but thinking (planning) allowed, whereby thinking is not put on the
same footing as speaking?'

XI

1. Our oppressors reckon from the Book of Daniel (Cf. Dan.
   9.24-27)
2. The (time of) the destruction of the most holy sanctuary

3. And the time when your 'anointed one shall be cut off'
   (Dan. 9.26).
4. The things which they assert are not to be found in the
   scriptures
5. But of their own imagining they invent what is false.
6.   Let us reply to them: 'It is your own chrism (Unction)
   that will be cut off.'
7. Let the sons of the living God answer and say:
8. 'Where was the Anointed One (Messiah) in Daniel's day?
9. For did not the Anointed Ones (Messiahs) come to an end
10. At the hands of Nebuchadnezzar—may his blood be upon
   him—
11. Many years before Daniel?'
12. But Thou O God wilt hasten to send us a redeemer
13. And Thou wilt proclaim: 'I am the Lord your God.'

1. Lit. *the oppressors.* The sentence might be understood as: they (the Christians)
reckon from the Book of Daniel the oppressors (or rulers).
6. *your own chrism.* So Wagenseil's text—krizmakem. Davidson emends the text
by reading kriztekem = *your Christ.* Kaufmann (op. cit.) suggests *Kristos shelakem* =
your Christ, saying that there is nothing like *krisma* = *chrism* in Lipmann's *Nizzachon.*
But Wagenseil's text presents the more difficult reading and is to be preferred; see
Introduction (above).
7. *sons of the living God.* Cf. Rom. 9.26.
9. Cf. Stanza viii.8 f.

CHAPTER V

THE POLEMIC OF THE POEM

T HE first three stanzas of the poem show the author engaged in combating the Christian doctrine that there is a plurality of persons in the Godhead. The belief that the doctrine of the Trinity was involved in certain passages of the Old Testament was already ancient in the fifteenth century when Meshullam ben Uri may have composed the Zikron. The belief of the Church in the divinity of Christ and the consequent development of Trinitarian doctrine had effected a difference in theological thought between Christianity and Judaism that has remained fundamental. And in an age when the interpretation of scripture in its literal sense was only one among other methods of interpretation, it was inevitable that biblical words, phrases or sentences were invested with a new or particular significance that made them useful in the establishment or defence of religious tenets which had become subjects of dispute. The plural form which the Hebrew word *Elohim* (God) possesses seemed to the Christian apologist to shed a new light on the verse: 'In the beginning God created the heaven and the earth' (Gen. 1.1). It appeared to him that in this plural form of the word for Deity a good debating point was offered by which he could substantiate the view that the Old Testament from the very first foreshadowed or indeed actually taught that there was a plurality of persons in the divine Unity. Also the very striking use of the plural pronoun in the verse Gen. 1.26: 'And God said, Let *us* make man in *our* image, after *our* likeness' made this passage of great polemical importance in 'proving' a Trinitarian conception of the being of God.

The Babylonian Talmud, completed in the sixth century, and the Midrash Rabbah on Genesis, of about the same date, reflect very adequately the controversy which was waged by Christian and Jew on the texts above mentioned. The Midrash (I, § 7; VIII, § 9; see Freedman's translation—Soncino Press 1939), points out, as does the Zikron, that the verb *created* in Gen. 1.1 is in the singular and that therefore its subject, *Elohim* (God), must also be regarded as in the singular number. Further, this Midrash represents that when scripture says that God said 'Let us make man', it is not to any person within the Godhead to whom these words are spoken but that 'when He came to create Adam He took counsel with the ministering angels, saying to them "Let us make man" ' (VIII, § 4) and that no man should be too proud to ask permission, for some proposed action, from an inferior but should 'learn from thy Creator, who created all that is above and below, yet when He came to create man took counsel with the ministering angels' (VIII, § 8). Another view given in the same work is that of Joshua ben Levi who says that God consulted about the creation of man 'with the works of heaven and earth' (VIII, § 3). But the Midrash felt that the verse Gen. 1.26 was an extremely awkward one from the stand-point of the Jew who was brought into discussion with those who questioned the Jewish concept of the Divine Unity. For it hands down the tradition that 'when Moses was engaged in writing the Law, he had to write the work of each day. When he came to the verse "And God said: Let us make man", he said: "Sovereign of the Universe! Why dost thou furnish an excuse to heretics?" [viz., to say that God had a partner or partners in the making of man] "Write, replied He, Whoever wishes to err may err." ' The Talmud also shews an awareness that in Gen. 1.26 there lurked a semblance of support for anti-Jewish polemic, for it reports (Sanh. 38a) that the Rabbis taught that 'Man was made on the day preceding the Sabbath . . . for the reason that the Minim might not say: the Holy One, blessed be He, had one who assisted Him in the work of creation' and that, according to Rabbi Jehudah 'when the Holy One . . . wished to make man, He first made a class of ministering angels and said to them: Is it your will that we make man in our image?' (38b). Indeed R. Jochanan (ibid.) held that God 'does not do anything before He consults with His heavenly company, for it is said (Dan. 4.17): The sentence is by decree of the watchers [i.e. the angels] and the demand by the word of the holy ones' (ibid.).

The statement that the Hebrew word for God (*Elohim*) de-notes that in the Divine Unity there is a plurality of persons is met by the Zikron in the only way such an assertion could then be met, namely, by reference to Hebrew idiom and grammar. Nevertheless, the belief that in the plural form of *Elohim* and in the *us* and *our* of Gen. 1.26 there are elements of a Trinitarian concept of the Deity has survived the polemics of the antique world and come to light even in modern times. According to E. L. Allen (*A Guide to the thought of Karl Barth*, Hodder and Stoughton, 1950, p. 30) Barth's teaching is that 'it was because of his nature as three-in-one that God created man in His image', and that 'the peculiar language of Gen. 1 at this point, where the plural is used, need not be pressed too far, nevertheless the old commentaries were not wholly wrong when they saw in it an allusion to the Trinity.' It is difficult to understand why, if there be an allusion to the Trinity in Gen. 1, the commentators were not wholly right in saying so.

Fortunately the history of religion can give some account of the beliefs of the Hebrews before the Mosaic age and can to some extent illuminate the religious background from which the word *Elohim* arises. Earlier than the polytheistic stage at which there are many divine beings with well-defined personalities and functions there is the so-called polydemonistic stage of beliefs where man feels himself to be surrounded by mysterious powers with ill-defined personality. 'It would also seem' says Adolphe Lods (*Israel from its beginnings to the Middle of the Eighth Century*, 1932, p. 251), 'that the simplest explanation of the very peculiar use of the plural *elohim* to denote *a* god lies in this early lack of differentiation between the various supernatural powers. In Hebrew, the word *elohim*, literally meaning *gods*, in the plural may be used to denote either several divine beings, or in speaking of a single god or goddess. And even when it has a singular meaning it may be construed with a plural adjective and verbs. The Phœnicians used the plural *elim* in the same way, while the Babylonians also applied the plural *ilani* to a single god. [The Moon God] Sin was called *ilani ša ilani*, "god(s) of gods".' From this account which draws upon the evidence of comparative religion it will be seen that the words for God in Hebrew, Phœnician and Babylonian use have the same character and that the polytheistic Phœnicians and Babylonians offer in their use of *elim* and *ilani* in every way as substantial and honourable a foundation for proof of an 'allusion' to the Trinity as does the Hebrew *Elohim*.

The plurals *us* and *our* in Gen. 1.26, if they be not, as they are best explained as in fact being, remnant fossils of the legendary polytheistic, mythological material behind the narrative of the Priestly Code to which Gen. 1 belongs, cannot be held to have had in the mind of the writer of this, the latest of the pentateuchal sources, even the smallest shade of reference to a doctrine of a Trinity. The interpretation that is given to the *us* and *our* in the Midrash on Genesis, the Talmud and the Zikron, namely that these plurals include the angels (bene Elohim. Cf. Job 1.6 'sons of God'), comes as close to the sense of these words in their Jewish context as it is possible to come. But there can be little doubt about the sort of source from which these plurals originally derive. The sixth canto of the Babylonian Epic of the Creation, which may date from as far back as two millennia B.C.,[1] preserves in its description of the making of man the scene in which the gods all consult together about the proposal of the God Marduk 'to produce a man'.—

> Marduk assembled the great gods, he entered and delivered
>   the decision,
> He opened his mouth, to the gods he spoke.

In the third stanza of the Zikron the argument is not clear, but it appears to detect some inconsistency between the teaching that Jesus as Logos or Word, operative in the work of Creation, had at the beginning of the world a personality distinct from God the Father and the doctrine of the incarnation, which implies, according to the Zikron, the taking on of a personality distinct from the Father at the time of Jesus' birth. Also the author of the poem asserts that the consequences of the incarnation, namely the suffering and death of Jesus—whose actual name does not occur once throughout the whole poem—cannot be reconciled with the claim that Jesus, before the incarnation, was appointed—presumably by divine decree as foretold by the prophets—to fill the role of counsellor and prince (cf. Isa. 9.6). This polemic seems to be based upon some acquaintance with

---

[1] See *Altorientalische Texte zum Alten Testament*, Gressmann, 2nd ed., 1926, p. 121. Also *Archaeology of the Bible*, G. Barton, p. 298 and *Ancient Near Eastern Texts*, J. B. Pritchard, p. 68.

the New Testament (cf. John 1.3; Col. 1.16; 1 Cor. 8.6; John
1.14, 16.28, 17.5) and, on the subject of the distinction of persons
in the Godhead, recalls one of the three 'arguments of a Jew
taken from the words of Christians' which Nicolas de Lyra
(1270-1349) added to a treatise 'Against a certain Jew who
denounced the Gospel according to St. Matthew', where the
question is asked: Were the Father and the Holy Ghost separated from the Son at the Incarnation? (See L. Williams, *Adversus
Judaeos*, p. 415.)

In mentioning the teaching that God the Father consulted
with His Son in the work of creation (lines 3-4) and thus referring to the Logos of the prologue of St. John's Gospel, the writer
of the memoir touches very lightly a theme that was capable of
becoming more fruitful of serious reflection upon the doctrine
of the Trinity than were the types of current Christian exegesis
which he had hitherto described. The Logos conception, however much it may have gained from Greek thought, shows very
markedly the influence of the Jewish conception of Wisdom
who in Prov. 8.22-31 is represented as assisting the Deity in
Creation and as being 'a master workman'. (Cf. Rendel Harris,
The Origin of the Prologue to St. John's Gospel, Cambridge Univ.
Press, 1917.) Within the O.T. there had developed the thought
that God availed Himself of intermediaries, such as the Malak
Jahweh (the Angel of Jahweh), the Kabod (Glory), the Name
and Wisdom, and this tendency was continued in Judaism (e.g.
the Shekinah or Divine Presence). It might seem that by
evaluating this body of ideas which speaks of beings which
occupy a mediating office or are manifestation-forms of the
Supreme Being, it was possible to modify the rigid Jewish concept of the Divine Unity. We find this being attempted by the
Christian author of the 'Dialogue of Athanasius and Zacchaeus'
(*c.* A.D. 325. See L. Williams, op. cit., p. 177) who argues that
the Divine Wisdom is the equivalent of what is called in Christian theology the second personality in the Divine Unity. Nor
was this direction of thought entirely eschewed by Jewish
thinkers. In the philosophy of Solomon ibn Gabirol (1021-1058)
the divine will is conceived of as mediating between God and
the world and is identified with the Wisdom and the Word of
God (cf. I. Husik, *A History of Jewish Mediaeval Philosophy*, p. 71)
But while mediation plays an important part in the O.T. and the

F

Judaism that follows it, the Synagogue later departed from the use of the idea. To account for this, we must suppose that it was felt that the supposition of intermediaries of a hypostatic character endangered the religious belief in the divine unity. It has also been held that 'an important factor' in the attitude of Judaism 'will have been opposition to the teaching of the Church, which made mediation an absolute necessity'.[1] In Judaism the shyness of speculation implying the existence of powers mediating between God and man becomes increasingly marked. Kohler, in a chapter on 'God and the intermediary powers',[2] after describing the intermediary powers of the O.T. and later Judaism and their waning in acceptance, at length states that 'the only real mediator between God and man is the Spirit of God'. Later, he states that in the course of development of thought the rabbis exerted themselves to 'avert the deification of either the Holy Spirit or the Word', and finally he says that to modern Judaism 'God is the only moral and spiritual power of life. . . . Hence we need no intermediary beings and they all evaporate before our mental horizon like mist.'

The divergence of thought which appears between Judaism and Christianity on the subject of the Divine Unity becomes also apparent when the content of another idea common to both faiths is examined, namely, the concept of atonement. In the thought of the Church atonement is connected with the person and the death of Christ the mediator between God and man. What this meant in the terms of the Church theology is appreciated in the Zikron in the fourth and fifth stanzas. The author there draws attention to a particular doctrine which might be estimated to place the Christian idea of atonement in the eyes of Jews in a most unfavourable light, that is, the dogma of *limbus patrum* or *limbus Inferni*, which concerns 'the place in the underworld where the saints of the Old Testament were confined until liberated by Christ on "His descent into hell" ' (see *Ency. Brit.*, 9th ed., art. Limbus). The teaching of the Church was that on account of the first man, Adam, having eaten the forbidden fruit, all mankind, including the righteous men of Israel, had at death descended to the underworld, there to await

---

[1] Jakob Jocz, *The Jewish People and Jesus Christ*, S.P.C.K., London, 1949, p. 279.
[2] K. Kohler, *Jewish Theology*, New York, 1918, pp. 197-205.

the atoning death of Christ which set them free and paid the
penalty due by them for sin, in as much as in Adam all men had
transgressed and were under the wrath and curse of God. Already in the fourth or fifth century the Gospel of Nicodemus
(see Vol. XVI of Ante-Nicene Lib.) gives an account of Jesus'
descent into Hades and of the release of the just men of the Old
Testament dispensation, Adam, David, Isaiah, Jeremiah and
others, from the power of Satan and of death, and of their being
led into 'the glorious grace of paradise'. Apparently, if we may
judge from the Zikron, the Christians of the author's day seem
to have cited as a 'scriptural type' of this liberation the story of
the prophet Samuel being summoned from the grave (1 Sam.
28), a story singularly inept and unsuitable, as the memoir does
not fail to show.

The writer of the Zikron reveals something of the scorn which
the theological speculation of the Church must have raised in
the minds of Jews, to whom it was represented that their revered
forefathers had been detained in Hades as though they were the
'seed of evil-doers' awaiting liberation through the atoning
death of Jesus. Yet it has to be observed that no theological
answer is given in the poem to the Christian dogma. There is
only offered instead the practical considerations that Jesus was
only a man, as he himself had admitted himself to be, and that
one who could not deliver himself in the day of distress and
death was not able to redeem or save others. But the fourth and
fifth stanzas must be read in the light of elements in Jewish
thought which are pivotal in Judaism and which are irrecon-
cileable with the theological conceptions of Christianity. These
elements concern sin and atonement.

The foundation of the dogma of the *limbus patrum* is the doctrine of original sin, which has been defined as 'that guilt and
stain of sin which we inherit from Adam who was the origin and
head of all mankind'.[1] This doctrine of an inherited guilt and
stain of sin is in agreement with St. Paul's teaching (Rom. 5.12);
and in Judaism the connection between the sin of Adam and the
power of sin and its consequences in death and misfortune has
come to expression (cf. IV Ezra and II Baruch). In the Book of
Genesis the penalty of death is visited on Adam and on all

---

[1] Cf. *A Catechism of Christian Doctrine*, approved by the Cardinal Archbishops and
Bishops (published at R. and T. Washbourne, Ltd., London), Question No. 115.

mankind because of Adam's disobedience. But 'a real or proper doctrine of an inherited or original sin (*Erbsünde*) is not known to Judaism except perhaps only in tentative beginning' (Bousset-Gressmann, *Die Religion des Judentums*, 3rd ed., p. 406). The view of dogmatic Christian theology that the sin of Adam worked in human nature a principial change is quite alien to Jewish thought. It is not without cause, states Lindeskog,[1] that a Jewish author (Dienemann[2]) has specified the realm of anthropology to be that in which the greatest disparity between the Jewish and Christian religions is revealed and that 'were a Jew to endeavour to illustrate his anthropological concepts in contrast to those of Christians, his natural starting-point would be the Christian teaching about original sin'.

Also in regard to atonement, while in both Judaism and Christianity this is an act in which God and man co-operate, the emphasis in Judaism lies upon the work of man in effecting atonement through his own effort and by repentance. The will of man is perfectly free to obey God. Man is not destined to sin. '*Die Möglichkeit der Sündlosigkeit is jedenfalls da*' (Lindeskog, op. cit., p. 83). On the other hand, in the Christian doctrine of atonement, whatever effort the Christian may put forth to effect his salvation, the emphasis is upon divine grace in saving and upon the work of a mediator (Christ).[3] We have seen that the growth of the conception of intermediaries as found in the O.T. waned in the course of Jewish religious history under the pressure of the need of expressing an uncompromising belief in the Divine Unity. Another reason for its waning is that it does not accord with the Jewish idea of atonement for sin. Characteristic of the viewpoint of Judaism are the words of the late Dr Adler: 'We require no Mediator to save us from the effects of our guilt. Our own sincere repentance suffices to achieve for us Divine forgiveness.'[4]

Describing the expansion of Christianity in the first three centuries of our era, Harnack presents a vivid picture of how the 'historical and political consciousness of the Christian community' led to the formulation of a number of claims over

---

[1] G. Lindeskog, *Die Jesusfrage im neuzeitlichen Judentum*, Leipzig und Uppsala, 1938, p. 81.
[2] *Judentum und Christentum*, Frankfurt am Main, 1919, p. 9.
[3] J. Jocz, op. cit., pp. 273-278.
[4] Oesterley, *The Jewish Doctrine of Mediation*, p. 157.

against Judaism.[1] The Christian religion was represented as being Judaism in its perfected form; the Christians were the people of God, the true Israel (cf. 1 Pet. 2.9). Even before the middle of the second century, in sermons, apocalypses and letters, there had grown up the Christian conviction that 'everything in the world is subject to us and must serve us.' Similar claims had been made by the Jews, but now the strife between both claimants became intense. The new people, the true Israel regarding themselves as inheriting all the promises that had been made by God to the ancient people of Israel; the promised Messiah was their Lord; even the O.T. itself was theirs; Judaism had been superseded. Harnack exclaims: 'The Gentile Church . . . takes from Judaism its sacred book and while the Church itself is nothing other than a transformed Judaism, it cuts off all connection with the same: the daughter rejects the mother after she has robbed her of all' (op. cit., p. 70). The position of Judaism in the world of the time, without temple, city or state, and dispersed among the peoples, added to the impression that she had been overcome and had become effete. The Gospel of St. Matthew had handed down a saying of Jesus concerning the Jews: 'The Kingdom of God shall be taken away from you and shall be given to a nation bringing forth the fruits thereof' (21.43). In the portion of the memoir which now follows (viz. stanzas VI-XI) the Jewish polemic has in view the strength of this conviction on the part of the Christians that they have entered into the heritage of Judaism and that they are the people to whom, in the purpose of God, the future belongs.

Behind stanzas VI and VII we must understand, though it is not actually stated, that the claim that is here being combatted is that the Christians are 'the true Israel' who are to take the place of Israel who has now been rejected. As in the days before the flood, when God saw the wickedness of men, He changed His mind concerning them and determined to destroy them all with the exception of Noah and his family, so God has reversed His judgment in regard to His people Israel and has chosen another people for Himself. A suitable text for the expounding of this view was the verse in Genesis (6.6) where it is said: 'And it repented the Lord that he had made man on

---

[1] *Mission und Ausbreitung des Christentums*, Vol. 1, 3rd ed., p. 68 f, p. 238 f.

the earth, and it grieved him at his heart, And the Lord said, I will destroy man whom I have created from the face of the ground.' Such was the Christian argument. The Jews who were once 'the sons of the Kingdom' had forfeited their position. The author of the poem admits that God may alter His plans and may repent of doing what He once intended to do. Man's relationship to God is subject to man's free-will, and when man disobeys God, God is capable of grief. God does destroy men who are disobedient to Him and it is wrong to bewail the destruction of such men. But in regard to Israel, though there have been ups and downs in its history, times for gladness and times for mourning, God has chosen Zion for His dwelling, cares for the welfare of David's brethren and has promised that He will not destroy Israel (Deut. 4.31). The Gentile adversary cannot destroy Israel, for Israel's enemies present themselves in the eyes of God only as a means whereby God can reveal His disciplinary action, as He did when He punished Pharaoh and the Egyptians.

The messianic claim which Christianity made on behalf of Jesus was naturally a central issue in the disputes of Christians with Jews. The account which St. Mark's Gospel (8.27-33) gives of St. Peter's confession of Jesus as Messiah shows that Jesus' messianic ideal was not that of the disciple, and while He did not reject the confession of His follower, His messianic consciousness was not a state of mind that was calm, clear, certain and unvarying (see Johannes Weiss, *S.A.T.*, ad loc., Vol. 1, p. 147). In such circumstances it may seem to have been inevitable that without any greater understanding of Jesus' mind than St. Peter had, without any qualification or enquiry into the sense in which Jesus understood the title to apply to Himself, all the messianic passages which occur in the O.T. should in the course of time be regarded as describing Jesus' work and character or as foretelling His actions and the events of His life. The O.T. was expected everywhere to witness to Jesus.

Two passages in particular seem to have had great popularity as providing proofs of Jesus' Messiahship: Gen. 49.8-12, from the poem describing Jacob blessing his sons, and Isa. 7.14, 9.6. The Genesis passage, which, though messianic, has no ethical content, was explained by Christians as envisaging a time when the sovereignty of Judah would come to an end and Shilo (v. 10)

—interpreted as the Messiah and equated with Jesus—would take over the kingdom. In other words the passage was understood to predict the supersession of Judaism by the new Israel, the people and kingdom of Christ, or, as Justin Martyr says to Trypho the Jew (*Dialogue*, Ch. 52): 'After the manifestation and death of our Jesus Christ in your nation, there was and is nowhere any prophet: nay, further, you ceased to exist under your own king.' Also the words in Isa. 7.14, 8.6 seemed to be a clear prediction that Jesus would be born of the Virgin Mary and would be of a messianic character and of a divine nature.

The notes that are given on stanzas VIII and IV (in Ch. IV) suffice to show that the author of the Zikron, in dealing with the above-named passages of scripture, employed at least the elements of the critical-historical method of exegesis. If we are right in placing him in the fifteenth century he was a forerunner not only in time but in spirit and outlook—along with the authors of the two Nizzachons—of the Karaite Jew, Isaac Troki (1533-1594), whose book 'The Confirming of Faith', particularly in regard to its criticism of the N.T., is spoken of by Lindeskog (op. cit., p. 21) as having anticipated those protestant theologians of a much later date, who adopted the historical method of biblical study. The writer of the memoir brings philological evidence from the Targum (cf. Z (VIII, 1.12)) to shed light on the word *shilo* and chronological data from Israel's history to prove that the time when Jesus lived precludes him from being considered the successor of the last of the kings of Judah. It is true that the exposition which he himself offers of Gen. 49.10 requires much more to be said than he himself says, but he is restricted by having to put his thought briefly and in poetic form. As to the Isaianic passages, his view that the young woman in 7.14 is Isaiah's wife has been shared by ancient (e.g. by Rashi) and modern commentators. There is no interpretation of this verse that can be regarded as certain. The author of the memoir shows himself somewhat reckless in combining verse 7.14 and 8.2 f, but he is well aware that the question of who the child in 7.14 is and who the child in 9.6 is, if it is to be solved, must be solved by a study of the texts and in light of the conditions and events of the age in which the prophet Isaiah lived. It is quite obvious to him, as it is to the serious expositor of to-day, 'that Isaiah could not possibly have intended to convince Ahaz and his unbelieving retinue . . . by a sign[1] which would not take place till more than seven centuries had elapsed.'

Another phase of the argument that Judaism was but a pre- paratory stage leading up to the establishment of Christianity and to the Christian ascendency appears in the last stanza (XI) of the memoir. Here it is stated that from the Book of Daniel the Christians reckoned the time of the destruction of the temple and the cutting off of 'your [i.e. the Jewish] anointed one'. The passage in the Book of Daniel that has relevance to such a reckoning is ch. 9.24-27 where the happenings within the 'seventy weeks' (i.e. the 70 Hebdomads = 490 years) are des- cribed. It would seem that Christian interpreters of this passage saw in it a prediction of the destruction of the temple in the year A.D. 70, in the war against Rome, when the power of the Judean state was finally broken. We see from the exposition which Tertullian in his 'An answer to the Jews' (Ante-Nic. Lib., Vol. xviii, p. 221 f) gives to Dan. 9.24 f how Christians under- stood the predictions there made. Tertullian's words are as follows: 'In the days of their [i.e. the Romans'] storming, the Jews fulfilled the seventy Hebdomads predicted in Daniel. . . . There afterwards ceased in that place [viz. the sanctuary] "liba- tions and sacrifices" which thenceforward have not been able to be in that place celebrated: for "the unction" too was ex- terminated [cf. Heb. = cut off] in that place after the passion of Christ. For it had been predicted that the unction should be exterminated in that place; as in the psalms it is prophesied: "They exterminated my hands and feet" [cf. Ps. 22.16 (17 LXX)]. And the suffering of this extermination was predicted within the time of the seventy Hebdomads under Tiberius Caesar' (op. cit., p. 224 f).

Later on Tertullian continues: 'Now, if according to the Jews

----

[1] 'The Century Bible' on Isaiah, p. 132, where seven principal interpretations of Isa. 7.14 are discussed. In a text from Ras Shamra describing the wedding of the goddess Nikkal with Yareach the Moon God (lines 7 f) the following words occur:

Lo! a lass shall bear a son
See that ye bring sustenance for his use.

The word translated *lass* (ğlmt) is the same word as the Heb. *Almah*. Cf. Isa. 7.15 on the sustenance of the child. A millennium or more before Isaiah's time, the above words would seem to have reference to the representation of the *hieros gamos* or 'sacred marriage'. I am indebted to J. Wilkie (Durham) for referring me to the lines above mentioned and for their translation.

He [the Messiah] is hitherto not come, when He begins to come, whence will He be anointed? For the law enjoined that in captivity it was not lawful for the unction of the royal chrism to be compounded. But if there is no longer "unction" there [i.e. in Jerusalem or Judea] as Daniel prophesied (for he says "unction shall be exterminated") it follows that they [the Jews] no longer have it, because neither have they a temple where was the "horn" (of oil) from which they were to be anointed' (p. 247).

These excerpts from Tertullian, especially the second, together with the section from the Old Nizzachon cited above in Ch. III, give much significance to the Zikron's last stanza and to the reply which Jews are exhorted to make to Christians: 'It is your own chrism (or unction) which will be cut off.' The Zikron of necessity is only able to give fragments of the fuller argument which is contained in Tertullian's polemic and which had evidently been valued by Christians of later days. The argument of the Christian apologist was that in the year A.D. 70 the means of performing the rite of the royal chrism had ceased in Jewry with the destruction of the temple and the disappearance of the horn of sacred oil that was kept there,[1] and that, even if it were true, as the Jews say, that Jesus was not the Messiah but that the Messiah was yet to come, the rite of chrism could not be performed, since the Jews' chrism had been cut off. Possibly Christians who in the time of the author of the Zikron advanced this argument reflected that the Christian rite of the royal chrism was very evident in the ceremony of the anointing of the Emperor by the Pope as the Vicar of Christ. The answer which the memoir proposes should be made to the disparagers of the Jews is that their interpretation of the Daniel passage is arbitrary and does not accord with what the Scriptures say; that long before Daniel's day the Jewish kings, 'the anointed ones', had ceased and that in course of time the rite of chrism as exercised by Christians would also be brought to an end. The last lines of the poem suggest that in the mind of the writer there was the same thought as is found in the Old Nizzachon, namely, that at the time of the redemption, in the messianic age

---

[1] In 'The discussion concerning the Law, between Simon a Jew and Theophilus a Christian' (c. A.D. 400?) Theophilus (cf. L. Williams, op. cit., p. 301) uses the phrase *unctio Samariae defecit* which, though applied to the Northern Kingdom, seems to have the same polemical content as has the argument used by Tertullian.

that is to come, all kings and dominions will cease and God alone will reign.

The tenth stanza is related to the others in so far as the subject of which it treats, the practice of lending money on interest, had much to do with the relative influence and power of the Jewish and Christian communities. But this stanza is quite removed from the others in spirit, for it is occupied with a question of moral action rather than with religious belief. Next to matters of religious belief nothing had so differentiated the Jews from their fellow citizens as their engaging in usury, the lending of money on interest. In the Europe of the middle-ages, Jews had acted as pedlars and hawkers in the country districts, exchanging town-wares for rural products. When they could maintain themselves in cities, they often became money-exchangers, for the places where coinage was minted were numerous, and thus they rendered a very necessary service to society at a profit to themselves. The next step, the taking of interest, was a natural one. When the products of agriculture, upon which the greatest value was formerly laid, sank in comparison with the value of fluid money, Jews acquired the position of money-traders, money-lenders. Times of dearth, famine and war made dependance on those who had money indispensable. The Jew, excluded from the trade-guilds, was also, by force of circumstances, encouraged to take to the profession of lender and at this he became adept, while the Christian, however commercial his instincts may have been, was subject to the ecclesiastical canon-law forbidding the taking of interest. But it must not be thought—so R. H. Tawney in his *Religion and the Rise of Capitalism* (Pelican Series, p. 41) warns us—that there was any violent conflict between the teaching of the Church and the policy of the world of business. Both Church and business world accepted the same assumptions which had arisen from the same environment. 'The suspicion of economic motives had been one of the earliest elements in the social teaching of the Church, and was to survive till Calvinism endowed the life of economic enterprise with a new sanctification' (op. cit., p. 38).

The ordinary rate of interest in the middle ages was often high. In Italy, by an edict of Frederick II, it was reduced to ten per cent; in France it was repeatedly fixed at forty per cent;

in Austria it was 'limited' to sixty-five per cent in the fourteenth century; in Regensburg in 1392 to seventy-five per cent on loans 'under a pound'.[1] These conditions naturally led to attacks being made upon Jews and to feuds between Christian and Jew which could only be assuaged according as advance was made towards modern methods of trading and of credit. But over how lengthy a period these feuds and debates persisted may be judged when we compare the Zikron's statement upon usury with that of the great Jewish commentator David Kimchi (1155-1235) of Narbonne two or more centuries previously. We see on comparison and also from the two Nizzachons, that the form of argument throughout the years had remained the same, namely, that the law as contained in Deut. 23.20 is specific and that what is said in Ps. 15 is only general and does not conflict with the specific law. What the latter forbids is the lending on interest to an Israelite, but it permits lending on interest to a Gentile. To this argument, common to all the documents mentioned, Kimchi (commenting on Ps. 15) adds that the rate of interest taken from a Gentile must not be extortionate, but that the Jew is not bound to lend his money for nothing to a Gentile 'for, in the mass, the Gentiles hate Israel'. Kimchi also allows us to see more clearly what the Christians' argument from scripture was, for he writes: 'I have written at length in order that you may have at hand a ready answer to Christians who say that David (Ps. 15) did not distinguish between Israel and the Gentiles but that all usury is forbidden—for it cannot possibly be maintained that David forbad what Moses, our teacher, permitted by the command of God.'

How strong the feeling against the Jews had grown, how easily the smouldering of hatred and jealousy could be fanned into flame against a class of citizens who were permitted to prosper in a trade forbidden to others, may be estimated by the protest· voiced by Luther: 'Put into the hands of the young strong Jews and Jewesses, flail, axe, mattock and spade, the distaff and the spindle and let them earn their bread in the sweat of their nostrils as is prescribed for the children of Adam in Genesis III. For it is not good enough that they would let us accursed Gojim (Gentiles) work in the sweat of our faces, and

[1] Cf. Professor Diestel, 'Geschichte des Mittelalters' in Spamer's Illustrierte Weltgescihchte, Vol. IV, Part II, p. 335.

they, the holy people, sit behind the stove, passing idle days fattening and pampering themselves.' The legislative enactments in Germany in the sixteenth century likewise mirror the disturbance and disorders in the body politic which were caused by the religious strife between Jew and Christian over the economic question that had troubled the previous centuries. An edict passed at Augsburg in 1530 speaks of distress and misery among the people caused by the Jewish usurers, of the high security demanded, of the Jews taking stolen property as pledges. The edict ordains that no person give such Jews admittance to any house he owns or maintain them with him; that they receive no assistance in claiming debts of an usurious nature in the law courts; that if any person desire to have Jews living with him, he must be responsible for their living by honourable trading and by manual labour. At Frankfurt (1577) it is ordained that documents relating to loans from Jews must be composed in the German and not in the Jewish language and that all relevant details of the nature of the loan must be stated. Further the bonds must not be sold to Christians as third-parties. But in order that Jews may earn their livelihood they are allowed to exact usury at not more than five per cent. Another Augsburg edict of the reign of Charles V (1519-1556) is perhaps the most revealing, for it states that since the Jews of both sexes have been assessed for state-taxes, in person, property and goods at a higher rate than Christians and have not any considerable property beyond their ready money, it is enacted that, in proportion to the sums that they have given to the State, they be allowed to exact a higher rate of interest for their loans of money than Christians are permitted to demand.

These three edicts—the full German text of which is contained in Wagenseil's *Tela*, op. cit., p. 538 f—provide an excellent example of the vicious circle. The last, with its rather peculiar sense of justice, shows perhaps more clearly than the others how effectively this one question of usury had, in the course of centuries, poisoned the whole stream of Jewish and Christian relationships and had vitiated legislation itself.

Even as late as 1807, in the Synedrion of Paris summoned at the dictate of Napoleon, the subject of loans, among the topics affecting the position of Jewry within the State, occupies a central place. Among the decrees issued by the Synedrion, usury—now taken to mean excessive interest—is forbidden altogether. In regard to interest, the texts of scripture on the subject are now declared to apply between Jews and fellow-citizens in precisely the same way as between Jews and Jews. (Cf. Israel Davis, art. 'Jews (modern)' in *Ency. Brit.*, 9th ed.)

PART III

POLEMIC IN LETTERS

CHAPTER VI

INTRODUCTION TO THE LETTERS OF RITTANGEL AND OF THE JEW OF AMSTERDAM

(A DISCUSSION ON GENESIS 49.10)

IN Johann Christoph Wagenseil's (1633-1705) polemical work the *Tela Ignea Satanae* (Altdorf, 1681)—*The Fiery Darts of Satan* (cf. Eph. 6.16)—containing records of Jewish religious debates with Christians and other writings which had their origin in conflict with the Christian religion, there is appended to the author's 'confutation' of the 'Memoir of the book of Nizzachon of Rabbi Lipmann' (R. Lipmanni Carmen memoriale) a collection of letters in Hebrew in which the scholar Johan Stephan Rittangel and a certain Jewish citizen of Amsterdam discuss the famous 'Shiloh' passage, Gen. 49.10. These letters Wagenseil translates into Latin under the title *Rittangelii cum Judaeo altercatio*. Apart from the religious and exegetical question under debate, this epistolary correspondence has a great human interest and as a record of the times and of discussion between Jew and Christian in the seventeenth century is in form and content without rival. I have therefore given it an English translation from the Hebrew, and can only hope that its English dress is likely to make it more attractive than the poor Latin dress in which hitherto it has been known. Though included in Wagenseil's book, this collection of letters is not regarded by him as one of the fiery darts which he has stowed away in his quiver, but the element of fire is not wanting in them. The debate exhibits piety, scholarship, even formal attempts at politeness; but ere long sarcasm appears, misunderstandings arise and at length, like many debates before and since, it degenerates into the *argumentum ad hominem*. On this low level the correspondence is by no means the least interesting. A quarrel in Amsterdam in the year 1642, originating in a discussion of a difficult point of exegesis in which the Bible, the Targum and Kabbala, Hebrew and Aramaic, Jew and Christian play their parts—upon all this the details supplied by the letters shed light and enable the reader to draw a very colourful old-world picture. But old-world though the picture be, it holds fast a phase or stage of the history of the dialogue between Jew and Christian which will continue as long as creeds conflict and which before it touches the deeper issues must first settle questions of the interpretation of scripture.

Johann Stephan Rittangel was born at Forchheim near Bamberg. The date of his birth does not appear to be known, though Blau (see below) gives his dates as 1606-1652. Those who assert that he was first a Roman Catholic, then a Jew, then a Calvinist and lastly a Lutheran (see Rose's *Biographical Dictionary*, 1853) or first a Jew, then a Roman, Calvinist and Lutheran in turn (cf. *Jewish Ency.*) would seem to be following some biassed account of his history. For Wagenseil, who was a younger contemporary of Rittangel, in his *Tela* (p. 327) speaks of the latter as being of Jewish origin, *a Judaeis genus trahens*, and as having somewhat tardily been drawn to Christianity, *ad proselytismum Christianum animum appulit tardiuscule*. It is fairly certain that not the adoption of the various modes of Christianity but the protracted period of reflection between his break with Judaism and the adoption of Christianity was what was characteristic of Rittangel's religious history. In 1642 he is described on the title page of his translation with commentary of the *Sephir Jeçira* (the *Book of Formation*) as Professor-extraordinarius of oriental languages in the university of Königsberg (viz.: *in Electorali Acad. Regiomontana. Prof. E.*). We have no reason for supposing that the Lutheran Professor had ever been Roman or Calvinist. The year of his death was in or about 1652.

In 1642 Rittangel visited Amsterdam to arrange about the printing of his translation and interpretation of the *Sepher Jeçira*, doubtless highly elated at the completion of what was apparently his first book, his *magnum opus*. Such exalted moods are proverbially fraught with danger, and while thus engaged in the city and meeting with some who were evidently interested in his venture, he is prevailed upon by men of position among them to enter upon a debate with a Sephardic Jew of the town upon a touchstone of Jewish-Christian controversy, the Shilo-

passage of Gen. 49. Thus the correspondence on this subject
which, as Rittangel tells us, he insisted should be in writing was
likewise a product of this year. Whether the condition that the
discussion should take an epistolary form damped the zeal of
the eminent patrons and promoters of the debate or whether
they whetted their love of argument by reading the letters at
leisure, we cannot tell. Nor, since the date of his birth is not
certainly known, can we tell whether in 1642 Rittangel was a
young man. In the years that followed there came from his pen
other works, the *Libra Veritatis*, the *Bilibra Veritatis* and his
Veritas Religionis Christianae (see Steinschneider, Cat. Bodl. Nos.
2146-2148). In these last two works his attempt to prove that
the Targums support the doctrine of the Trinity show the cast
of his mind. But the work for which he is known is his exposition
and rendering into Latin of the important mystical book, the
Book of Formation.

In the correspondence, the occasion and nature of which
have been described, we may observe from the letters of Rittangel how his mind is still moving in the atmosphere of the
Sepher Jeçira, the *Book of Formation*, and is still occupied with its
ideas. He employs a passage from this book (ch. IV, § 1—Rittangel's edition, p. 203) to score a point against his opponent,
namely that contraries cannot be predicated of one and the
same subject. Apart altogether from logic, the point made is
duly conclusive, since the patriarch Abraham, the reputed
author of the book, is speaking. Again, there appears both in
Rittangel's commentary to the *Sepher Jeçira* (p. 132 f) and in the
letters—in the latter because of a reference to the Shilo-passage
—a very lengthy quotation, with by no means perspicuous symbolism, from the Kabbalistic work the 'Supplements of the
Zohar' (see below). This quotation bears with it the authority
of Simeon ben Jochai (*c.* A.D. 150) saint and teacher, who had
intimate knowledge of the divine mysteries. It was evidently
felt, at least by those of the intellectual world of the time to
whom mystical thought appealed, that to be conversant with
the *Sepher Jeçira* and the *Zohar* required, as indeed is true, no
mean scholarship and that the traditional authors of these
works possessed an authority which none could question or
gainsay without incurring the charge of impiety. Rittangel took
this view. Next to these supreme and saintly persons came the

Targumists, who had clad the scriptures in the vernacular, and after them the great commentators held rank. These all were 'the pillars (or mainstay) of the world'. The task of the teachers (the Ḥakamim, lit. *the Wise*) of the succeeding generations was to expound faithfully what the great predecessors had said. It is in the light of this thought we must view that which Rittangel had written in his Hebrew preface to his work on the *Book of Formation* and reiterates in the controversy with the Jew of Amsterdam in the letters, namely that the interpretations which he offers are not the result of his own predilections but are the judgment of the commentators whom he cites. The language in which this thought is couched in the preface 'to the Reader' in the *Sepher Jeçira* is practically identical with that employed in the correspondence and is striking in its form. 'I have placed in their due order', he says (p. 2 of address 'Benevolo Lectori' in *Seph. Jeç.*) 'the statements of the authors whom I have named, each man by his standard, according to his host (i.e. camp, group, regiment) with ensigns and signs—for they (i.e. these statements) are not products of my own invention.' This language, breathed upon by the mystical spirit of the Zohar, is adapted from the Book of Numbers (1.52, 2.2) and Rittangel intends to say by it that he has placed his authorities in their due order and given place and page, chapter and verse, for each quotation. It is curious that in the letters we find the attraction for books of mystical thought and teaching, which is of necessity free and liberal in its interpretation of scripture, bound together with a rigid adherence to tradition and authority which cannot move freely and, when it does move, has to give paragraph and page to legitimatize every step it takes. But these two approaches to scripture are very divergent and the realization of this divergence contributes much to the appreciation of the letters with which we are concerned and also to the understanding of the religious thought and controversy of the age in which they were written.

In his explanatory comments throughout his translation of the *Sepher Jeçira* and of the prefatory adjunct *The Thirty-two Ways*, particularly in his notes upon the ten *Sephiroth* or grades of emanation intermediate between the Absolute Being and the material world, in the authors whom he quotes, the Rabbi Simeon ben Jochai of the Zohar-Supplements, Moses Botril

(Botarel) and others, Rittangel reveals himself as a student of *Kabbala* as, since the thirteenth century, the system of Jewish theosophic teaching was called. Further, as we have indicated, in the correspondence with the Jew of Amsterdam written in the same year as the publication of the *Jeçira* (1642) Rittangel draws support from, at least in part, Kabbalistic sources. Thus in virtue of his *Jeçira* and the letters, Rittangel appears as the immediate forerunner of the best known of Christian Kabbalists, Christian Knorr, Baron von Rosenroth (1636-1689), the author of the *Kabbala Revealed* (*Kabbala Denudata*, 2 vols., Sulzbach 1677-1678, Frankfurt, 1684). In this work Rosenroth provided a Latin translation of important portions of the Zohar (*Sepher ha-Zohar*, i.e. *Book of the Splendour*) the chief monument of the Jewish Kabbala, namely, the portions known as the Introduction, the Book of Mysteries, the Great Assembly and the Small Assembly. By this translation Rosenroth set the coping-stone upon the work of his immediate predecessor Rittangel, the translator and commentator of the *Jeçira*, and on that of his earliest forerunner, the first Christian mystic to be attracted to Kabbalistic teaching, the *Doctor illuminatus*, Raymund Lully (1236-1315).

Upon Rittangel's writings, particularly upon the letters in which he debates upon a scripture-passage which had apparently for him some dogmatic interest or implication, some light is cast by consideration of the aims of his younger contemporary, Rosenroth. According to Karpeles (*Geschichte d. Jüd. Literatur II*, 349) Rosenroth strove to combine German mysticism with the mystic teaching of the Jewish Kabbala and, from this combination, to construct a Christian philosophy. On the other hand Waite (*The Holy Kabbalah*, p. 478 f) describes the motives of Rosenroth's studies and writings in another way. Rosenroth, he says, 'did not want the Christian to become a Kabbalist, but he longed very much for the Kabbalistic Jew to become a Lutheran.' Single motives no doubt occur seldom. Possibly Karpeles' view of Rosenroth's interest being the reconstruction of a Christian philosophy represents the major motive, although the missionary interest may in fact be regarded as also present. But Waite (op. cit.) also draws attention to those reasons which Rosenroth himself gives in justification of his Latin edition of Zohar-portions. These reasons in brief are that the Zohar con-

tains a philosophic system which flourished in the time of Christ
and the apostles and from which the sacred oracles have largely
drawn; that the sanctity and sublimity of the Kabbalistic teachings give them the character of revelation and that they are of
use in explaining the books of the Old and New Testaments.
It is the latter reason which helps us to appreciate the letters of
Rittangel, although all three reasons would appear to be acceptable to his mind. The Zohar is actually a *midrash* or commentary on the Pentateuch though it is of a mystical order, purport-
ing to be the teaching of Simeon ben Jochai and his school. In
the letters which Rittangel writes in the discussion on Gen.
49.10 we have the incursion into the exegesis of the scriptures
of a new kind of authority alongside of the old, though the new-
comers come with every mark of antiquity. Beside the Targum
and the well-known commentators Rashi and Ibn Ezra we
have now the mystics Abraham and Simeon ben Jochai, the
mystics among the scribes, men of prophetic temper among the
grammarians and teachers, but now clothed with the authority
of the scribes, nay with even greater authority. In the letters
we see the mystics harnessed to the scribal chariot and Rittangel's opponent is charged by him with disrespect and impiety,
not so much for gainsaying Abraham and ben Jochai—for
that would be a very heinous offence—but for by-passing them,
that is, by remaining silent in regard to what they say. In their
own element the mystics, as allegorists, are distinct from scribes.
The spirit of the Zohar is a liberal exegesis and a variety of
interpretation. A refreshing and a quickening wind has always
blown upon the mind and heart of the Zohar-lover and this
accounts for the book as standing high in the esteem of those
who consciously or unconsciously protest against Rabbinism,
traditionalism and the letter of the law. But Rittangel has
mystic exegetes and scribal commentators all 'arranged in
order', 'each man by his standard, ensign and sign' all members,
in various ranks, of one new disciplined army. The letters of
Rittangel, though referring to only a single but important passage of scripture, are an interesting historical document testifying to the experiment, in behalf of Protestant thought in a
particular age, of making Kabbalist teaching useful in the explanation of the scriptures, the authority of which having overcome the authority of an Infallible Church had yet to assert

itself against individual intuitions and subjective interpretations given by individual minds.

When we compare Rittangel with his fellow-disputant something more than a mere contrast of personalities appears to be involved. The letters constitute a most entertaining example of Jewish-Christian debate. The Jew is obviously not disposed to undertake a long discussion. He would settle the matter of the interpretation of the Shiloh-passage rather by interview and conversation than by writing. He may have been ready enough with his tongue in word of mouth encounters with his opponent alone or in an audience of a small group, and his opponent may have been quicker and subtler with the pen than in verbal discussion. The latter tells us why he insisted on the correspondence being conducted in writing. Besides the reasons which he gives, one can well understand how long quotations from Simeon ben Jochai could hardly be repeated in the course of conversation. That mode of communication was hardly fitting for the abstruse thought of the Abraham of the *Book of Formation*. The Jew seems to have been a peace-loving man to whom argument was not congenial. His letters are woven through and through with scripture passages and he shews a certain skill in employing biblical language as a vehicle of mild invective and rebuke. A less pious man would have taken his terms of abuse from other sources. Why the patrons of the controversy chose him as controversialist it is difficult to conjecture. He was a Spanish Jew—it would seem, a wealthy man—and possibly he was a leading person in the Sephardic community of the town.

But the correspondence of Rittangel and the Jew of Amsterdam reveals more than the lighter side of debate. The latter has a view of the nature of exegesis which is different from that which is allowed or entertained by his partner in the controversy. Rittangel summons all his authorities to speak, however variously they may speak, in favour of *one* interpretation of the Shiloh passage, Gen. 49.10 (R.V. The sceptre shall not depart from Judah, nor the ruler's staff from between his feet, until Shiloh come, etc.). He proceeds upon the proper assumption that the author of the biblical passage had the intention of expressing by it one definite thought, or, if more than one thought, at least thoughts which were consistent and coherent with one another, and that the purpose of exegesis was to set forth the original idea of the author's mind. The Jew on the other hand gives two different explanations of the word which in the English versions of Gen. 49.10 is rendered *sceptre*, and he justifies the giving of a variety of interpretations of Bible texts on the ground that though some explanations of texts may be wiser, fitter and better than others, all explanations given may be in their degree acceptable. In the Word of God, even in one verse, there are many facets of truth. Indeed, it used to be the practice, he points out, that anyone who, in the discussion of Bible passages, gave a new interpretation or teaching that seemed to his listeners to discover a new vein of truth or ray of light was congratulated with joy and kissed. The only interpretation which the Jew will not hear of is present to the minds of both disputants but not set forth in as many words, namely that the Christian Messiah is Shiloh whose kingdom will succeed the old kingdom of Judah, the new Covenant succeeding the old.

The procedure of Rittangel's correspondent in regard to the biblical passage, the meaning of which is debated, corresponds entirely to the method of exegesis adopted by the *Midrashim*, that class of Rabbinic literature which, on the basis of the Bible text, gives homiletic (*haggadic*) or juristic (*halakic*) interpretations. We have seen (see above) that the Zohar itself is a *Midrash* on the Pentateuch. Now although the Jew appears to have had little more than a hearsay acquaintance with the Zohar and seems to have had no leanings towards the mystic movement among his people, in his idea of the inspiration of scripture he is nearer to the spirit of the *Midrashim* and even of the Zohar than is Rittangel, the enthusiastic admirer of Simeon ben Jochai. The Zohar seeking to reveal the hidden meanings of the Biblical narratives revels in variant and not always consistent interpretations and 'other explanations'. For example, commenting upon the text 'And it repented the Lord that he had made man on the earth and it grieved him at his heart' (Gen. 6.6) the Zohar offers three explanations of the word *repented* as given by three teachers; *repented* in the sense (used in Exod. 32.14) of *change of mind*; in the sense of *be grieved about*; and in the sense of *was consoled* or *comforted Himself*. The older *Midrash* on Genesis (Bereshith Rabbah) offers on the same verse much the same definitions as the Zohar but in a less extended form. It will be seen at once that the second and third meanings of the word explained are not consistent. But expositions of scripture that were aware of hidden meanings in the sacred book and held that even the very consonants that formed the words were invested with a divine power and sacred mission (cf. Men. 29b) could not be exclusive or niggardly in their interpretations. Nor did one need to be a Kabbalist to share this view, though a mystical religious outlook would certainly encourage and promote it. Even the Talmud tells us in regard to a certain Halakah (juristic decision) that when the schools of Shammai and Hillel had disputed for three years about it, each giving a different opinion in regard to its form, a Voice from heaven announced: 'The words of both are the words of the living God' (Erub. 13b).

Bension ('The Zohar in Moslem and Christian Spain') writing of the Jews of Spain before and after their exile from that country says that tolerance is the Sephardic Jews' chief charm (p. 6). He speaks of their love of learning and their readiness to harmonize the claims of science and religion as marking the Spanish period. One incident he mentions as being memorable because fraught with evil consequence, namely the appointment of the Askenazi Talmudic scholar Asheri as Rabbi of the community of Toledo. The old tolerance was now banished from the city. The conflict between science and religion was revived. Authoritarian orthodoxy fortified itself with punishments and the ban. Though nothing of this conflict appears in the correspondence on the subject of Genesis 49 yet the tempcramental difference between Rittangel and his correspondent and between the Rabbi and his flock is analogous. Though it is Rittangel who is the Kabbalist, yet the Jew of Amsterdam who has forgotten or discarded the Zohar, the mystical Bible which in the thirteenth century came to fruition in the Spain of his ancestors, exhibits in large measure the tolerant spirit which that book, among his forefathers in the Peninsula, did much to foster. It is true that there is a limit to tolerance in matters of exegesis. It is also true that tolerance may be based on scepticism or lack of conviction. It is enough for us here to shew, concerned as we are with the letters as personal documents, that Rittangel's amusing, foolish and childish outburst against Spanish Jews, while inexcusable, is not so irrelevant as it might appear.

The subject of the interpretation of Scripture, which we have considered in connection with the Jew of the correspondence and the Midrashic writings, opens up the wider issue of the views prevalent in Judaism and Protestant Christianity concerning the inspiration of the Scriptures, that is of the Old Testament scriptures which are the common property of both faiths. In spite of the position taken by orthodox Judaism that both the written Law (the Pentateuch) and the oral Law, that is, the Law which afterwards came to be codified in the Mishna (*c.* A.D. 200), were given to Moses at Sinai and are complete and unalterable for all time, there has resided within Judaism an effective corrective which mitigates this orthodox mechanical theory of inspiration. This agent has been the Midrashim whose free and liberal exegetic method has made room for development of thought throughout the ages. The character of the Midrashim is thus described by Zunz (quoted by E. Levine, *Judaism*, p. 44): 'The value of Midrashic literature lay not on literal interpretation and in natural hermeneutics, but in the application of scripture to contemporary views and needs. . . . This method of free exegesis was manifested in many ways; the obvious sense of the biblical passage was followed; or the inner meaning of the text, to the exclusion of the literal sense, was considered; or recourse was had to the traditional agada. But this liberty wished neither to falsify Scripture nor to deprive it of its natural sense, for its object was the free expression of thought and not the formulation of a binding Law.' Since the other books of the Old Testament were regarded as of a lesser degree of holiness than the Pentateuch it is obvious that the Jewish and the Protestant Christian views of the inspiration of the Old Testament have never coincided. The orthodox Jewish mechanical theory of inspiration extends only to the first five books of scripture and even here, due to the Midrashic freedom in interpretation, a wide liberty of discussion exists in all matters outside the area of Halakah (juristic decisions) and on all subjects apart from the belief in the unity of God, His supreme goodness and power and His moral government of the world. Dr K. Kohler (*Jewish Theology*, p. 14) who treats very fully of this freedom says that 'as a safeguard against arbitrary individualism there was the principle of loyalty and proper regard for tradition', a sense of 'historical continuity'. The fear of the consequences that might arise from the private intuitions of

individual souls has no doubt always been the cause of the
ascription of inerrancy to sacred texts. There is much that is
fanciful and even fantastic in Midrashic exegesis, but Midrash
saved Judaism from a greater peril than is constituted by an
exegesis of this kind, through mitigating or rendering innocuous
the primitive and semi-magical notions of the Divine activity
which are in the background of the doctrine of verbal inspiration.

It has been stated (see A. Miller, *The Problem of Theology in
Modern Life and Thought*, p. 60) that, although Protestantism in
its historic manifestation has given, at times, to scripture the
low and narrow estimate of which we have been speaking, 'in
all the great Confessions of the Reformation the authority of
Holy Scripture was placed on an absolutely sound basis'. In
behalf of this statement the Westminster Confession (ch. I, § v)
is cited, especially the paragraph where it is said that while by
its own qualities Scripture doth abundantly evidence itself to
be the word of God 'yet, notwithstanding, our full persuasion
and assurance of the infallible truth and divine authority thereof
is from the inward work of the Holy Spirit, bearing witness by
and with the Word in our hearts'. The reference to the testimony of the Holy Spirit certainly appears to be safeguarding
against any extreme and narrow teaching concerning Scripture,
but it cannot be said to make the position clear or to place the
authority of scripture on a sound basis. The sentence in which
the words concerning the Holy Spirit occur in the Confession
takes away at once what the mention of the Holy Spirit seemed
to be about to bestow; there remains only a statement that the
Holy Spirit will corroborate man's persuasion and assurance of
the infallible truth and divine authority of scripture. The words
of the Confession here are a dictate to the Holy Spirit who cannot be dictated to and who when 'bearing witness by and with
the Word in our hearts' is very far from affirming the infallible
truth of certain parts of scripture, or the wholeness of certain
truths of scripture or the divine authority for much that is in
scripture. It is because the Holy Spirit refuses to do this that
there have arisen those inner conflicts in the souls of men which
G. A. Smith (*Modern Criticism*, etc., p. 28) speaks of as resulting
in disasters 'innumerably repeated'. When, further on, the
Westminster Confession (ch. I, § x) states that the supreme
Judge in all religious controversies is 'the Holy Spirit speaking

in the scripture', this hardly makes amends for having before-hand placed the testimony of the Holy Spirit in an almost sub-ordinate position by the declaration that 'our full persuasion and assurance of the infallible truth' of scripture is 'from the inward work of the Holy Spirit'. Additional evidence, apart from that given in the Westminster Confession itself, that the Confession did not, as has been alleged, 'place the authority of scripture on an absolutely sound basis' is that Protestantism appears never to have been restrained by the Confession from accepting the narrow verbal inspiration doctrine. In fact (ch. I, § III) the Confession directly encourages such a view by dis-tinguishing the Apocryphal books from the scriptures by calling the former *human writings*. That no other distinction than this is offered is significant.

Defenders of the Protestant tradition regarding scripture resent it being said that the Reformers placed the Bible as an infallible Book over against the infallible Church which they abjured. But nevertheless the fact that the elaborated and rigid form of the mechanical theory of inspiration so speedily ap-peared and 'is characteristic of the scholastic theology of the seventeenth century' (Paterson, *Rule of Faith*, 1932, p. 64) has to be explained. The Reformers distinguished between the word of God which is 'contained' in the Scriptures and the Scriptures in which it is contained, but it was not said how the word of God is contained in scripture, that is, whether the doctrinal and ethical element is to be separated from matter of a narrative sort which has no such bearing, or whether strata of religious truth have to be distinguished, or whether there is a central core of truth and teaching which has to be distinguished from the rest, or whether the 'letter' or husk is discernible from the spirit of truth which it enshrines. Luther exhibited by his criticism of the biblical books and of the narratives therein a freedom of literary and moral judgment. But if the Reformers' position had been clear and unambiguous, Protestantism of the very next century would not have lapsed into the doctrine of verbal inspiration, elaborating the same with the result that Protestant history revealed the consequences. T. M. Lindsay in his *History of the Reformation* (Internat. Theol. Lib., 1907, Vol. I, p. 464) says in describing the Reformation religious principles: 'The authoritative character and infallibility belong really and primarily to the word of God, and only secondarily to the Scriptures—to Scripture only because it is the record which contains, presents, or conveys the word of God. . . . The Reformers and the Confessions of the Reformation do not recognize any infallibility or divine authority which is otherwise apprehended than by faith. If this be so, the infallibility is of quite another kind from that described by mediaeval theologians or modern Roman Catholics, and it is also very different from what many modern Protestants attribute to the scriptures when they do not distinguish them from the word of God.' A reader of these sentences may reasonably conclude that the Reformation position as so described would necessarily lead to its being misunderstood by the modern Protestants to whom reference is made and that such a description is not without that casuistry which these Protestants must also employ in the interests of their doctrine. The idea of an infallibility of a secondary sort —'only secondarily'—belonging to Scripture cannot be entertained by anyone desirous of avoiding confusion, and explains perfectly the confusion and uncertainty which it wrought.

In Judaism, the influence of the Midrashim, which in their interpretation cf scripture admitted (see Zunz, in Levine, op. cit. above) an inner meaning beside the literal meaning and the traditional homilletic exposition, facilitated the overcoming of difficulties which were presented to man's reason and conscience by the acceptance of the authority of scripture. This manifold interpretation of scripture was in its origin a recognition that there were such difficulties. In the correspondence of Rittangel and the Jew of Amsterdam, documents of the same decade to which the Protestant Westminster Confession, as ratified, belongs, one of the writers is a Christian Kabbalist who believes that the new found treasure of mystic teaching and interpretation may be employed, with advantage, in the explanation of scripture, while the other writer is a Jew who is apparently long accustomed to applying the Midrashic method to the sacred text. In the early Church the Midrashic and the mystical methods of interpretation had been in use. Origen (Hom. V. on Leviticus) says: 'Analogous to body, soul and spirit in man there is a threefold sense of scripture—the historical (literal), the moral and the mystical.' It is clear from Origen's thought in this connection (cf. *Princ.* iv.i.xi.) that the development of a

threefold method of scriptural exegesis served as a door of escape
from the awkwardness occasioned to reason and feeling by the
literal meaning and actual intention of many scriptural passages.
It was a method which successfully established the authority of
scripture while allowing freedom and development of thought,
as Judaism also shows.

Protestantism did not follow the system of interpretation
known to Origen and the early Church, nor the fourfold scheme
(literal, moral, allegorical and anagogic) of the mediaeval
Church. Rather, through declining to accept the temptation of
adopting the method of free exegesis, it inevitably exposed itself
to the danger which arose in what has been described as the
doctrine of verbal inspiration. In speaking of 'the sense of any
scripture', that is the meaning of any passage of scripture, the
Confession (ch. I, § ix) says that it, namely the sense, is *not
manifold but one*, that unclear passages are to be explained in the
light of other passages of scripture which are clearer and that
while all things in scriptures are not plain, even the unlearned
can attain to a sufficient understanding of them (ch. I, § vii).
The conclusion that God's word to mankind lay in the plain
meaning of scripture, despite the problems that such a conclusion had raised and was still to raise, was at least less fraught
with evil consequences than was the affirming of a manifold
mode of interpretation. For such a mode may afford temporary
relief but in the end, in an enlightened age, would lead, if
generally adopted, to the disintegration of scripture and the
undermining of its authority, more rapidly than could ever be
the case through individuals applying dogmatic or arbitrary
judgments in their scriptural expositions.

In the recognition of the importance of the knowledge of the
written Word for *all men*, not only for scholars, by the setting and
the answering of the question how that Word was to be interpreted, by the beginning of criticism in regard to the trust-
worthiness of traditions that had come down through Church
and Synagogue, the Reformation made the way clear for the
accumulation of more knowledge of the Old Testament. The
Humanists (in particular Reuchlin 1455-1522) had drawn attention to the importance of the Hebrew language in equipping
the student for the study of the scriptures. Translations of the
scriptures into the vernaculars appeared. Old Testament Science

was born but was a long time in coming to manhood. Its task was necessarily a hard and slow one. The way was often beset and obstructed by the children of the Reformation themselves through their crude notions of inspiration and infallibility. Rittangel the Kabbalist and scholar still stands only on the threshold of Old Testament scholarship. Throughout the next two centuries and a half the real discovery of the Old Testament is gradually made. A few of the steps toward this may be roughly indicated. H. G. Witter (1711) of Hildesheim, a fore-runner of the French physician Jean Astruc (1733) the so-called father of Pentateuch-criticism, perceived that different sources in the books of Moses were disclosed through the different names given by them to the deity; Eichhorn (1780) who saw that Isaiah, chapter 40 f was a different book from the rest of the book of that name has been called the pioneer of the criticism of the prophetic writings; De Wette (1805) who identified the Book of Deuteronomy with the book discovered in the reign of Josiah (622 B.C.); Julius Wellhausen (the author of *The Prolego-mena to the History of Israel*, Berlin, 1878; English ed. 1885; *The Composition of the Hexateuch*, 1876, 3rd ed., 1899) whose view of the history and growth of the Pentateuch is the general working hypothesis of modern scholars; William Robertson Smith (*The Religion of the Semites*, 1889, 3rd ed., 1927, with notes, etc., by S.A. Cook) regarded as the founder of the modern Comparative Study of Religion, and even, as Cook says, of the Science and Theory of Religion—these scholars sufficiently represent the stages on the way to what is called the historical-critical method of the interpretation of the Old Testament. Nor is it inappro-priate or presumptuous to speak of Old Testament *Science* for the literature, the religion and people of Israel are here studied with the same methods as would be applied to other books and subjects. 'Old Testament Science justly claims to be a fully qualified member of the circle of historical sciences' (H. Gunkel, *What Remains of the Old Testament*, p. 19). And if its character as such is in large measure owing to the initial advance made by Humanists and Reformers, it has repaid the efforts of the latter abundantly by answering some of the difficulties which arose out of the conceptions of inspiration and authority, by making it no longer a matter of prime necessity to use these conceptions as terms of definition. The knowledge acquired by Old Testament study of the history, teaching and chronology of the books, the light it sheds upon the history of the religion of Israel, its growth and content, upon the background of this religion, upon the influences which affected it from outside, upon the theological ideas developed throughout the centuries, make clear what the religious values of the Old Testament are. The measure of the certainty with which these values are made clear to the mind and received as values is the measure of the *authority* they possess. 'What we call Inspiration and Revelation depend on the receptivity and response of men and of their age' (Stanley Cook, *An Introduction to the Bible*, p. 184).

The description of the Old Testament as the word of God is not a description that can be held only by those who hold the mechanical theory of inspiration. Robertson Smith who was assailed by those who held this doctrine frequently referred to the Old Testament as of Divine origin (cf. G. A. Smith, op. cit., p. 115). The propriety of our calling the book 'holy' does not stand or fall with the claim that it possesses perfection and infallibility. Hermann Gunkel, who had the finest feeling for the beauty of the Old Testament literature and the deepest insight into its religious truth, points to that aspect of the revelation of the Divine in which man sees not a finished achievement but a picture of struggling growth. He writes: 'The mind that has undergone historical training sees not only beautiful incidents —he sees the History. To him it is clear that in every human effort and attainment there is and must be both "great" and "small", the sublime beside the ordinary. The inferior element does not repel the historian; indeed, he loves history because, as a faithful picture of human nature, it contains, and must contain, these features.' (op. cit., p. 55.) The Old Testament has its manifest imperfections but in the light of history, of which God is both Lord and Interpreter, the book would not be *improved* by their removal. Both Jew and Christian have defended sacred scripture in whole or in part as being perfect, but the former, trained by the Haggadic interpretation of the text, was anciently aware that the truth about scripture had to be otherwise expressed. It therefore represents God as saying to His people: 'Not I in My higher realm, but you with your human needs fix the form, the measure, the time and the mode of expression for that which is divine.'

Old Testament study is prolific in the discovering of subjects of investigation for it covers many centuries of the development of religious thought. Not all the questions as to the meaning of scripture passages can be answered with certainty by the method above described. There is still, for example, a number of competing opinions on the meaning of the Shiloh-passage in Genesis and of the Almah-passage in Isa. 7.14 f, the virgin-birth of the Isaianic Messiah being upheld even to-day by Professor Procksch in his *Kommentar zum Alten Testament* (1930 ed., Sellin). But the application of the historical-critical method of interpretation has the effect of limiting the number of arguments offered in regard to the meaning of a debatable passage and of distinguishing among them the more probable and defensible, from the point of view of language, of history, of history of religion and of chronology.

Additional Note on Gen. 49.10

See the notes given under Stanza VIII of the Zikron.

In addition attention should be paid to the following renderings of Gen. 49.10:

The Greek version (LXX B): 'A prince (archon) shall not fail from Judah, nor a ruler from his thighs, till that which is laid up for him come; and he shall be the expectation of the nations.' This presupposes that this version read instead of *Shilo*, the word *Shello*, lit. = 'that which is his', or 'what things belong to him'. Some MSS of the Greek version read 'until he come for whom it is laid up'.

The Vulgate: *donec veniat qui mittendus est* (until he come who is to be sent). Cf. *shalach* (send) in Heb.

The English renderings of the Targums are contained in the letters.

Moffat's translation:

> The sceptre never passes from Judah,
> nor ever the Staff of sway,
> till he comes into his own
> and makes the clans obey.

Gunkel's translation:

> Nicht weicht das Szepter von Juda
> noch der Stab zwischen seinen Füssen;
> bevor der Geruhige kommt,
> dem die Völker gehorchen.

H

Gunkel (cf. Göttinger Handkommentar zum Alten Testament) reads instead of *Shiloh* the word *Shalev* = peaceful or prosperous one, the one at ease, as name of the prince of peace. Gunkel takes *ad ki* (R.V. *until*) as = *before* and adds: '*ad ki* does not mean that Judah's rule ceases with the Messiah's advent, but that then it is right firmly established. Cf. Ps. 112.8.'

The Revised Version (with transliterated Hebrew words in brackets): 'The sceptre (*shebet*) shall not depart (*lo' jasur*) from Judah, nor the ruler's staff (*u-mehoqeq*) from between his feet, until (*ad ki*) Shiloh come (*jabo' Shiloh*); and unto him shall the obedience (*jiqqehath*) of the peoples be.'

See also Kittel's *Biblia Hebraica*, 3rd ed., ad loc., and Spurrell's *Notes on the Hebrew Text of Genesis*, Oxford, 1896.

THE LETTERS

translated from the Hebrew text
in Wagenseil's *Tela Ignea Satanae*, pp. 328-373

CHAPTER VII

RITTANGEL

LETTER No. 1[1]

MY DEAR FRIEND,

May the Lord preserve you from all ill, from every adversary and misfortune and may He let no plague befall your dwelling. I have taken note of your arguments upon the verse, Gen. 49.10: '*The sceptre shall not depart from Judah, etc.*' And because I am bound by the bonds of love and truth to defend the words of the Law of our Lord which was given by Moses, the man of God, I have spared no effort in the examination of the authentic text of scripture, as it is witnessed to by all the interpreters, who, for many centuries, even millennia, have exerted their powers to give trustworthy interpretations. These expositors have stood, for ages now, as men of repute, men of good standing, of absolute and genuine sincerity (1). But compared with the opinion of Jews in general and as must be evident to any person competent to judge, your opinion, standpoint and arguments run counter to those of these men, since indeed not a single one of them agrees with you in interpreting this verse in Genesis in the way you explain it.

As you will observe on page 53, column 2 (2), the Targum [Onkelos] (3) on the above-mentioned verse explains as follows: '*Dominion shall be in the beginning; and in the end a king of the house of Judah shall become great etc.*' Then, after this, the same Targum continues: '*He who exercises dominion shall not pass away from the house of Judah, nor the scribe from his children's children for ever, until the Messiah come, whose is the kingdom, and whom the peoples shall obey.*

Next, Ibn Ezra (4) who interprets thus: 'The sceptre shall not depart from Judah (nor the mehoqeq [A.V. a lawgiver; R.V. the ruler's staff] from between his feet, until Shiloh come).

---

[1] See Appendix A 'Notes on the Letters'.

This means that the sceptre of greatness shall not depart from [*the tribe*]
*of Judah until David come who is the beginning of the Kingdom of
Judah.* Nor the meḥoqeq—*that is the scribe who inscribes* (*jaḥoq*)
ordinances in a book. And the significance of the words from between
his feet *is that so was the custom of every scribe to sit between the feet
of the prince.*'

Rashi's (5) exposition is: 'The sceptre shall not depart from
Judah—*This signifies: from the time of David and onwards thereafter*
[*i.e. even after the house of David ceases to reign*]. *For this refers to the
Chiefs of the exile in Babylon* (6) *who ruled over the people with the
shebet* (=*rod or sceptre*) *having been appointed by the government.* Nor
the meḥoqeq from between his feet—*This refers to the scholars of
the Law, the princes of the land of Israel.* Until Shiloh come *means
until the king Messiah will come, whose will be the kingdom. Thus
also does the Targum Onkelos render it. A Midrashic interpretation is:
Shiloh is the same as shai lo = a present unto him—as it is said in Psalm
76.12: Let all . . . bring presents* (*shai*) *unto him that ought to be
feared.* And unto him shall the jiqqehath [R.V. obedience] of
the peoples be. *This word means the gathering* (7), *namely, of the
peoples, a sense which accords with the words of Isaiah 11.10: Unto
him shall the nations seek.*' Thus far Rashi. And be it that I have
found grace in your eyes, do not refrain from returning me a
frank reply. For, for this reason have I come, through the
transaction of these letters, into the presence of your excellency,
that you may satisfy my hunger and satiate my thirsty soul with
the dew-drops of your response. Thereby you will bring healing
to him who is affectionately disposed to you, by letting him see
a letter of reply, showing your own handwriting (8). And I,
on my part, am prepared so far as possible to bring my mind
into conformity with the verity of the Law of the Lord our God,
to explore its depth (9), to probe it and its thought, uprightly
in pursuit of the exact meaning. Therewith I bring what I have
said to a close. Only gladness and joy rest upon you and upon
all your family and those who come under the shadow of your
roof. Written in speed with a metal pen (10).

A Jew of Amsterdam (Letter No. 1)

My Dear Sir,

Thanks be to the bounty of your excellency for all the honour
you have done me by writing me. Although your name has not

been disclosed to me, may a thousand greetings convey to you from me my earnest desire for your welfare. Your voice indeed I have heard through your epistles (11); and your words read as here cited:

'I have spared no effort in the examination of the true intention of scripture (12) according to what all the interpreters have said, who for many centuries, even millennia, have exerted their powers to give trustworthy interpretations. These expositors have stood for ages now, as men of repute, men of good standing, of absolute and genuine sincerity. But compared with the opinion of Jews in general and as must be evident to any person competent to judge, your opinion, standpoint and arguments run counter to those of these men, since indeed not a single one of them agrees with you in interpreting this verse in Genesis in the way you explain it. As you will observe on page 53, column 2, the Targum [Onkelos] on the above-mentioned verse explains as follows, etc.'

Among the interpreters whose names are cited (13) in your highly esteemed letter you mention Rashi and Ibn Ezra, and also what our Ḥakamim [Wise, sages] have said in the Midrash Aggadah (14). To sum up, your view is that these men who are regarded by us as authorities all explain the word *shebet* [= sceptre, rod, staff,] in the verse under consideration, in the sense of rule and kingdom. Now, although, of the interpretations which I gave with stringent brevity or merely indicated, one of them was after the analogy (15) of chastisement and suffering, the other interpretation which I offered, as you may observe, had regard to the idea of greatness and sovereignty, as my words will testify and shew if they be studied closely. Furthermore this latter interpretation not only does not run counter to the writers which you have mentioned but is itself taken from Onkelos the Targumist, some of whose words your excellency adduces but not them all. For since Onkelos paraphrases thus: 'He who exercises dominion shall not pass away from the house of Judah, nor the scribe from his children's children *for ever* (16) (Aramaic = '*ad* '*alma*)' he gives the same sense to the word *ad* of Gen. 49.10 as is given to that word in Ps. 132.14 where we read: 'This is my resting place *for ever* (Heb. = '*ade* '*ad*)', and the meaning of the verse in Gen. 49 is that the kingdom will not *ever* have ceased when (17) the Messiah will come. So that, as I have

said, one of the interpretations which I offered is actually taken
from Onkelos. Rabbi Bechai (18) also, in the name of his
teacher of blessed memory, offered it; and this was the view of
our honoured Ḥakamim as well. Wherefore, if this be so, I have
not said anything opposed to that interpretation of the passage
which is given by the expositors (19) whom you cite. But on
the contrary the position is rather this: What you have said is
what some of these expositors have said, and what all of them
have said is in agreement with what I have said in previous
exposition (20).

In regard to the second interpretation, this was given by my
esteemed master and teacher of blessed memory who was a man
of distinction and of wide learning, as was apparent to all who
had knowledge of him, though he himself considered his own
abilities as small. I call heaven and earth to witness that I am
speaking with all my heart and soul, when I say that in spite of
all that the above-named interpreters and the rest have said, I
regard everything that is consistent with truth and righteousness as being wholly a gift of divine knowledge. Nevertheless
among things that are good there appear that which is good
and that which is better; and accordingly it seems to me that
that interpretation which was given by my teacher, who was
my own father, is the sounder exegesis (21) in as much as it is
in agreement with the opinion of both the earlier and the later
writers, as my father himself said. But leaving aside the fact
that this interpretation does not run counter to the other interpretations, it readily allows (22) that in Gen. 49.10 the purpose
of the words 'ad ki is to define a limit of time, in the manner in
which they do in Gen. 41.49 where it is said: '(And Joseph laid
up corn) . . . until (Heb. 'ad ki) he left numbering (23).'

As Ps. 19.8 says: 'the law of the Lord is perfect . . . the
testimony of the Lord is sure' and there is evidence to prove that
the interpretation that was [first] mentioned is in accordance
with the literal sense of scripture. For you can take shebet in its
real and original significance [of rod] side by side with matṭeh
(= rod), which a man may use to chastise and discipline his son,
or his servant, or for the leading and governing of a people.
Hence sometimes the word chastisement [chasten] appears in
such a connection as 2 Sam. 7.14: 'I will chasten him with the
shebet [R.V. rod] of men', an example which I brought as proof

in my letter. Sometimes too the word *shebet* appears for the purpose of describing sovereignty and kingdom, as in Isa. 14.5: 'The *shebet* [R.V. *sceptre*] of the rulers.' Under these circumstances it is, that whenever the original sense of *shebet* is given, it coheres with the views of the earlier and later expositors as I have stated and as may be seen explained at length in the commentary of my father, my teacher. From this book it becomes apparent that I have been unduly induced, out of regard for your excellency, to hold to the side-issues of the main question upon which you have entered. This then is what I have seen fit briefly to bring to your attention. And if there be any doubtful or difficult matter remaining I shall discuss it by word of mouth, with demonstration of proof and not in riddles. Ever observant of your commands, I incline my ear in attention to your voice—Written on 9th Nisan 5402 [= 1642].

Rittangel (Letter No. 2)

To the man for whom this epistle is written with all my heart I say: may honour dwell in his sanctuary (24). Pure and upright may his actions be. May his wisdom remain with him. May the Lord bless his substance, to exalt and make him great, with riches and honour (25) in his left hand. Because he has deemed me worthy to see a letter, the work of his own fingers, may God preserve him and grant him a long and happy life.

I have received the letter you have composed in defence of your views and from it I perceive the great efforts you make to justify certain interpretations of Gen. 49.10: 'The sceptre shall not depart from Judah, etc.' In case this would be so, I pointed out to you, with clear and plain reasoning, in my first letter, the gross errors and inconsistencies (26) which were incidental to and grew out of your exegesis. Further I shewed that of all your Ḥakamim who were expressly named—each man by his banner (27), with signs and signals, stationed at the head of their hosts to set out to do battle for their Law—not a single one of them attempted to set his foot to the crooked and tortuous path which you have chosen, nor dared to lend the power of his intelligence to explain and interpret the verse referred to in the manner in which you have interpreted and explained it. But when I saw that the plague of false judgment continued as before (28) and that you still obstinately held to your opinion,

alleging that your opinion and the opinion of your father was
the same as that held by Onkelos and all the commentators
who were cited in my first letter, then, while combining friend-
ship with the love of holiness, I bestirred the thoughts of my
bosom and girt my loins to chastise you for your dreamings and
futile arguings. I am very astonished that you have assailed
Onkelos, a man who was skilled in interpreting accurately, in
accordance with the intention of holy writ, and in an upright
and trustworthy manner. I am amazed also that you gainsay
the other commentators and from their chaste and perspicuous
statements bring to birth false conclusions, false reasonings and
ill-founded premises which are wrong and cannot possibly be
represented as right, unless one enters into a conspiracy against
humanity to rank these expositors with infidels. You have
struck them upon their pates, advancing evidence that is utterly
worthless. Even the opinion of your father you have introduced
to place it in a false light. And with how much idle protracted
talk you have sought to establish your own view! Surely you
know how to bridle your tongue and not to pervert the reliable
findings of knowledge or to turn light into darkness! It is from
these features of your letter that I perceive that you no longer
have the power of expressing a rational religious belief, for in
all that you say there is no proof, or even semblance of such, to
shew that your view is the same as that of Onkelos and all the
other commentators who were mentioned in my first letter.
And now from your own statements I shall demonstrate to you
that the contrary is the case, namely, that your view is not theirs.

In the first place it must be evident that all these commentators explain the word *shebet* in the above-named verse as
intending sovereignty and rule and this explanation is agreed
on by them, settled, established and firmly based. Whoever
then impugns the truth of their doctrine on this point denies the
substance of the faith and his end is Sheol, the bottom of the pit,
eternal perdition, death and the fire of Gehenna.

But now I shall shew you briefly that not even one of the
commentators explains the Genesis passage according to the
interpretation which you first submit, namely, that the word
shebet takes here the sense of chastisement and affliction; also
that not one of them explains in accordance with the view you
submit in the second place, that the word *'ad* in this passage has

the meaning of *eternity* (or *for ever*). In regard to the former of these two interpretations it is clear and manifest that none of the commentators mentions it by devoting to it even so much as a vowel-point, far less a single letter of the alphabet, as you may observe from my letter where all is more fully set forth. 'The *shebet* shall not depart from Judah' was paraphrased by Onkelos as meaning: *He who exercises dominion shall not pass away from the house of Judah,* and explained by Ibn Ezra as meaning: *The* shebet *(sceptre) of greatness (eminence) shall not depart from Judah.* Also when Rashi, commenting on the same text, says: *'Thus also does the Targum Onkelos render it',* he is saying in effect that Onkelos' view of the meaning of the text is the same as his own view which as you will observe is as follows: 'The *shebet* shall not depart from Judah—this signifies: *from the time of David and onwards thereafter. For this refers to the Chiefs of the exile in Babylon who ruled over the people with the shebet* [rod or sceptre] *having been appointed by the government, etc.*' The view of the Midrash Aggadah also is in accordance therewith. If what has already been quoted is not sufficient for you, look at what the Jerusalem Targum (29) has to say, namely: *'Kings shall not cease from the house of Judah, nor scribes teaching the law from his children's children until the time that the King Messiah shall come, whose is the kingdom and to whom all the kingdoms of the earth shall be obedient.'* Likewise the Targum of Jonathan (30) ben Uzziel: *'Kings shall not cease, nor rulers, from the house of Judah, nor scribes teaching the law, from his seed, till the time that the king, the Messiah, shall come, the youngest of his sons, and on account of him shall the peoples flow together.'*

Besides these explanations we have that given by the Talmud (31) tractate Sanhedrin (5a): 'The *shebet* shall not depart from Judah—*this refers to the Chiefs of the exile in Babylon who ruled over Israel with the shebet* [rod, sceptre]. Nor the *mehoqeq* [lawgiver] *from between his feet—this refers to the children's children of Hillel, who taught the law publicly.*' Rashi's commentary on this Talmud passage runs thus: '*Shebet means sovereignty—nor the mehoqeq— this denotes a lesser sovereignty of those who ruled the people, for the power and authority to do so was bestowed upon them by the kings of Persia. The children's children of Hillel—this refers to Hillel, who was Prince* [President of the Sanhedrin, an office to which his family is said to have succeeded] *as is said in the tractate Pesachim*

(66a): They then set him (Hillel) at their head and chose him as Prince over them.'

The Tosaphoth (32) also agree that *shebet* signifies sovereignty. Rabbi Hazzekuni (33) says: 'The shebet shall not depart—*that is, from the kingdom of David and onwards, government shall not depart, to be given to another tribe* [shebet Heb. = tribe]; *in the manner that the kingdom of Saul departed, to be given to David.'* And Rabbi Joshua Ibn Schuaib (34) (p. 19, col. 3) writes: '*Thus you will find written in regard to Judah, on the subject of the kingdom and of the Messiah, that the shebet shall not depart from him. Accordingly it has been explained by those of blessed memory that these words refer to the Chiefs of the exile in Babylon who came of the seed of Judah, on the father's side and who ruled over the people.* Nor the meḥoqeq—*this refers to the princes who remained in the land (of Palestine) and were of the seed of David on the mother's side.'* And in the book Rabboth (35) (p. 113, col. 3) we read: 'The *shebet* shall not depart from Judah—*this refers to the throne of the kingdom, for it is said* [Ps. 45.7, R.V. v. 6]: "Thy throne, O God, is for ever and ever a *shebet* [R.V. sceptre] of equity." *To what time do the words* "Nor the meḥoqeq from between his feet" *refer? To the time when that one shall come whose is the kingdom, for it is written* (Isa. 28.3): "With feet shall be trodden down the crown (of pride, the drunkards of Ephraim)" [cf. A.V.]. Until Shiloh come—*this is he whose is* [shello] *the kingdom.* And unto him shall the *jiqqehath* [R.V. obedience] of the peoples be—*This is he who shall blunt* [from Hcb. root qahah] *the teeth of all the peoples, for scripture says* (Mic. 7.16): "They shall lay their hand upon their mouth, their ears shall be deaf." *Another interpretation of the words* "and unto him shall the *jiqqehath* of the peoples be" *is: He to whom the peoples of the world will gather* [cf. Heb. qavah] *for it is said* (in Isa. 11.10): "the root of Jesse, which standeth for an ensign of the peoples, unto him shall the nations seek." ' The opinion of the author of the book Kebod ha-Ḥakamim (fol. 59, col. 1) (36), who brings also the view of the Ḥakam Rabbi Moses ben Nachman (37), is of a like tenor. He writes: 'The *shebet* shall not depart from Judah, *because Jacob bequeathed the kingdom and rule to Judah and blessed him so that the kingdom should not depart from the tribe (shebet) of Judah to go to another of the tribes.'* Further, the author of the book *'Aqedath Jiṣḥaq* (Binding of Isaac) (38) comments: 'The *shebet* shall not depart from Judah nor the meḥoqeq from between his feet—*As those of blessed memory say, these are the Chiefs of the exile in Babylon, the Chiefs of the exile who continued in office throughout the whole time. For this reason Jacob (in Gen. 49.10) [when he blessed Judah] did not say the word king [but shebet and mehoqeq] for it was revealed and foreknown to him that their kings would not remain continually.'*

There now I have brought forward, in addition to those expositors to whom I referred before, explanations given by these Ḥakamim to whom no specific reference was made in my first letter. In all that they say they preserve a literal agreement with those who preceded them, in whose footsteps they follow, and not one of them deviates from the straight path of understanding by interpreting the word *shebet* in Gen. 49.10 in accordance with the view which you set forth as your first interpretation, namely, that *shebet* means affliction and chastisement.

And now I shall exert myself to shew you also that none of the commentators explains the verse, of which we are speaking, as you explain it in the second interpretation presented by you. For you divide the verse into two parts, detaching the word *'ad* [which you render as =*for ever*] from the latter part of the verse and attaching it to the first part, so that the first part of the verse would read thus: 'The *shebet* shall not depart from Judah, nor the *mehoqeq* from between his feet *for ever*.' That is, you give a variant meaning to the word *'ad*, giving it the sense of eternity. No other expositor has done this, but all of them join the word *'ad* to the latter part of the verse, as you may see from all their commentaries. For the Commentators, after interpreting and expounding at length, and as behoves, the first part of the verse [The sceptre . . . his feet], then begin next to interpret *'ad ki jabo shiloh* [R.V. until Shiloh comes], which is the latter part of the verse, separately. And however much these commentators among themselves may vary in the manner of their explanations, they at least do not interpret in accordance with your view, since they do not separate the word *'ad* from the word *ki*, but in regard to the division of the verse they are entirely at one in attaching *'ad* to the latter part of the verse, as you may observe in all the expositions that now follow.

Ibn Ezra comments on the word *'ad* twice, the author of Kebod ha-Ḥakamim as many as five times, and Rabboth twice;

and all of them join the word to the latter part of the verse and do not separate it from the word *ki*. The Jerusalem Targum renders *'ad ki* by *up to the time* (*'ad zeman*) and so also the Targum of Jonathan. And this corresponds to the view of all the other commentators as you may see from the Concordances, where all the meanings of *'ad* are given and where five senses of that word are distinguished as follows. First *'ad*, by itself, without specifying what is signified [i.e. *ad* as conjunction = *until* = *up to the time that* without further reference; and *'ad* as prepositional particle without pronominal suffixes added to signify its reference = *up to, to*]; secondly, *'ad* meaning words or mouth (39); thirdly, *'ad* meaning *eternity* (*for ever*) or *a long time*—but here the concordances differentiate the words of our verse *'ad ki jabo shiloh* from all other passages where *'ad* appears in the sense of *eternity* (*for ever*), in order to indicate that the *'ad* of the verse *'ad ki jabo shiloh* does not have the meaning of *for ever*. Fourthly, the word *'ad* may mean *booty*; and fifthly it may have the significance of *worn or ragged cloths* (40). That, then, is the sum of the whole matter, and what is firm, durable and never can be shaken is the fact that all the authorities cited connect the word *'ad* with *ki jabo shiloh* and that not one of them interprets the *'ad* in the significance of *for ever* but according to the plain sense it bears as in the phrase *'ad hennah*, i.e. *up to* (*till*) *now*. What came into your mind, when you fled for support to renderings made by Onkelos, contending that *'ad* in Gen. 49.10 was to be understood as in Ps. 132.14: 'This is my resting place *for ever* (*'ade 'ad*)', was that Onkelos' Targum renders the *for ever* of this Psalm by its Aramaic equivalent *'ad 'alma*. But here you have gone far astray, for Onkelos' rendering of this Psalm has, for Gen. 49.10, no semblance of relevance, to say nothing of proof, since Onkelos renders the *'ad ki jabo shiloh* of Genesis by *'until* the King (41) Messiah come' and thus his interpretation is the same as that of the other Targums which give to *'ad ki* the meaning of *up to the time that* (*'ad zeman*). Hence you will perceive that Onkelos and the other Targums and all the commentators as well did not explain the *'ad* of our passage in the sense of *for ever*.

As to the word *ki*, Onkelos paraphrased it usually throughout scripture by *d* (*di*) and accordingly you will observe from his words and those of the other Targums that *ki* is rendered by *d* (*di*) in Gen. 49.10—e.g.

Scripture:	'ad	ki	jabo	shiloh
	until (till)	that	(will) come	Shiloh

Onkelos:	'ad	d	jethe	malka (42) meshiha
	till	that	(will) come	the king Messiah
Targ. Jerus:	'ad zeman	d	jethe	malka meshiha
	up to the time	that	(will) come	the king Messiah

Targ. Jonathan	'ad zeman	di	jethe	malka meshiha
	up to the time	that	(will) come	the king Messiah

Moreover in the interpretations of these words of the verse by the other commentators you will not find any changing either of letters, far less words [e.g. by moving 'ad to the first portion of the verse], since essentially in the same sense do all of them interpret. And in respect of the words 'ad 'alma (for ever) which Onkelos employs immediately before 'ad djethe (till he come), the words 'ad 'alma are not his interpretation of 'ad ki (see above) but are an expansion of his own making which does not correspond to anything in the scripture text. For it was his wont to make such expansions (43) as you may observe in many passages of his paraphrase. And if reference be made again to Ps. 132.14, the argument based upon this is altogether valueless for this verse has no similarity at all to Gen. 49.10 since the words 'ad ki do not appear in the verse of the Psalm but 'ade 'ad, the significance of which latter words is plainly 'ad 'alma as also Onkelos honestly and faithfully rendered. But surely the verse to which Gen. 49.10, upon which division of opinion has arisen, is analogous is Gen, 26.13: 'And the man waxed great, and grew more and more until (Scripture—'ad ki: Onk. 'ad di) he became very great (Scripture—gadal meod: Onk. reba lahada)', from which verse it appears what Onkelos rendering of the expression 'ad ki is. For all the Aramaic Paraphrases, as you may see from the two verses cited, render the word ki sometimes by di [e.g. Gen. 26.13 where the word is separate from the following word] and sometimes by the letter d only, in which case they join the d to the word following as, for example, djethe in Gen. 49.10. Finally the whole matter comes to this, namely, that it is not possible to shew by a single logical inference, far less to demonstrate by clear and cogent reasoning from Scripture, Targums or commentators that these writings interpret the words 'ad ki in accordance with your view. And in the event of your affirm-

ing that in Gen. 49.10 you do not propose to separate the word
'ad from the word ki and that these words thus taken together
would have, none the less, the meaning of for ever, then the
latter portion of the verse [from which ki as well as 'ad would
now be taken and be attached to the first portion] would be
bereft of all flavour and fragrance (44) and you would have
destroyed the whole inner structure of the verse from top to
bottom.

The viewpoint which you bring in the name of your father,
and which you describe as your second interpretation of Gen.
49.10, you say was the result of his own meditation and you
extol it above the expositions of all the other commentators.
That is a grave mistake on your part. For as the old proverb of
the Ḥakamim says: 'The man who is still seeking wisdom is
wise but when he thinks that he has attained its perfection he
is a fool." This explanation of yours I read already twelve
years ago in a book entitled Be'er Moshe (The Well of Moses)
(45) in which the difficult sayings of scripture are explained in
German through the medium of Hebrew characters, in order
that these difficult sayings might be understood by women,
boys, girls, maid-servants and grandmothers. Possibly your
father read this explanation there or in the Kebod ha-Ḥakamim
(Honour of the Ḥakamim) for the author of this work also
introduces it in the name of his teacher. However, their reasoning is not without blemish nor is it adequate to shew that this
explanation is the viewpoint of scripture or of any of the ancient
authors, much less of all of them, that is, of both ancient and
later exegetes. Further, you write that I have adduced some of
the words of the commentators who have been mentioned but
not all their words. But you are perfectly well aware that I
cited what was needful to the question under discussion and
their other statements, which were not applicable, I left where
they were. But here is a tangled skein (46), one of the Ḥakam
Rashi's contriving, which I still have to set before you and you
will speedily unravel it. I refer to what he writes on Gen. 24.33
[which says: 'I will not eat until (lit. till if—Heb. 'ad 'im) I have
spoken my words']. Rashi here states: ' . . . (so you will see
that 'im has the meaning of both asher and ki) an example of
the latter usage being (Gen. 49.10) "ad ki jabo shiloh", and
that is what our sages of blessed memory have said: The word

ki is used in four meanings. One of them is *'i* which is the Aramaic for the Hebrew word *'im* [=if i.e. involving a condition].' And now how can you be so foolish as to employ your tongue to offend the Holy Spirit of Him who liveth for ever, by explaining this verse of Gen. 49 in a way so perverse and misleading and in so contradictory senses, alleging that your viewpoint is that of the scriptures themselves.

In your first interpretation you say that the word *shebet* has the sense of chastisement and affliction, that it contains an allusion to the captivity (47) in which you and those of your faith at present are. And in your second interpretation you say the opposite, namely, that the meaning of *shebet* is sovereignty, kingdom and dominion. But now, that chastisement and affliction, that is, servitude, and sovereignty and dominion, which imply kingdom, are direct opposites you will see clearly demonstrated in the *Book of Formation* (48) (*Sepher Jeçira*), Ch. 4, § 1. There we read: 'There are seven twofold expressions (49). The seven letters *b, g, d, k, p, r, t* have customarily two modes of expression (pronunciation). [Corresponding to these letters] life and prosperity, wisdom and wealth, beauty and seed (fruitfulness) and sovereignty have customarily two modes of expression. [In regard to the seven letters the second mode of pronunciation] is represented by *bb, gg, dd, kk, pp, rr, tt*, for there is a soft form [e.g. *b, g, d*, etc.] and a hard form [*bb, gg, dd*, etc.] a strong form [*bb, gg, dd*, etc.] and a weak form [*b, g, d*, etc.] of pronunciation. [These seven letters and the seven conditions of existence] are twofold for they have their counterparts (lit. changes). The counterpart of life is death, the counterpart of prosperity is misfortune, the counterpart of wisdom is foolishness, the counterpart of wealth is poverty, the counterpart of beauty is ugliness, the counterpart of seed is desolation and the counterpart of sovereignty is servitude.' So far the *Book of Formation*. Further, Moses Botarel (50) in his commentary on this book (p. 75, col. 4), says in the name of Rabbi Aaron the great Kabbalist, the head of the school in Babylon: 'These counterparts are called twofold (*kephuloth*) because they are ancillary (51) to the scale (*kaph*) of merit and the scale of demerit, and we find that they have two divergent aspects, the first aspect being that of a mode of goodness indicating the scale of merit, the second aspect being that of a mode

of evil indicating the scale of demerit. In this light they are
ancillary to the concepts of good and evil.' And later on he says:
'In *bb, gg, dd, kk, pp, rr, tt* (52), each expression has a twofold
form, in which one letter represents goodness, the other evil—
that is, the soft and the hard. The mode of goodness which is
the scale of merit is called soft. The mode of evil which is the
scale of demerit is called hard. For the counterpart of prosperity
(*shalom*, peace) is war, etc.' And hence it is as clear as the light
of the sun that sovereignty or kingdom, on the one hand, and,
on the other, servitude, which is the result of chastisement and
suffering, are two opposite things. In these circumstances, the
two interpretations which you bring are opposed the one to the
other; and were you to ask even persons of no erudition they
would, without doubt, testify and declare to you that it is not
possible that two contraries persist in one and the same subject,
in the material world, far less in the mind of the Most High
which is hid from mortals and beyond the power of their intellect to comprehend. For 'out of the mouth of the Most High
proceedeth not evil and good' at the same time [cf. Lam. 3.38].
'God is not a man, that he should lie; neither the son of man,
that he should repent' [Num. 33.19]. And do you not perceive
what a great disgrace it is even for men, who are but flesh and
blood, when they let proceed from their mouths contradictory
accounts in respect of one and the same actual fact? I therefore
admonish you not to speak perversely against God's holy Spirit.
For His seal is truth and in Him is found no changeableness or
contradiction and His words are not as our words.

We [Christians] (53), on our part, interpret the above-named
verse Gen. 49.10 as your own ancient and later Ḥakamim who
lived many centuries, even millennia, ago, interpreted it.
Thereby it is not our view that you [Jews] will not be redeemed.
God forbid! For we await with great joy the day of your redemption, the end of your captivity and the coming of your
salvation. But this will come in a way other than you expect,
namely, by ransom and freedom from the angel of death, to
bring you under the kingdom which enriches the King Messiah
whose kingdom is for ever. This will also be freedom from the
Law which is 'in the letter' (54), that is, from the kings and
powers who rule the Israelite people after the order of the law
of Moses which is 'in the letter'. The lawgivers who are the

I

Ḥakamim, the public teachers of the law of Moses, will cease, since, in the time of the King Messiah, the whole earth will be full of knowledge. For He Himself will break 'the shells' (55), that is, the Law which is 'in the letter' and will bring forth marrow therefrom.

Mark what Rabbi Simeon ben Jochai (56) says in the book of the *Supplements of the Zohar* (Tiqqunē Zohar—Tiqqun 21, fol. 52, col. 2) in his interpretation of our verse Gen. 49.10, '*ad ki jabo shiloh*: 'He [Simeon] said to them: That Serpent with whom you wage warfare, how can you be rescued from him who swallows up and kills not only at the present time but was the very same who killed the first man and all the generations which have come after him! And the [King's] Daughter is on the Tower that flies in the air, and every day proclamation is made in the firmament that whoso kills that Serpent, to him shall be given to wife "the King's Daughter within, whose clothing is inwrought with gold" [Ps. 45.13, see Heb., A.V., R.V.]—which gold signifies the seven days of Creation. And because of this proclamation which is made, how many strong men and how many men armed with shields have gathered in College to do battle with the Serpent on her account and how many shields have been broken in behalf of the King's Daughter!—"And he [Moses] looked this way and that way and he saw that there was no man" [Exod. 2.12]. He saw that none had killed the Serpent (for men waited) until there should come that one concerning whom it is said: "And he looked this way and that way . . . and he smote the Egyptian." The reference is to Shiloh-Moses whose is the inheritance and of whom therefore Scripture says: "Until Shiloh come" (Gen. 49.10). His task assuredly it was to kill the Serpent. "And unto him shall the *jiqqehath* (i.e. obedience, or gathering) of the peoples be"—because he is an Anointed one [cf. 1 Chr. 23.12; Zec. 4.14—lit. son of Jiçhar = son of oil], descended from Qehath (E. V. Kohath). Also he was a son of Amram, which means son of a high people ('am ram) concerning which it is written (1 Chr. 23.17): "but the sons of Rehabiah were many, upwards." Therefore he slew the Serpent and his forces on sea, on land and in the firmament and many were the warriors who along with him waged battle upon the sea. Thus Ps. 104.26 says: "There go the ships", which signifies that they go upon the sea of the Law, for these ships are the eyes of those who reflect upon (or have become enlightened by) the Law. And how many of those ships have been wrecked and perished in the sea, until he came whose is the inheritance (var. lect. until its lord came)! For he cleft the sea of the Law (cf. Exod. 14.16, 21)—And "the horse and his rider hath he thrown into the sea" (Exod. 15.1). This refers to the Serpent and his spouse which is his horse. He [i.e. Shiloh-Moses] brought Israel across the sea that they should not sink in it, as Exod. 15.19 says: "but the children of Israel walked on dry land in the midst of the sea." In the first instance deliverance was effected in the sea of the material world but the deliverance that was to follow was altogether in the sea of the Law. The staff with which he cleft this sea was a reed [pen] because thereby was revealed the *Arm of the Lord* of which Isaiah (53.1) speaks: "And to whom hath the arm of the Lord been revealed?" Whenever the evil Serpent was removed from the sea, the holy Serpent ruled and from that time "therein are things creeping innumerable, living creatures (hajjoth) both small and great" (Ps. 104.52). Ships now voyaged in confidence on the sea, since they do not sink, for behold, the wind of the tempest has been caused to forgo its dominion over the sea of the Law. Since that time "creeping things innumerable are there . . . there go the ships, there is Leviathan whom Thou hast made to sport therein" (104.25-26). Then there was rejoicing among them. As Ps. 48.13 says: "Set your mind upon her *rampart* (lehelah)" but instead of *lehelah*, write *leholah*—set your mind upon the chorus of singers and dancers. Further Ps. 104.27 says: "These wait all upon thee that thou mayest give them their meat in due season", which indicates the seasons of the Law—in accordance with the precept of the Ḥakamim of blessed memory that a man should set apart fixed times for the study of the Law [cf. Sabl. 31a]; for this is the season of the Zaddik (the Righteous).—"That Thou givest unto them, they gather" (Ps. 104.28). This means the manna of which it is said (in Exod. 16.26): "six days ye shall gather it." It is gathered from the domain of the Central Column which comprehends the six lateral grades.—The Leviathan which is above is *Ẓaddik* for he is as a small fish by the shore [or at the bottom, lit. on the rock] of the sea. Later on, Rabbi Simeon added this explanation: The Shekinah which is above is the sea. The Shekinah which is below is the way of a

ship in the *midst* [Heb. *leb*] of the sea. For there are thirty-two
[leb. = 32] divine powers (Elohim) active in the work of creation' [The word *Elohim* (= God) appears thirty-two times in the
account of creation in Gen. 1]. Also in the Supplements of
the Zohar cited above (fol. 53; col. 1) we read that the Leviathan of the sea is *Zaddik*, the culmination of the Central Column.

From these citations it is plain that your Ḥakamim and your
early Fathers were of a different mind and persuasion in regard
both to the substance of belief in the King Messiah and to your
redemption. That is, they believed that the Messiah would
abolish and destroy the ancient Serpent in order to effect the
reconciliation of the human race with the Lord its God, as you
may see from the Targum of Jerusalem (57) on the verse Gen.
3.15: 'It shall bruise thy head.' The Targum says: 'And it shall
be when the sons of the woman consider the law and perform
its instructions they will be prepared to smite thee on thy head
to kill thee; and when the sons of the woman forsake the commandment of the law and perform not its instructions, thou
wilt be ready to wound them in their heel and hurt them.
Nevertheless there shall be medicine for the sons of the woman,
but for thee, Serpent, there shall be no medicine: but it is to be
that for these years there shall be a remedy for the heel in the
days of the King Messiah.' Wherefore I again warn you to forsake and abandon those bewildering views of yours that are so
confused and entangled and to hold by the accredited views of
your early Fathers—those stalwarts who have ever served you
as brazen pillars and as iron ramparts.

Doubtless it is well known to you and clear as sunlight that
many of your later Ḥakamim (58) busied themselves with de-
fining the time and season of your redemption. But some of
them departed from the path of truth and knowledge observed
by the early Ḥakamim and went astray because they adduced
opinions that were alien and false, which denied the coming of
your Messiah and were contrary to the intention of holy writ
and to the opinion of the early writers. And in error themselves,
they led into error others who, following in their steps, became
as blind men groping about in the full light of noon.

You say in your letter that the word *shebet* has two meanings.
I am quite aware of this and, not only so, but that this word
may have many meanings. But the discussion in which we are

here engaged is not about how many aspects of meaning this
word may have, but in what manner it is interpreted in the
verse Gen. 49.10 by all the Ḥakamim, early and later; whether
in fact the word is given by them the significance of chastisement, affliction and servitude or that of sovereignty, dominion
and kingdom? And when finally you write that your two interpretations are in agreement with what the commentators have
written, whose names are indicated in my first letter, I have to
say in short that two contraries cannot possibly be predicated
of one and the same subject. On which account you should bear
in mind that this belief which you profess is highly capable of
effecting your being driven stage by stage to lapse into the
uttermost depth of misery and gloom. For how is it that you
are not afraid of the Most High, the God who tries the hearts
and the reins of men, that you extol to the height of heaven
false opinions which deny the true faith, and abase to the lowest
regions of the earth the opinions of those who ride upon the
heavens, who embrace the everlasting arms, whose words,
gentle and pure, are in agreement with the intention of
scripture?

With reference to what you further say, your statements are
pointless and merit no reply, for they contribute nothing at all
to the subject at present in debate. But this reflection only
would I make, namely, that you have forsaken the law of the
Lord your God and the decisions of all the ancient and the later
Ḥakamim and that the principles of their firm belief have been
renounced by you. Rather, these principles should have served
you as foundations prepared for battlements, as bolts and stout
staples fixed in position securely and for ever immovable.
Awake! Why do you sleep? Take heed, for your own good, to
understand the hidden mysteries of your salvation and the
many things, marvellous and blessed, which are conducive of
eternal welfare. And they will be an ornament upon your neck
and will bring you under the shadow of the Ancient Wisdom
(59) which, for the righteous man, is the chief thing and which
indwells him with power. As Rabbi Simeon ben Jochai testifies in this regard: 'There thou shalt be satisfied with the bread
of Mighty ones and with the spiritual Leviathan (60)—thou,
together with the tribes of Jah (cf. Ps. 122.10) who go up to
judge the high mountains and the hill-summits in behalf of the

sons of the Shekinah (61).' May the Lord take you under the
cover of His wing and keep you and yours from all evil. May
He pour upon you the spirit of His mercy, the spirit of His
knowledge, the spirit of counsel and understanding. May He
enlighten your mind and may He draw over you and all who
come under the shadow of your roof the line of His compassion,
that you do not abhor, refuse and reject the Corner-Stone of
your salvation (62) which comes from the palace of His mercies
—that stone which is without dimension or measure and which
is sunk in the utmost depth of the foundation (Heb. Jesod) of
Salvation and Love. And I also cast myself down in prayer, in
complete prostration upon the ground, before the Most High
God, beseeching Him to bring you to a knowledge of Himself
and into the possession of wealth and happiness and of the
heavenly treasure which faileth not, which the Lord has reserved
for all His saints and prepared for all them that fear Him. As
the languid earth opens its mouth for the latter rain, so am I
expectant of a sincere reply from you and therewith you will
oblige me who am your servant ready to serve you and who
shall be attentive to all your behests.

A JEW OF AMSTERDAM (Letter No. 2)

I had thought that perhaps you would go out for a walk and
that we might catch a glimpse of each other. But there you sat
still 'in the covert of the steep place' (Songs 2.14) (63) and kept
yourself hid. Surely you are afraid to render a reply in person,
for you have again, through the medium of a friend of mine,
sent me a letter—a letter full of 'strong reasons' (Isa. 41.21) (64).
And were it not that I respect the honoured messenger, God
forbid that I should write you an answer. 'For a dream cometh
with a multitude of business; and the voice' of your letter (65)
'with a multitude of words' (cf. Eccles. 5.3) which do not affect
(66) the question under discussion in the least and which, in my
estimation, are worth nothing.

'In the multitude of words there wanteth not transgression'
(Prov. 10.19) and especially in your letter you go beyond the
bounds of propriety and put your tongue to evil service. And
'thou thoughtest that I was altogether such a one as thyself:
but I will reprove thee and set in order before thine eyes' (Ps.
50.21) my judgment of this, your attitude (67), lest I also should

become like you. I shall indeed reply to your arguments, that you be not wise in your own eyes. And don't imagine that you can drive me off 'with a bruised reed' (68), for as when a man dreams 'and behold he eateth; but he awaketh and his soul is empty' (Isa. 29.8) so shall be the multitude of your words when you awake from your slumber.

At first I was remiss in not answering you at once, immediately after I had received your letter, for I delayed in giving it to be copied and to be turned from your script into our script, for yours was not in Hebrew characters but in characters that are foreign. And now, although I have already answered you I write once again, and, unlike you, I shall reply with brevity and in order to the relevant substance (69) of what you say.

You state that none of our Ḥakamim attempted to set his foot to this path which I have taken, which you call crooked and tortuous, or to lend the power of speech and intellect to explain and interpret the verse, 'the *shebet* shall not depart from Judah' in the manner in which I have interpreted it. Further, you write that I said that my opinion, and the opinion of my father of blessed memory, was the same as that held by Onkelos the Targumist. Also you state that I have done violence to the said Onkelos by saying that his interpretation is the same as mine.

Truly, what I am much astonished at is the amazing thing that has befallen your understanding, which is so confused and perverse that, not content with not comprehending my words, you foist upon me false statements which I did not write and which did not enter my mind. For 'that which my lips know they shall speak sincerely' (Job 33.3) and are as the sun in the height of heaven in making matters clear. For I did not assert that my opinion and the opinion of my father was the same as that held by Onkelos, but I said that one of the interpretations which I brought in regard to the aforesaid verse in Genesis was in fact the view of Onkelos, that our teacher Rabbi Bechai also offered it and that our Ḥakamim of blessed memory held the self-same view. This was the purport of the beginning of my letter and of my opening remarks on the subject. It also accords with fact, since in one of the interpretations which I gave I explained the word *shebet* in the sense of greatness and sovereignty and by dominion and kingdom, citing as an example 'the sceptre (*shebet*) of the rulers' [Isa. 14.5]; and I explained the word '*ad* in the sense of eternity, citing as example 'that inhabiteth *eternity*' [Isa. 57.15 *shoken 'ad*] and 'This is my resting place *for ever*' ['*ade 'ad* Ps. 132.14]. This interpretation is the same as that of which our teacher Rabbi Bechai, whom I mentioned, wrote as follows: 'My preceptor Rabbi Solomon explained that the word '*ad* in this passage [Gen. 49] was the same as *la'ad* [=*for ever*] and that therefore the accent (70) fell upon the *ad* to indicate that this word was not to be attached to the following words *ki jabo shiloh* [=for (or when) Shiloh comes (or will come)]. Hence Onkelos paraphrases the Hebrew *ad* by the Aramaic *ad alma* [=for ever] and paraphrases the Hebrew *ki jabo shiloh* by the Aramaic *djethe meshiḥa* [=for (or when) the Messiah comes (or will come)]. Thus whoso would explain the text by rendering it '*ad djethe meshiḥa* [*until* the Messiah come] would be in error, for the meaning of the text is that *when* the Messiah has come the kingdom shall not ever have lapsed from Judah. In the Book of Daniel (2.44) we have words of the same significance namely, "(a kingdom) which shall never be destroyed".'

From what has here been said three things now emerge. Firstly, that you have pronounced a verdict contrary to truth when you say that none of our Ḥakamim attempted to set foot to the path trodden by me, if you are making a general statement about the two interpretations which I offered. Because the teacher of our Rabbi Bechai offered an explanation of the very same kind as I have given. In the second place, and by this may be tested whether your words can be confirmed, you say also that not a single one among the commentators interprets the word '*ad* in the sense of *eternity*. Thirdly, you have likewise made a pronouncement contrary to the truth by alleging that I have done violence to Onkelos. For now you see that I did not simply invent the statement that my explanation was the explanation which Onkelos gave. But rather, my view is in accordance with the opinion of eminent men of former days; and here is the above-named teacher (R. Solomon) who asserted as well that this was the view which Onkelos himself held.

Now to suppose that he (Onkelos) was to misunderstand (71) the use (the rule) of the word '*ad* (by translating it '*for ever*'), yet without this affecting what was his opinion (of the meaning of the verse) compels protest, on the ground that two contraries cannot be present in one and the same subject. After he had paraphrased the word 'ad by 'ad 'alma (for ever), which signifies that which is lasting and eternal, that which is without limit or cessation, there was no point in his introducing 'ad yet again (72), namely before djethe meshiḥa that it should indicate limitation and a fixed period of time

Apart from what I have so far said, there is still another argument that may be urged with a view to a complete understanding of the passage in question. Even if the second 'ad in the phrase ad djethe meshiḥa be retained, this admittedly accords with the style of scripture itself when it speaks in the same language as the Targum [viz. in Aramaic, as in Daniel]. For you will find in Dan. 7.9 the words: 'I beheld till ('ad di) thrones were placed' (R.V.) and in 7.4 'I beheld until ('ad di) the wings thereof were plucked' (R.V.), the meaning of which is, when the thrones were placed . . . when the wings thereof were plucked, I beheld, etc. But on the whole subject see what RaLBaG [i.e. Rabbi Levi ben Gerson 1299-1344] has to say, for he also interprets the words 'ad ki of Gen. 49 as meaning for ever, though otherwise his treatment of the passage is different. Here is what he writes: 'The intention of the passage is not that the sceptre shall depart from Judah when Shiloh comes but is to the effect that complete dominion (73) shall not depart from Judah—so that there may be someone of Judah's seed who will become ruler over many nations. And my learned father brought as close parallel to this his explanation of the verse, the words of Deut. 7.24: "there shall no man be able to stand before thee, until ('ad) thou have destroyed them." The text here does not mean that after he has destroyed them they shall be able to stand before him, but it is clear in itself what is intended.'

And now take note how very untruthfully you spoke when you said that faithfulness (74) had been cut off from my mouth. For I have brought against you to-day faithful witnesses [cf. Isa. 8.2] and they shall be for me for a sign and manifestation [cf. Isa. 8.18] that righteousness has been the girdle of my loins and faithfulness the girdle of my reins [cf. Isa. 11.5] that faithfulness has not been cut off nor will be cut off nor move away from my lips nor from the lips of my seed and seed's seed now and forever.

Next, in answer to your second point. You say that all the

commentators interpreted the word *shebet* in Gen. 49 in the sense of sovereignty and dominion, that this explanation is agreed on by them, settled, established and firmly based, and that whoever impugns the truth of the view of the ancient expositors on this point denies the substance of the faith and his end is Sheol, the bottom of the pit, eternal perdition, death and the fire of Gehenna. Those are your words, and truly more and more I marvel at them and laugh and shake my head over the shortcoming of your intellect and disposition (75). Wherefore listen to me while I speak; and gird your loins like a man while I question you [cf. Job 40.7]. Tell me, in regard to the sum total of what the commentators, known and little known, have said to us in exposition of the verses of scripture or handed down to us, is it the case that nothing can be added to it and that nothing can be taken from it? Has no one the right or power any more to offer other explanations of these verses? And who is he or where is he who has set limit and bounds, by declaring that no man dare further reveal the hidden things of the Torah, which is illimitable in its mysteries and in the profundity of its hidden verities? Was it not concerning this that Job [11.9] said: 'The measure thereof is longer than the earth and broader than the sea', in reference to the numerous interpretations of the Torah and the wealth of its expositions? 'And canst thou put a rope into' its 'nose? or pierce' its 'jaw through with a hook?' [cf. R.V. Job 41.2] (76). No indeed, except stupidity, folly and grave disorder should ensue.

But go and read what RaMBaM [Maimonides, i.e. Rabbi Moses ben Maimon 1135-1205] wrote on the matter of interpretation. His statement is that while in the interpretation of the precepts which Moses received on Sinai we cannot change anything or give other interpretations as to the manner of obeying them or perpetuating (77) them, nevertheless, these precepts being excepted, it is permissible for anyone whomsoever to give, on other themes, as many and as varied interpretations as he will, according to his intelligence, knowledge and regard for truth. That is also what our preceptors of blessed memory meant by the saying: in Aggadoth (i.e. the homiletic interpretations of scripture, in contrast with Halakah, the juristic interpretation) (78) there is no restriction [viz. on exegesis].

But one other question I would have you answer is whether, in all that the commentators have claimed in their writings as being true, there is no difference between the assertions of one commentator and those of another? Is it not an established fact that, times without number, one commentator has said one thing and another another and that on various occasions exegetes have opposed and contradicted each other? The conclusion to be drawn from this is that no one, unless he be bereft of knowledge of understanding or sense, can say that the homiletic interpretations (Aggadah) cannot be supplemented. Indeed rather, it was usual for anyone who rendered a new and fitting interpretation of a text to be the recipient of kisses on his lips (79). And if such be the case, the lips of my father of blessed memory murmur in the grave (80) [see note and Jab. 97a] and his soul rejoices over that interpretation which he brought, more precious and more choice than rubies, on account of its harmonizing the earlier exegetes and their successors. Moreover, as I have said already, his explanation is in agreement with ascertained truths of scripture and above all does not deny admittance or close the door to any of the other explanations that are given of the verse we speak of. For such explanations as have been given of it are alike divine utterances, all of them holy and sincere, every one of them deriving its purpose 'from one Shepherd' [cf. Eccles. 12.11]. David had this truth in mind when he wrote: 'God hath spoken once, twice have I heard this' [R.V. Ps. 62.11] and the prophet [Jer. 23.29] alludes to this very same truth when he cries: 'Is not my word like as a fire? saith the Lord; and like a hammer that breaketh the rock in pieces?'

This is now the third time I have written you on this matter and I wish that I had not undertaken the useless task. To the rest however of what you have said in your lengthy and wearisome epistle, especially in regard to that about which you are proud and conceited, and to your statement that you put yourself in a suitable attitude to pray in my behalf to God that He may enlighten my countenance, I shall not take upon myself the trouble of further reply. But I conclude by saying that: 'Also the Strength of Israel will not lie' [1 Sam. 15.29] and He testifies to me and to us and to the rest of Israel that they should not do iniquity nor speak falsehood and that the tongue of deceit be not found in their mouths. As the psalm of David affirms [148.19]: 'He sheweth his word unto Jacob, His statutes and his judgments unto Israel.' In his mercy he will confirm Scripture where it is written for your sake [Jer. 19.16]: 'the nations shall come from the ends of the earth, etc.' So be it. Amen.

RITTANGEL (Letter No. 3)

Irrespective of what I might say, God will reply to the salutation (81) of your last letter. What should I say, or what should I, so poor in sacred learning, communicate to the Great Eagle (82) of the mighty wings? I who am but a wisp of straw, a grain of dust (83), but you 'a dove covered with silver'! [R.V. Ps. 68.13].

You assail me with many feeble arguments, which, like women's and old wives' tales, are crammed with inaccuracies. You put cord to cord without binding them in any concord, you place patch on patch to cover the bareness of your reasoning, but without succeeding. And I had thought that you would be 'wonderful in counsel' and excellent in resource [cf. Isa. 28.29] and would strictly weigh every word and consonant, term (84) and point with a view to justifying the ideas and thoughts of your Ḥakamim on the subject of our debate and that you would give me a proper answer, one, namely, consistent with the mind of Scripture, in respect of the pronouncements of those writings which have proceeded from my hands. And now I have received your letter which is lacking both in taste and fragrance.

When I perceived that you were inhibiting yourself from paying attention to the contents of my letters, in particular to the statements of Abraham our teacher, of Rabbi Simeon ben Jochai, the Targums and the other commentators, who 'are expressed by name' [Num. 1.17] in my letter, 'every man by his own standard' [Num. 2.2] with ensigns and signals (85), I reflected that your mental grasp and power of comprehending anything correctly (86) would perhaps be failing or that, since you were disregarding what did not accord with your wishes, you had come to the opinion that there was no one among us who was able to arbitrate between us.

Alas, that upon a single thread of hair are suspended your mountains of error and that as hail dissolved by the sun in its strength your fortified ramparts have fallen to the ground, your strong pillars, in which you trusted, demolished! Alas that presumptuous persons have arisen and cast the fire of wrong opinion throughout all the camps of Israel, setting ablaze all the mighty cedars of Lebanon, even to the hyssop of the wall! Awake, awake, for the flame of error has taken hold of the Garden of God [cf. Ezek. 31.8] and of the Forest of Lebanon! Alas that you think that, since cruel Death has devoured, is devouring and will devour those who have been the glory of mankind, who rode upon the heaven, who embraced the Everlasting Arms [cf. Deut. 33.26, 27] in the purity of their thoughts, Death will likewise devour their creative works, their precious and honoured writings!

You have tried to cut down the cedars on which men in early times relied, in order that sycamore-trees might 'renew their strength' [Isa. 40.31; cf. 9.10; 1 Kings 10.27]. But you have gained nothing by the attempt. You have imputed to these ancient authorities wrong notions, which they never entertained and for which not a particle of evidence is to be found in what they said, with a view to misrepresenting their views. As you have ignored the statements of Rabbi Simeon ben Jochai and the Targums, you imagine that I shall imitate you by adopting your method. But although you have deviated from the straight path by contradicting the reliable commentators who have always been held in high repute in respect of the exposition of the subject we are speaking of, and, although you have condescended, by no means worthily, to the folly of light and empty persons, I shall answer a few of your many misapprehensions. These I shall deal with *seriatim*, whether they have to do with your absurd notions or with your remaining assertions and wrong arguings.

First of all, you write that you had thought that I would surely go out for a walk and that we might see each other but that I continued to stay 'in the covert of the steep place' [R.V. Cant. 2.14] and kept myself hidden as though I was afraid to render a reply in person. Well then, you may know that you were in grave error; for I did not come to the city of Amsterdam to argue with you on the subject of our present discussion but to have the text of the *Sepher Jeçira* (*Book of Formation*), along with some of its supplements, put into the hands of the printer.

While I was thus engaged, certain persons of note begged of me that I would discuss with you on the subject of the coming of the Messiah and the other fundamentals of belief. I refused to do so, but afterwards, on their insisting, I at last subjected my own inclination to their demand, howbeit on the condition that this discussion should not be in each other's presence, *viva voce*, but by letter. For as unstable water [cf. Gen. 49.4] and as birds in flight, so are the utterances of man's mouth. On the other hand, what things are written are fixed and permanent, for what is put into writing is not subject to alteration in the same way as are the fleeting words of speech.

In the second place, you state that I again sent you a letter, through an acquaintance of yours as messenger, and that my letter was full of עצמות [in the intention of Rittangel's correspondent = עֲצֻמוֹת = açumoth, in Isa. 41.21 R.V. 'strong reasons' i.e. ironical for *specious arguments, tours de force*. See note.] You may notice that, when it fell to your fate to write עצמות your pen was in advance of your intelligence, for this word, when provided with the needful vowels [namely עֲצָמוּת i.e. açmuth = *substance, essence*] signifies that my letter was full of the *essence* (87) of verity and probity.

Thirdly you write: ' "A dream cometh with a multitude of business, and the voice" of your letter "with a multitude of words" [cf. Eccles. 5.3] which do not affect the question under discussion in the least and which in my estimation are worth nothing. "In the multitude of words there wanteth not transgression" [Prov. 10.19] and especially in your letter you go beyond the bounds of propriety and put your tongue to evil service. And "thou thoughtest that I was altogether such a one as thyself: but I will reprove thee and set in order before thine eyes" [Ps. 50.21] my judgment of this, your attitude, lest I also should become like you. I shall indeed reply to your arguments, that you be not wise in your own eyes. And don't imagine that you can drive me off with "a bruised reed" for as when a man dreams "and behold he eateth: but he awaketh and his soul is empty" [Isa. 29.8] so shall be the multitude of your words when you awake from your slumber.' Having quoted the full text of your words, I would now reprove you for your own dreamings, your so idle assertions, your defaming an innocent man like myself, your propagating of mendacious conclusions (88) and wrong beliefs which it would be difficult for anyone to ascribe even to the followers of Epicurus. For the statements which I made in my letter were made in the name of Abraham your father and of R. Simeon b. Jochai, of the Targumists and the other expositors, both early and later. They were not products of my own invention but are excerpts from these authors' works and are faultless, flawless, clear as noon-day's sunlight. It was obvious that I did not adduce them in my own name but in theirs; but you, on your part, have put forth a thesis which is void of both substance and truth, destructive, disruptive and false, in opposition to Abraham your father, the friend of the eternal God, and to those other pillars of the world. Nor have you set the fear of God before you in applying your tongue to reproach and malign them.

Now, any possessed of sight and hearing may judge for themselves whether the things which you have written opposing the chief and father of them that believe [cf. Rom. 4.11], the friend of God, Abraham our father, are not vicious opinions and subversive beliefs and whether it befits us to have sympathy with a person of this sort who subverts and misconstrues. Who writes, as you have, against his own Ḥakamim who are the foundations of the pillars of the world, his disgrace and perfidy are not to be glossed over. And, as it is, I have already closed my eyes to much that you have said, for fear of the length of time (necessary to reply to it). It is quite apparent to anyone who has a particle of sense that it is nothing but sheer badness of heart that can call Abraham, the friend of God, 'a bruised reed', as appears when it is stated: 'I shall indeed reply to your arguments, that you be not wise in your own eyes. And don't imagine that you can drive me off with a "bruised reed", for as when a man dreams "and behold he eateth: but he awaketh and his soul is empty" so shall be the multitude of your words when you awake from your slumber.' That is the actual text of your own words. And as to the other foundations of the pillars of the world, you have referred to them in the same strain when you write that ' "a dream cometh with a multitude of business, and the voice" of your letter "with a multitude of words" which do not affect the question under discussion in the least and which in my estimation are worth nothing. "In the

multitude of words there wanteth not transgression." ' I call
heaven and earth to witness that, letter for letter, word for
word, as I found what was said, in the book of our father Abraham or in the book of R. Simeon b. Jochai, or the works of the
other celebrated pillars of the world, so I have quoted in my
letter. I added nothing to their statements and subtracted
nothing from them. He who wishes to get at the root of the
facts can examine the books of those I have cited for himself
and put his mind at ease. On what ground then did you make
not a vestige of reply to the important statements of these
authors which my letter conveyed? The only reason is because
you had constructed your misinterpretations and your false
opinions upon a certain misleading fiction, as we shall see in
due course at the end of this letter.

Fourthly, you write: 'At first I was remiss in not answering
you at once, immediately after I had received your letter, for I
delayed in giving it to be copied and to be turned from your
script into our script, for yours was not in Hebrew characters
but in characters that are foreign.' Now this about your being
delayed hitherto on account of giving my letter to be transcribed is the greatest of all falsehoods. You must surely perceive
that the two letters which, previous to the letter referred to,
proceeded from my hand are witnesses which declare against
you what the honest truth was. Members of your household
testify that the books of the expositors from which I quoted in my
letter were not all at your disposal and that you had to pester
other people for loans of them and also that your intellectual
resources did not extend to understanding Abraham our father
in the work, the *Book of Formation*, or R. Simeon b. Jochai in the
book of the *Supplements of the Zohar*. Indeed the works of these
authors are very difficult to understand, although, by (89)
scholars maturer than you are, their thoughts, expressed in
pregnant and unprolix writing, are highly valued. May the
wise reader ponder them and pay attention to them, for, upon
the verse in Genesis of which we are speaking, these writers
have recorded the words of the living God. But you have passed
over their explanations altogether and make no response to them
either by sign or syllable. Yet that is not to be wondered at,
because this missive of yours makes it evident that you are not
of the race of warriors, of mighty men and champions of the

true faith, but that in those matters with which these have to do you are not able to distinguish right from left.

Besides, your own letter gives you away. For there you say: 'Were it not that I respect the honoured messenger, God forbid that I should write you an answer.' This shows that at the beginning you decided not to write me in reply. Thus it is the greatest falsehood to say that hitherto you were kept from writing on account of giving my letter to be transcribed. Anyone can see that the composing of contradictions and untruths is your daily bread; just as, in your first letter about the word *shebet* in the Genesis passage, you wrote that this word had the meaning kingdom and sovereignty as well as that of chastisement and affliction. Finally, my own two first letters likewise bear testimony that your having been delayed by giving that letter of mine (which followed them) to be transcribed is a lie, for the two first letters that I wrote were in cursive (90) script with rounded characters after the fashion of those who write what is called in our parlance *current* style [Kurrentschrift]. But the letter which followed the two first was written in square characters in the same form as appears in print so that not a single consonant or word should be too difficult for you. Hence then if you are able to read printed works you should also be able to read that letter of mine. Why was it that you did not give my two previous letters to be transcribed, since these were written in cursive script and rounded characters? Or have you never read that he who wishes to plead a lie must first remove the witnesses and further, that a successful liar (91) needs to have a good memory? And yet you write to the effect that the characters I employed were not as Hebrew characters but were foreign! That is the worst lie of all. Tell me please: who was it who transcribed for you that letter of mine? Was he a Jew or was he not? And further, the square characters which are used in the printing of Hebrew characters, was it or was it not in accordance with their form that I wrote that letter to which you refer? But fit as you are to continue lying, I would have you know that I have written many hundreds of Hebrew letters to Jews of pure stock domiciled in Poland, Russia, Lithuania, Germany, Turkey, Egypt, Constantinople, Cairo, and all of them read my epistles without difficulty. Nor did I ever hear from a single one of them, when I had written to them in the

K

self-same handwriting as I wrote to you, that the characters I
used were foreign and not Hebrew. But now in your case the
opposite appears to be true—for you Spanish Jews are not of
pure Jewish stock but are of a mixed type and this is not only
borne out by your style of writing but also I have heard from
eminent and leading men in Poland, Germany, Lithuania and
Russia that you are sprung from an impure and mongrel strain.
They say that were a wealthy Spanish Jew of high position to
have an only daughter, heiress of all his wealth, the poorest man
in all the regions I have mentioned would not take her to wife
because of the corrupt nature of your descent. That is the
answer that is to be made to the charge that I wrote a foreign
script and not a Hebrew one—but this might be added, namely,
that concerning me men of note in Israel testify: 'From John
to John (92) there has arisen none to be compared with John
Rittangel.' Far be it from me to glory in their opinion, but I
wish to subjoin it in case you might say that I wrote you in
German or Polish and not in Hebrew. So far then for my reply
to your untrue and trivial assertions, your dreams, imaginings
and delusions, that even the unlearned of the house of Israel in
the various countries where they are, might not remain in
ignorance of them.

Now you began to answer me on the ground of statements
which I had cited in your name from your letter, statements
which you term 'a rigmarole' [Toref—see note] (93) of words.
That is a quite true description for they are your words not
mine, time after time reiterated by you without tact or taste
and oftentimes repeated in folly, false presentation and hostility
against Abraham the father and chief of them that believed and
against the other pillars of the world. For I said nothing on
my own authority but everything was said in their name and I
set each one of them by his own standard, with signs and signals.

At the outset of your reply to me you quote my letter to the
effect that none of your Ḥakamim attempted to set his foot to
the path which you have taken and which I called crooked and
tortuous or to lend the power of speech to explain and interpret
the verse 'the *shebet* shall not depart from Judah' in the manner
in which you have interpreted it. You can take it that this
claim remains true until you can bring proof that it is not so.
Moreover, when I wrote that you had asserted that your own

opinion and the opinion of your father was the same as that of Onkelos the Targumist, what I wrote was likewise the truth. And now I shall shew you the authentic words of your first letter. In your second interpretation of the verse you wrote (94): 'There is a second meaning of sceptre according to which it is said that the sceptre shall not be taken from Judah nor the teacher from between his feet eternally (that is, never) when the Messiah shall have come. In this second meaning, the words *until that* [Heb. *ad ki*] are translated *eternally when*, as in various passages of Holy Scripture is the usage. For several words of this verse are ambiguous, that is, they have a double sense.' This then was the view you set forth in your second interpretation, namely that the word *ad* has here in the verse Gen. 49.10 to be taken in the sense of *eternally*. Now we have before us your actual words and the same view as was held by your father. . . .

CHAPTER VIII

RITTANGEL, THE MYSTIC

THE ZOHARIC PASSAGE IN THE LETTERS[1]

THE Supplements of the Zohar were published by Jacob ben Napthali at Mantua in 1557. Apparently they date from about the same period as the *Sepher ha-Zohar* (the *Book of the Splendour*) itself and are identical with the Zohar in teaching. The latter work, the chief monument of Kabbalism, is, as are also the Supplements, written in Aramaic and appeared in the late thirteenth century in the possession of Moses ben Shemtob de Leon (1287) of Avila in Spain. The Zohar is in form a midrash or commentary on the Pentateuch which is made by it the vehicle of a comprehensive mystical teaching and speculation. It was widely regarded as the work of Simeon ben Jochai (*c*. A.D. 150) who in its pages is the exponent of this mystical thought. But examination of the text shews that Simeon cannot possibly be the author and that it is improbable, if not indeed impossible, that Moses ben Shemtob himself or any single person composed it. The Zohar was published simultaneously in Mantua and Cremona in 1558-1560.

In the fourteenth century the word 'Kabbalah', meaning *received* teaching and which had been of old applied to the Talmud, was now applied to Jewish mystical, hidden or theosophic teaching. This teaching, however, goes further back than the extant manuscripts which convey it. And it is generally agreed that whatever be the date of the Zoharic writings, the roots of this mystical thought go back beyond the beginnings of our era. E. Müller (*Der Sohar*, p. 9, 1932—Selected passages) sees the roots of this teaching in the writings of Philo, in Apocalyptic, in Gnosis and in Aggada (Jewish homiletic) and traces it to the early Alexandrine Period. Bension (*The Zohar*, p. 24, 1932) agrees that 'the Zohar in its actual form was com-

---

[1] See pages 121-124 above.

piled and composed in Spain in that highly mystical period marked by the thirteenth century, but that its beginnings are rooted in the mysteries of antiquity' with the reservation that the sources are Jewish sources, namely the Pentateuch, the Prophets, Daniel and the Book of Enoch. But E. R. Goodenough in his brilliant book *By Light, Light. The Mystic Gospel of Hellenistic Judaism* (Yale Univ. Press, 1935, p. 369) in which Philo's writings are brought under contribution, speaks of 'the process by which the ideas of Philo survived for a thousand years and reappeared in the Kabbalah'.

One of the results of the re-awakening of mystical Jewish thought in the thirteenth century was that the Zohar, with its teaching of God, of the archetypal or Heavenly man, the Messiah, with its deeply earnest moral tendency and spirit and its disquisitions on the Law, proved to be a means of *rapprochement* between enthusiastic Jewish Kabbalists and Christians who were attracted to the book. Especially the so-thought discovery in the Zohar of Trinitarian passages led to the propagation of the Christian faith among Jews and during the sixteenth and early seventeenth centuries there was a wave of conversion to Christianity. Among these converts or 'cabalistic apostates' as J. L. Blau (*The Christian Interpretation of the Cabala*, New York, 1944) calls them were Paul Ricci, author of *De coelesti agricultura*, and John Stephan Rittangel (1606-1652) who was a descendant of the famous Isaac Abarbanel (1437-1508) and author of 'the most valuable early Latin translation of the Sepher Yetzirah' (see Blau, op. cit., p. 75). The descent of Rittangel from Abarbanel, if this be granted, is of much interest from two points of view, for Abarbanel claimed to be 'of the stem of Jesse of Bethlehem, of the royal house of David' (see Karpeles, op. cit., Vol. II, p. 183) and secondly, according to Bartolocci (Vitae Rabbinorum in Reland's Anal., p. 113 f), Abarbanel, though consorting with Christians and coming to high office among them, was very hostile to Christians in his writings (*quod atramenti commixtum liquore contra Christianam religionem evomuit in chartas*). Further since Abarbanel was a Spanish Jew, the disparaging remarks of Rittangel upon Spanish Jews appear all the more remarkable.

In the following notes an attempt is made to explain briefly the more obscure portions of the passage which Rittangel quotes both here and in his *Sepher Jeçira*, from the Supplements of the Zohar, so far as the teachings of the Zohar and its interpreters can be made to shed light on the questions involved. In addition to the books of Waite, Müller, Bension, Bischoff, Goodenough, already mentioned, references will be made to 'The Zohar, translated by Sperling, Simon and Levertoff, Soncino Press, 1931-1934'; J. Abelson, *Jewish Mysticism*, London, 1932; Ad. Franck, *La Kabbale ou la philosophie religieuse des Hébreux*, Paris, 1889; D. H. Joel, *Die Religionsphilosophie des Sohar*, Leipzig, 1849.

That Serpent. The Serpent which brought death upon our first parents by tempting them to evil and upon all who have descended from them is ever active. Simeon's pupils as also the pupils of the Ḥakamim and saintly teachers of every age are summoned to do battle with the power of evil and many warriors set out with zest and fervour to the campaign against the arch-enemy of mankind. The Serpent of this passage of the Supplements is masculine, though sometimes in the Zohar (cf. Waite, p. 274) the Serpent is feminine, the wife of the Death-Angel Samael who rides upon her back. But here the Serpent, apparently representing Samael or Satan, rides on the back of a mare which is his spouse. For according to Kabbalistic thought the male and female principle prevails everywhere and in all things, in evil as well as in goodness. Also according to the Zohar everything that is conceived of as being here below or which takes place here is but an image of what takes place above in the supernal world. There is an earthly man and a heavenly man (cf. Bension, p. 137; Franck, p. 163). As there is an Evil Serpent in the world below who works iniquity and seeks to enslave and destroy man, so there is a *Sacred or Holy Serpent* in the world above which restrains the power of the Evil Serpent and protects men. The Philonic mystical thought also differentiated two kinds of Serpent. The serpents which attacked the Israelites in the wilderness symbolize the love of matter and pleasure and are of the same character as the serpent which tempted Eve. But the Serpent which Moses made at the command of Jehovah is the Serpent of self-mastery (see Goodenough p. 219 f).

The [King's] Daughter is on the Tower that flies in the air. Mankind has a vision of the romantic figure of the King's Daughter summoning men to do battle in her interests and in their own against evil. The King's Daughter or simply, as she is called, The Daughter, is the *Shekinah*, that is, the Divine Presence, of whom Waite (p. 342) says: 'She is now the Daughter of the King; she is now the Betrothed, the Bride and the Mother and again she is the Sister in relation to the world at large. There is a sense also in which this daughter of God is—or becomes— the Mother of man.' The Shekinah also has these aspects: she is 'the architect of the worlds' and 'the Oral Law is in her image, while the image of Jehovah is the Written Law' (ibid., p. 343), the inward Law being Life, while the outer is the Body of Life.

The relation of the Shekinah to the Law and the description of her as King's Daughter who is on the Tower that flies in the air receive some explanation from a portion of the Zohar called 'The Small Holy Assembly' (p. 185, Bension). There we read: 'Behold there is a Tower that elevates itself above all the others! This Tower symbolises the Law. . . . There are three hundred doors that give access to it. . . . When the doors of the Tower are opened, the cherubim spread their wings, so as to cause the heavenly light to shine forth, and cry out: "How great is the goodness that thou hast reserved for them that fear thee!" When the scrolls of the Law are returned to the Tower, a light comes from above. . . . The Cherubim are silent and the flying Tower returns to its place above the other Towers.' It is the Shekina as intimately associated with the Law who moves man to combat with the Serpent. The proclamation of war and of the reward of victory comes from the firmament which no doubt is symbol of the upper world, but in the list of Zoharic technical terms (given in Vol. I, Sperling, pp. 387 f) appears as 'a reservoir of light and illumination'. The reward of successful warfare with the Serpent is that he who overcomes the Serpent will be given the King's Daughter or Shekinah *to wife*. The term 'to wife' refers to that *grade* or *degree* of emanation of the Supreme Being called *Binah*, i.e. *Understanding* (see Diagram below and Sperling, Vol. II, Glossary of technical terms).

The King's Daughter within, whose clothing is inwrought with gold *—which gold signifies the seven days of creation.* Ps. 45.13 is usually translated: 'The king's daughter is all glorious within: her clothing is of wrought gold' (A.V.). The Zohar renders: 'All the glory of the daughter of the king is within' (cf. Waite, p. 19).

The Supplements (above) say that whoso kills the Serpent shall be given 'to wife' the *King's Daughter within*, which statement may be interpreted to mean that whoso overcomes evil is rewarded with *Understanding* (cf. above) and the indwelling of the Shekinah, that is, with the Divine Presence. The clothing of the King's Daughter is inwrought with gold. The gold is apparently the symbol of the light of creation, the Divine Presence having a vesture of the kind that is mentioned in Ps. 104.2: 'Who coverest thyself with light as with a garment.' In Zohar I, 2a (Sperling, Vol. I, p. 7) it is said 'God is "above the heavens" in respect of His Name, for He created a light for His light, and one formed a vestment to the other.' The first light, the created light, here mentioned is a vestment for the purer uncreated Light of the Deity. So the *gold, the light, of the seven days of creation*, is light created as a garment for the King's Daughter, the Shekina. Philo when he speaks of the golden candlestick in the Temple being the symbol of the heavens says that it is made all of gold because the heaven is made up of a single element, the 'fifth' in contrast to the constitution of the rest of the universe from the four elements (Quaestiones in Exodum 73; Goodenough, p. 112). Another passage from the Zohar (see Franck, p. 191 f) narrates that when Adam lived in the garden of Eden he was clad with a vestment made of the upper or supernal light and when he and his wife were expelled from the Garden they were provided garments of skin. It is also said in the same place (Zohar, II, 229b; Sperling, Vol. IV, 281) that 'a man's good deeds done in this world draw from the celestial resplendency of light a garment with which he may be invested when in the next world he comes to appear before the Holy One.'

Shiloh-Moses. In our passage the task of killing, or as it would be perhaps better to say, of overcoming or defeating the Serpent pertains to Moses. Light is shed upon this portion of the Supplements by the following statement which appears in the Zohar (I, 25b; Sperling, Vol. I, p. 101): 'According to another explanation, the words [Gen. 2.5] "no shrub of the field was yet in the earth" refer to the first Messiah and the words "no herb of the field had yet sprung up" refer to the second Messiah. Why had they not shot forth? Because Moses was not there to serve the Shekinah—Moses, of whom it is written "and there was no man to till the ground". This is also hinted at in the verse "the sceptre shall not depart from Judah nor the ruler's staff from between his feet", "the sceptre" referring to the Messiah of the house of Judah, and the "staff" to the Messiah of the house of Joseph. "Until Shiloh cometh": this is Moses, the numerical value of the two names Shiloh and Moses being the same. It is also possible to refer the "herbs of the field" to the righteous or to the students of the. Torah.' This passage from the Zohar is a very complete commentary to the excerpt from Supplements which Rittangel quotes in his letter. Its exegesis is quite clear. The *sceptre of Gen. 49 is the Messiah ben David* of the house of Judah to whom the sovereignty and kingdom belong, the *staff is the Messiah ben Joseph* or ben Ephraim who in Rabbinic literature is called the 'Anointed for war' and whose task it is to conduct the great battles which precede the coming of the Messiah ben David. The Messiah ben Joseph will lose his life in these wars. He is a 'dying Messiah' (see Strack-Billerbeck, *Komm. zum N.T. aus Talmud und Midrasch*, Vol. II, p. 292). Neither of these two Messiahs will appear, says the Zohar passage, until after Shiloh comes. *Shiloh is Moses,* and a hint that the prophecy of Gen. 49 is so to be understood, is, it is suggested, that the numeral value of the consonants of the words Shiloh and Moses—for the Hebrew letters are also indications of number —is the same, each word totalling 345.

Moses-Shiloh is represented by this Zohar-passage as a fore-runner of the two Messiahs. He had first to till or prepare the ground for them. It is said that they could not shoot forth as plants 'because Moses was not there to serve the Shekinah', to answer the call, as the Supplements-passage narrates, of the King's Daughter. He fulfils his task by overcoming the Serpent at the Red Sea, slaying his hosts on land and sea and in the firmament, effecting deliverance from the power of evil in the moral and intellectual spheres by giving to Israel and mankind the Law and thus revealing the Arm of the Lord.

The paraphrase of Gen. 49.10 given by the Zohar-passage therefore runs as follows: The Messiah ben David shall not go forth from Judah, nor the Messiah ben Joseph from between his feet, till Shiloh-Moses comes and to him shall the obedience of the peoples be. Neither Rittangel nor the Supplements-passage say anything of the Messiah ben Joseph. It might appear, however, that on the authority of Simeon ben Jochai whom he cites Rittangel believed that Shiloh referred to Moses, as Simeon in the Supplements teaches. But it is obvious that Rittangel's view is that Shiloh is the Messiah, for this is the view of the Targums and of the commentators who are in his first and second letters brought as evidence. His citation of the Supplements-passage hardly supports him in his explanation of Gen. 49.10 except so far as it is taken for granted that *ad ki* means *until* and has to be taken with the words that follow them, and also that sovereignty or kingdom is spoken of and not chastisement and affliction. Indeed from the standpoint of strict exegesis the citation is a digression. But Rittangel, in the paragraph preceding and in the paragraph following the citation, indicates why he has introduced Simeon ben Jochai at this stage, namely because the passage speaks of the redemption of Israel. Thus the careful method of textual criticism has been departed from and the religious-polemical motif which has been smouldering in the breasts of both the participants in the debate has blazed forth into flame.

From neither the Zohar-passage nor from the Supplements-citation must the meaning be extracted that Shiloh-Moses who defeats the Serpent and deals him many blows has utterly overcome the power of evil, for the Zohar in general reserves for the Messiah the destruction of the Serpent, for as long as death reigns among men the Serpent is active. 'The world will not be set free from the Serpent until the coming of Messiah the King who will cast down death for ever' (Waite, p. 276). 'Rabbi Simeon wept and said . . .: from the day that the Evil Serpent, having enticed Adam, obtained dominion over man and over the world, he has ever been at work . . . nor will the world cease to suffer from his machinations until the Messiah shall come' (Zohar, I, 114a; Sperling, Vol. I, p. 358).

Sea of the Law—Zaddik—Hajjoth (living creatures).

Central Column—Leviathan. The great deliverance wrought by Shilo-Moses was in the moral and spiritual realm here called the Sea of the Law. He drove the Evil Serpent and his forces from this realm, broke his dominion over the mind of man and made it possible for the Holy Serpent, the friend and protector of man, to rule. As the Red Sea at the Exodus was severed by the staff of Moses, so Moses' reed (calamus, pen) with which he wrote the Torah made a path in the spiritual world for men to

walk in; or, to change the picture, Moses and his warriors, that
is the scholars of the Torah, have driven from the Sea of the
Law their spiritual enemies. Or again, those who study the
Torah are themselves compared with ships which since Moses'
victory can ply now in peace upon the Sea. 'For these ships are
the eyes of those who reflect upon (or have become enlightened
by) the Law.' (Cf. Tiqqunē Zohar-passage translated above.)
Since Shiloh-Moses has come and made the Sea of the Law free
and open, the multitude of beings who live in and by the spiritual and moral law of God, both in the upper and the lower
worlds, now rejoice. Among those of the upper world are 'the
living creatures, both small and great' (Ps. 104.25), the *Hajjoth*
who, according to the Zohar (see Sperling, Vol. I, p. 388), are
members of the higher ranks of angels. As the storms of doubt
and debate, caused by the Evil One, upon the Sea of the Law
have ceased, the whole universe feels relief. To those who study
God's Law there is given in its season spiritual manna. The
regular time put apart for such study is the season of profit for
the *Zaddik* (the pious or righteous man). Such is the general
sense of the passage in regard to the effect of Moses' work. But
the Sea of the Law, the Central Column, the Zaddik and
Leviathan belong to a milieu of Zoharic ideas of more specific
content and sufficient notice must be taken of these in order to
make Rittangel's quotation more intelligible. The passage does
not simply equate the sea of the Law with the Torah or written
law of Moses, but rather it seems to mean that through the
Torah Moses made the Sea of the Law, the intellectual, moral
and spiritual realm, navigable. The deliverance that was effected 'in the sea of the material world', that is the Red Sea, is
contrasted with the deliverance which was to follow in the Sea
of the Law.

'*Rabbi Simeon added this explanation: The Shekinah which is above
is the Sea*' (see p. 123). The discussion of the meaning of this and
of the other terms (Central Column, etc.) mentioned above
requires the setting forth of the main doctrine of Kabbalism,
namely the doctrine of divine emanation. The fundamental
conception upon which the teaching of the Zohar is based is that
God manifests Himself through stages of emanation by the outpouring of vitality or power which is at first of a purely spiritual
order and then later of the physical order. The source of this

process of emanation is the Absolute Being, the unknown Ultimate (in Heb. 'En Soph = the Limitless) or First Cause and in
the course of His descent towards the material sphere certain
modes of His Being are manifested. God manifested and manifests His existence by the production of the universe and the
means by which He does so, the stages through which He does
so, are potencies or intermediary agents. These modes of
manifestation or emanations are called *Sephiroth* (lit. *numerations*),
that is, grades or spheres, and may be generally described as
attributes, forces, vitalities, powers or principles. The Sephiroth
(a plural form: singular—Sephirah) are ten in number and the
names they bear and their relationship to one another are
represented in the accompanying diagram (p. 154). The theory
of emanation bases upon Neoplatonic conceptions of God and
of existence. Already in the *Sepher Jeçira* (ninth century A.D.)
the ten Sephiroth are used in a mystical sense when the author
(I.1, 2) speaks of the numbers (Sephiroth one–ten and the
twenty-two letters of the Hebrew Alphabet) as constituting together the *thirty-two paths of Wisdom,* that is the thirty-two divine
agencies or principles active in the work of *world-formation* (as
distinct from world-creation or production) (see p. 123). But the
real Kabbalistic doctrine of the ten Sephiroth, or divine grades,
dates from the twelfth century. In the thirteenth century we
find it in the Zohar. There (I, 46b; Sperling, Vol. I, p. 146) in
a discourse which has in it an obvious allusion to the Sephiroth
as emanating from 'En Soph, the Unknown Ultimate, we are
given a reason for the conception of number or numeration
(Sephirah) being applied to the stages of emanation: 'There is
a certain point which is the beginning of number, and which
cannot be further analysed. There is one point above, un-
revealed and unknowable, which is the starting-point for numbering all entities hidden and recondite. Corresponding to it
there is a point below, which is knowable and which is the
starting-point for all calculation and numbering; here consequently is the place for all measurements.'

But besides the notion of the ten Sephiroth as ten successive
emanations from the Godhead, as 'ten lights' or as a stream of
light and life, this outpouring of energy and vitality is also
compared to the waters of the Sea, though even then the number ten plays a role. 'For the waters of the sea are limitless and

shapeless. But when they are spread over the earth, then they produce a shape (dimiōn) and we can calculate like this: The source of the waters of the sea and the force which it emits to spread itself over the soil are two things. Then an immense basin is formed by the waters. . . . This basin is filled by the waters which emanate from the source; it is the sea itself and can be regarded as a third thing. This very large hollow (of waters) is split up into seven canals. . . . The source, the current, the sea and the seven canals form together the number *ten*. And should the workman who constructed these tubes [canals] come to break them up, then the waters return to their source, and there remains nought but the débris and the water dried up. It is thus that the Cause of causes has created the Ten Sephiroth. (Cf. Abelson, p. 139-140; Sperling, Vol. III, p. 131, and cf. p. 110 f.) It is the supernal sea which is here spoken of and described in terms of the ten Sephiroth and which is referred to in Zohar II.20a (Sperling, Vol. III, p. 65): 'He [God] made this world corresponding to the world above, and everything which is above has its counterpart here below, and everything here below has its counterpart in the sea.' (Cf. ibid., p. 149, where there is a contrast between 'the supernal' and 'the lower sea'.) When Rabbi Simeon in the Supplements-passage says that '*The Shekinah which is above is the sea*', it is the Supernal sea which is intended and which has been hitherto called the Sea of the Law. In other words the Sea of the Law as equated with the Shekinah which is above, that is, with the Divine Presence, is nothing but that complex of emanations designated by the ten Sephiroth which flow from 'En Soph, the Cause of causes. In the latter part of Rittangel's quotation only 'the Sea' is spoken of and in the first part 'the Sea of the Law'. Without doubt the words *of the Law* only particularize those ethical and spiritual powers which are active in the redemption of man and which help him to overcome the Evil Serpent. For there are other energies besides the strictly moral and spiritual which flow from the Source of all being.

Corresponding to the Shekina which is above, there is the Shekina which is below (cf. Abelson, p. 133) which Rabbi Simeon in the Supplements-passage describes as *active in the work of Creation*. He indicates that this Lower Shekinah operates through *thirty-two divine powers*. This is a reference to 'the thirty-two paths of Wisdom' of which the *Sepher Jeçira* speaks (see above p. 148). The description of the activity of the Shekinah which is below as *the way of a ship in the midst of the sea* makes the reference to the thirty-two paths all the more emphatic since the word for *midst* or heart (Heb. leb) has the numerical value of thirty-two.

It [the Manna] is gathered from the domain of the Central Column which comprehends (or harmonizes) the six lateral grades. What the Central Column is, receives illustration in the diagram (p. 154) of the Ten Sephiroth, i.e. those stages of emanation or grades which descend from the Unknown Ultimate. The first three grades or manifestations of the Divine Being, namely numbers 1, 2 and 3 on the diagram, form a triad representing the world as manifesting the divine thought or the immanent thinking power of the Universe. The second triad, 4, 5, 6 represents the immanent moral power. The third triad 7, 8, 9 represents the physical, dynamic aspect of the Universe (die Schöpferwelt des Naturhaften, Müller, op. cit., p. 4). The tenth Sephirah, called 'the Kingdom', is the material world, the visible universe. The three triads are respectively the world of thought, the world of soul, the world of corporeality; and 'the Kingdom' may be said to be (cf. *J. Ency.* art. Sefirot, the Ten) 'the sum of the permanent and the immanent actuality of the Sephiroth'.

But viewed in another aspect (see diagram) the grades 1, 6, 9 and 10 are seen to occupy a middle position in relation to the other grades. The grades 1, 6, 9, 10 are therefore in the language of the Zohar called the Central Column or Central Pillar; while numbers 2, 4 and 7 form the Right Side or Right Column (being the Side of Compassion) and numbers 3, 5 and 8 form the Left Side or Left Column (being the Side of Severity), which two Sides or Columns represent respectively the counter-forces and joint-principles of Grace and Justice, light and darkness, good and evil, male and female, which are inherent in all existence. The Central Column reconciles and mediates between the right and left Sides. Thus Simeon ben Jochai says in the Supplements passage that the Central Column *comprehends, that is, harmonizes, the six lateral grades.* It mediates between 2, 4 and 7 on the one side and 3, 5 and 8 on the other. It effects a synthesis. As Waite says (p. 203): 'The Middle Pillar draws the right and left sides, the good and the evil together, in which union evil dissolves as

such and the good obtains entirely under the name of Benignity
—which is that of the Middle Pillar.' In the triad of the moral
order, the grades of 'Compassion' and 'Severity' are reconciled
in the Central Column in the grade 'Beauty'. Joel (op. cit.,
p. 213) quotes the Italian Kabbalist Menachem of Recanati
(1290-1330) as saying, in respect of the Pillar of Benignity, 'that
the world requires the divine Grace, but in view of sinfulness it
needs also the divine Severity, yet since neither of these principles must be allowed to operate in a one-sided manner, therefore
a mediating principle is demanded.' The mediating principle
is Benignity, the name of the Central Column, that is, 'Kindness' (Heb. *Rahamim*) which is the other name of the grade
'Beauty' (see Müller, op. cit., p. 4). It is this principle with
which the *Zaddik* or Righteous man will nourish his mind and
soul—the spiritual manna to be *gathered from the domain of the
Central Column*, which is composed of the harmonies of the three
triads above mentioned, and especially from the grade that
harmonizes the second triad and manifests to man the moral
quality of the Divine Mind.

The question which now remains to be answered is: what is
meant in the Supplements-passage by the statements that *the
Leviathan which is above is Zaddik for he is a small fish by the sea-shore*
(or on the sea-bottom) and that *the Leviathan of the Sea is Zaddik,
the culmination (or head) of the Central Column?* In the reference to
the Leviathan previous to these statements the Leviathan has
appeared along with the other inhabitants of the Sea of the Law
who rejoice because the Evil Serpent has been driven from the
Sea and the Sea is now free and its paths without obstruction.
The ships which now ply upon the Sea are interpreted by the
passage itself as meaning the eyes of those who are enlightened
by the Law and this may refer either to the students of the
divine and heavenly Torah or to the inhabitants of the world
above who likewise live by the divine Law. Likewise the living
creatures, *Hajjoth*, great and small with which the Sea is teeming
are, in Zoharic symbolism, the multitude of the angelic host
that is above. They form the joyous *chorus of singers and dancers*.
But what does the Leviathan represent, of whom Ps. 104.26
R.V. says: 'there is leviathan whom Thou hast formed to take
his pastime (sport. A.V. to play) therein'? This question is not
easy to answer for while the Zohar contains a few passages in

which 'the great sea monsters' and Leviathan are treated of, yet
the Leviathan of this Supplements-passage is a more clearly
defined figure and cannot simply be generalized away. He is
an occupant of the Supernal Sea, is Zaddik and head of the
Central Column.

We must first of all concern ourselves with the word Zaddik
which is a Hebrew word meaning *righteous* or *just*. In the Zohar
however this word has a variety of meanings. It may mean a
pious or righteous person. It may mean the divine or perfect
Man, the Messiah (see Müller, pp. 10, 18). Then again the
word is used to specify the ninth Sephirah, called Jesod or
Foundation or the Righteous One, that is, that grade which is
the harmony of the third triad of Sephiroth. The application
of the title Zaddik to the grade Foundation is based upon the
text Prov. 10.25 (A.V. 'The righteous is an everlasting foundation') which is translated as meaning 'The Righteous is the
Foundation of the world.' Already in the Talmud (cf. Hag. 12b)
we have this rendering—'Rabbi Eleasar ben Samua said: on
one pillar whose name is Zaddik (does the world rest) for it is
said—Prov. 10.25: The Righteous is the Foundation of the
world.' Although the ninth grade Foundation belongs to the
triad of Sephiroth (7, 8 and 9) which form the world of corporeality, yet it has to be noticed that the title *Zaddik* as name
of the ninth grade does not lose all spiritual significance, for the
Righteous One, the Foundation of the world, 'upholds God's
covenant with the earth and procures sustenance for the living
beings upon it' (Sperling, Vol. I, pp. 121, 382 f). Besides, from
the higher grades, from the world of thought and the world of
soul, there is a constant stream of vitality flowing down to the
world of corporeality. Speaking on the text 'And the gathering
together of the waters called He seas', the Zohar I, 33a (Sperling, Vol. I, p. 124) says: 'This is the upper reservoir of the
waters where they are all collected and from which they all flow
and issue forth. R. Hija said: "The gathering place of the
waters is the Zaddik".' There in Zaddik the flow from the
Supernal regions meets and is gathered. In another place (I,
26b) the Central Column is compared to or rather is said to be a
river. As the gathering place of the down-flowing waters of the
Supernal Sea, Zaddik is the *head or culmination of the Central
Column*. We might have expected that the tenth Sephirah called

Malkuth or the Kingdom would be described as the head of the
Central Column (on Malkuth see Waite, p. 197). But that
Malkuth is not here so called is not because the last of the Sephiroth has no apparent function (see Abelson, p. 152) but because the Supplements-passage has here the three other worlds
or triads in view. *Zaddik* is the harmony of the last of the triads,
which are all dependent one on the other. It is the gathering
place and place of issue of all the vitalities. As the Zohar says:
'Everything shall return to its Foundation from which it has
proceeded. All marrow, seed and energy are gathered in this
place. Hence all the potentialities which exist go out through
this' (III, 296 in Isaac Myer, *The Qabbala*, etc., p. 271).

Since it has been shewn in what sense the grade *Zaddik* can
be called the *head of the Central Column*, it may now be asked what
is meant by the assertion that *the Leviathan of the Sea is Zaddik*.
Zaddik or Righteous One is a name given to the ninth grade
Jesod or Foundation and we do not hear in the Zohar of this
grade receiving the name also of Leviathan, although in the
Gnostic system of the Ophites two of the seven stations or circles
which the soul has to pass in order to be purged and obtain bliss
have the names *Behemoth* and *Leviathan* (cf. *Jewish Ency.*, art.
Leviathan). It seems fairly evident however that in the Supplements-passage the Leviathan of the Sea is not given as
another name of the ninth Sephirah, but is rather the symbol
of the function which the Zaddik performs, that is of those vital
forces with which the grade Zaddik is associated. When the
analogy of the sea has been adopted to indicate the stream of
emanations which proceed from the ultimate Source no better
symbol of the natural forces could be devised, than that of the
mighty sea-monster who sports, plays and has his pastime in his
native element. But it must be remembered that the third triad
is still the world of Formation, not the actual world or world of
action (see Waite, 197 f); that in Zaddik (Foundation) are not
the forces of the materialized world but those elementary powers
(die zugrunde liegenden Urpotenzen) which are the foundation
or base of material nature and which have yet to develop. See
E. Bischoff, op. cit., Part I, p. 29 f. As Isaac Myer (op. cit.,
p. 271) says, these forces in *Zaddik* represent the *natura naturans*
not the *natura naturata*. The ninth grade 'creates the reproduc-
tive power of nature, endows it with, as it were, a generative

L

organ from which all things proceed, and upon which all things finally depend' (Abelson, p. 152). Leviathan in our actual, lower world offers a singularly appropriate picture of the fully developed forces and powers of nature. But in the supernal region the vitality and power which are symbolized by Leviathan are only in potentiality and are not fully developed. *The Leviathan which is above is* (that is, represents) *Zaddik*, but here above he is *a small fish by the sea-shore (or on the sea-bottom)*.

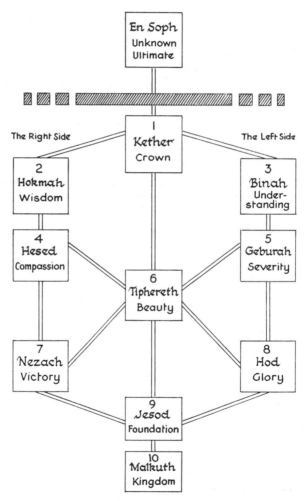

DIAGRAM OF THE SEPHIROTH

PART IV

POLEMIC IN DEBATE

CHAPTER IX

INTRODUCTION TO THE DEBATE BETWEEN NACHMAN AND FRA PAULO

I

NACHMAN (Nachmani, Nachmanides) whose full name and title, Rabbi Moses ben Nachman, is commonly abbreviated into RaMBaN, lived from about 1195 to about 1270. He was Rabbi in Gerona in Aragon. The description which Graetz (*Geschichte der Juden*, Vol. VII, p. 42) gives of him finds very exact confirmation in the account which Nachman has left us of his discussion with Fra Paulo in July 1263 in the presence of King Jayme I and his nobles in Barcelona. Graetz's description of the Rabbi of Gerona is to this effect: 'Nachman, or, as he was called in the language of the country in which he lived, Bonastrüc de Porta,[1] was a sharply defined personality, a mature character with all the virtues and defects of such. He was full of sound moral sense and conscientious religiosity, of mild temperament, of keen intellect; his religious belief being dominated by authoritative tradition. "The wisdom of the ancients" appeared to him to be unsurpassed and unsurpassable and their utterances as understood in their plain sense had not to be doubted or suffer any detraction. "Who steeps himself in the doctrine of the ancients drinks old wine" was Nachman's firm conviction. According to him the whole wisdom of later generations consists solely in their discovering the viewpoint of the great forerunners, in adjusting themselves to that viewpoint and in taking it as norm. Not only the scriptures in their whole range, not only the Talmud in its full extent, but also the Geonim [that is, the chiefs of the Babylonian Academies in the post-Talmudic period] and their immediate disciples up to Alfasi were for Nachman exemplary and infallible authorities. ... Nachmani was acquainted with philosophic literature but

---

[1] Bension, *The Zohar*, p. 20, gives the form BONASTRIC da Porta.

metaphysical speculation remained unfamiliar to him. He either could not or would not explore its depths. But the Talmud was for him all in all and in its light he viewed the world, the events of past history and that which the future would bring.'

To what Graetz says about Nachman being a Talmudist may be added that he was also a Kabbalist; indeed Dr Schiller-Szinessy (*Ency. Brit.*, 9th ed., xx, p. 264) calls him the most celebrated Talmudist and Kabbalist of his age in his own country. Though opposition to Kabbalism has sprung from Talmudic scholarship and rationalism, Nachman was an enthusiastic supporter of the new mystical doctrine which spread throughout Spain and it was his influence and authority which was largely responsible for its spreading. 'In enthusiastic letters to the communities of Aragon, Castille and Navarre, he averred that mysticism lies at the heart of Judaism. A Judaism without mystical interpretation he found inconceivable' (Bension, op. cit., p. 20). The commentary to the Pentateuch which, after his disputation with Fra Paulo was over, Nachman wrote in Palestine whither he had gone when expelled from Spain, is the most valuable of his extant commentaries and shews very strong Kabbalistic trends. In the preface it contains the following statement: 'As real tradition (Heb. Kabbalah) we know further that the whole Pentateuch consists entirely of the names of God, since the words combine with one another otherwise than appears in the text as we at present have it and so form divine names. . . . It appears that the divine original text of the Pentateuch was written without word-divisions, so that the consonants could be read together in that scheme which forms the divine names as well as in that ordinary scheme which gives the teaching and precepts of our present text. In this letter form Moses received the Law (Torah) as Scripture, while the reading of the text in the form which offers the names of God was only communicated to him orally' (E. Bischoff, *Die Kabbalah*, Leipzig, 1917, p. 69 f). Even in the disputation in Barcelona in circumstances where one would least expect mystical allusions, these are not altogether wanting.[1]

II

The causes leading up to the disputation of Nachman with

[1] Cf. p. 206, note 1, below on *Shining Mirror* (lucid speculum).

Fra Paulo were the plans of the Church for the conversion of Jews and Mohammedans and in particular the employment of Fra Paulo, as missionary to the Jews, by the Dominican Order. Fra (Fray) Paulo—otherwise known as Pablo Christiani—was a converted Jew and now a Dominican monk. As the result of the foundation of the Franciscan and Dominican Orders in the thirteenth century, great activity and zeal on the part of the Church in missionary efforts became manifest and to this enthusiasm was joined the recognition of the necessity and value of linguistic studies. The moving spirit in the furtherance of the study of Arabic and Hebrew, the tongues in which the religions of the two most conspicuous rivals of Christianity had expressed themselves, was Raymond of Pennaforte (near Barcelona) who from 1238 to 1240 was Master General of the Dominicans. Before entering upon this office Raymond of Pennaforte had been able to obtain permission for the training of twenty or more monks in Arabic, of whom it is reported that they had great success in the mission field among the Saracens. At the same time also his advice was taken in regard to giving some Brothers instruction in Hebrew that by mastering the original text of scripture they might be able to controvert the Jews and shew the agreement between the interpretations given by Jewish scholars of earlier days and those given by the Christian faith. (See Williams, op. cit., p. 244.) Bishop Francis Bosquet[1] (see Wagenseil's *Tela*, p. 2 of Introduction to the disputations of Jechiel and Ramban) speaks of Raymond of Pennaforte, when the latter was *Exmagister Generalis Ordinis Praedicatorum,* as having persuaded Jayme I to suppress by edicts the calumnies of impious persons. Then he describes Raymond as having employed for the enlightenment of Jews and infidels men trained in scripture and divine science at his institute for the study of Arabic, Hebrew and Chaldee. Now there can be little doubt that this institute represents a development of the work begun on a small scale before de Pennaforte held the post of Master General and it probably occupied his attention in the period after he had held that post. For, that his missionary interest, so far as Jews were concerned, did not wane is evident from the fact that, in 1263, twenty-three years after he had held the Master-Generalship of his Order, he is the chief figure next to

[1] In a prefatory letter to the *Pugio Fidei.* See below.

and behind the king when the king with the royal court are assembled to hear Nachman and Paulo at the Barcelona discussion. But apart from de Pennaforte's own efforts in organizing missions and linguistic instruction, one of his successors in the Generalship from 1254 to 1263, Hubert de Romans, 'gave an impetus to the establishment of missionary schools where languages were taught'.[1]

Of the men of the school of languages of whom Bosquet[2] speaks as being skilled in scripture and divine science, two are mentioned as being pre-eminent, namely, Frater Paulus Christiani and Frater Raymundus Martini (Ramón Martínez). The latter, Raymond Martin, was the most remarkable product of the linguistic training encouraged by the Dominican Order. He studied Hebrew, Aramaic and Arabic, and Graetz (VII, p. 163) regards him as being the first Christian to possess a knowledge of Hebrew that was greater than that attained by Jerome. Martin wielded his knowledge and scholarship with great effect, for the book of which he was author in 1278, *The Dagger of the Faith against Moors and Jews (Pugio Fidei adversus Mauros et Judaeos)*,[3] was a store-house of argumentative weapons at the disposal of preaching monks who discussed the claims of Christianity with Jews. He was teacher also. In 1281 when Hebrew and Arabic studies (cf. Daiches, op. cit., p. 101) were instituted at Barcelona, we find him as instructor in Hebrew— *lector ad studium ebraicum*. Of Paulo we are justified in concluding in lieu of more definite information about him, that his relation to the language-school and to Raymond Martin was that of teacher of Hebrew. Paulo's teacher in Hebrew before his conversion had been Rabbi Eliezer of Tarascon and it is to be supposed that Paulo performed that function later in the Dominican service. Graetz is of the opinion that the thorough grounding which Martin received in biblical and Rabbinic literature was *perhaps* given him by Fra Paulo. Dr Schiller-Szinessy (articles

---

[1] D. Daiches, *The King James Version of the English Bible*, p. 101.

[2] Bosquet (ut sup.) says: Raymundus viros sacrae scripturae, ac divinae scientiae peritos, sui instituti, linguarum Arabicae, Hebraicae, ac Chaldaicae studio applicuit: quorum opera ad docendos, ac convincendos infideles usus est. Inter caeteros Frater Paulus Christiani et Frater Raymundus Martini, oppido de Soubirato in Catalania oriundus, emicuere.

[3] Edited and published by Voison in 1651 (Paris); Carpzov's edit., Leipzig, 1687. L. Williams, *Adv. Jud.*, p. 248 f gives a brief account of the whole work. Martin had already, before the *Pugio* appeared, written a treatise *Capistrum Judaeorum (A Muzzle for the Jews)*.

on *Ramban* and *Talmud* in *Ency. Brit.*, 9th ed.) speaks with
certainty of Paulo having been 'the teacher of Raymundus
Martini'. Therefore we may assume that when in the year 1250
(see Williams, p. 248) Martini was chosen by de Pennaforte to
study Oriental languages, he came under the instruction of
Paulo. If this be so, then, whatever Fra Paulo may have accomplished as missionary, his greatest accomplishment was the
training of Martin. From the account of the disputation we see
that some time prior to 1263 Paulo had been making missionary
journeys in Aragon and possibly in other places. Little more is
known of him. The date of his birth is not known. It is thought
that he was born at Montpellier in Languedoc. He is said to
have died in Sicily about 1274.

In a moment of some intensity in the dispute in the presence
of the king, Nachman asks Paulo: 'Are you the one who asked
the king to assemble the Jewish scholars that they might debate
with you?' This suggests that Paulo was responsible for the
proceedings at Barcelona having taken place. And indeed this
suggestion would appear to meet the facts of the case, even although the influence and authority of Raymond of Pennaforte
may have gained the king's consent to Paulo and Nachman
being summoned to dispute in public. Raymond was the king's
confessor. But we must not rate the friar Paulo's influence with
Jayme as merely of a secondary character, resting upon the
support of de Pennaforte. Good historical evidence[1] vouches
that Jayme's contemporary, Louis IX of France, valued his
acquaintance with 'our beloved brother in Christ Paulo Christiani' and in the year 1269 followed Fra Paulo's advice to
enforce the rule that the Jews should wear a distinctive badge
—a disk of red felt or saffron-yellow cloth fixed on the garment
on breast and back—'in order that those so marked should be
recognized from all sides'. Considering that the account of the
disputation by Nachman is written by one who must have de-
tested Paulo as a '*meshummad*', an apostate Jew who had accepted
baptism, it is remarkable that there is nothing recorded in the
account which reveals any weakness in Fra Paulo's temperament
or character. Paulo preserves a spirit of restraint in the debate.
There are some remarks by Nachman of a depreciatory character upon Paulo's scholarship, even upon his understanding of

[1] De Laurière, *Ordonances des rois*, I, 294. Cf. Graetz, vii, 150.

Hebrew, but we need not regard these detractions as other than sparks engendered by the ordinary friction of controversy. Similar charges of ignorance and incompetence appear in the correspondence of Rittangel and the Jew of Amsterdam, and it is by no means a singular occurrence when an advocate in a law-suit accuses the counsel for the other side of knowing nothing of the principles of law. Dr Williams (p. 245) speaks of Nachman as being 'the protagonist put forward by the Jews' and suggests thereby that the Jews were consulted on the matter. In this case the command of King Jayme that Nachman should debate with Paulo would have been more or less a formality. But there is little inducement for us to accept this nicety as the background of the Barcelona conference. A few weeks after the debate, when the king (29th August 1263) issued a decree[1] facilitating the missionary efforts of Fra Paulo, his commands to the Jews to open their synagogues and houses to the friar for the purposes of discussion and conference, his demands that all Jews, in public or in private, separate or with others, should listen to Paulo favourably, shew him their books and answer his questions are very plain and peremptory. Graetz is of the opinion that de Pennaforte arranged the public meeting between Nachman and Paulo in the hope that the most famous Rabbi of Spain would be converted and in consequence there would be a wholesale turning to Christianity on the part of the Spanish Jewish communities. We cannot tell what the extent of the hopes of de Pennaforte or of the Dominicans was but there is little doubt that Graetz defines rightly the nature of these hopes and at the same time gives the most probable explanation of the presence of Nachman as the defender of the Jewish faith at the public discussion.

III

Next to Nachman, who in 1263 was a man of about sixty-eight years of age, and Fra Paulo, the persons of most significance present at the disputation were King Jayme and Raymond of Pennaforte. The king even plays some small part in the discussion and draws out from Nachman some of the latter's versatility and resource in debate. The Rabbi's explanation of the

---

[1] Cf. Wagenseil (*Tela*, p. 2—Introduction to disputes of Jechiel and Nachman) —decretum, quod est in Codice Legum Antiquarum Lindenbrogii fol. 235.

words of the Psalm (110.1) 'The Lord saith unto my lord' exhibits a subtlety that is sharpened by the king's approval of Paulo's question. King Jayme, born in Montpellier in 1208, the son of Pedro II of Aragon and the Lady of Montpellier, was fifty-five years of age when the Barcelona conference met. His Father-Confessor Raymond of Pennaforte (1176-1275), who had then attained the great age of eighty-seven, was a man of great scholarship and piety (see note below on text). Graetz, whose characterizations of men and events are often far-seeing and invariably trenchant, but who is apt to ignore the many shades, varied colours and variety of motives which are part of any true picture of human actions, describes de Pennaforte as a 'most ferocious persecutor of heretics', a 'gloomy monk', the 'fanatical Dominican General', the collector of Papal decretals who sought to subject the civil governments to the power of Pope and Church.[1] But even though de Pennaforte shared in what seemed axiomatic in the Middle Ages to both Christians and Jews, namely the reliance upon censorship and ban as a means of countering what was thought to be irreligious thought and writing, he did modify this method of response by a belief in the value of learning and discussion.

While the disputation was practically wholly confined to the two protagonists Nachman and Paulo, there were occasions on which, besides the king, others, by statement or question, joined in the discussion. De Pennaforte spoke at the opening of the proceedings very briefly on a matter of procedure, and at their

[1] Graetz, VII, pp. 27, 130, 163. Cf. *The Life and Times of James the First the Conqueror* by F. Darwin Swift, B.A., Oxford Clarendon Press, 1894, p. 245—'But the most remarkable churchman of the reign was the famous Ramón de Peñaforte, scholar, missionary and saint. Originally a student at Bologna, he was called to Rome in 1230 by Gregory IX and became the Pope's chaplain and penitentiary, in which capacity he undertook the collection of later decretals not included in "Gratian's Decree". In 1235 he declined the archbishopric of Tarragona and on returning home to Barcelona in 1238 was appointed General of the Dominicans —an order which he had entered some years previously. He soon however resigned his office (1240) and busied himself in founding schools for the study of Arabic so as to facilitate the conversion of infidels. A devoted missionary among the latter, towards heretics his attitude was very different, and, as we have seen, the introduction of the inquisition [cf. p. 243] into James' dominions was largely due to his influence.' Raymond died 6th January 1275. Advocating the mild treatment of Jews and Saracens by Christians Raymond says: 'Jews and Saracens ought again to be drawn to the Christian faith by the citation of authorities, by reasons and kindnesses rather than by asperities. They ought not to be compelled because compulsory services are not pleasing to God.' Summa lib. 1 de Judaeis et Saracenis. See Swift, p. 245, note 4. See note 7 on text of the disputation (below).

end, apparently at some length, on the subject of the Trinity. Raymond Martin, his protégé, took no part in the debate. But the king's Justiciary and Arnold of Segura and Fra de Genova had all something to say. The Justiciary elicits from Nachman the interesting distinction between the time of the Messiah's *birth* and the time of *his having come*. But it is the role played by the Franciscan scholar Fra de Genova which provides us, we may suspect, with an instance of that rivalry which at times obtained between the Dominicans and Franciscans (see Swift, op. cit., p. 242). Both of these Orders were, as Nachman tells us, interested in the discussion. When at a certain point in the debate, which took place àt various places on certain days at the end of July and the beginning of August, Nachman reported that pressure had been brought to bear upon him by various parties to discontinue the disputation, he mentioned especially Fra de Genova as urging him to discontinue. To close the disputation on the advice of a Franciscan would have been a blow, if not an insult, to the Dominican Order of de Pennaforte and Paulo. The king, very wisely, would not allow the debate to terminate in this manner. Whether there was anything beyond rivalry in Fra de Genova's interference we cannot tell but we are reminded of other times and places when the Franciscans opposed themselves to Dominican action. In England in the reign of Henry III (1216-1272) when the murder-of-the-Christian-child outcry had been raised and fury against the Jews had been fanned by Dominican preachers, the Franciscans used their influence to free many Jews from prison. Also in the beginning of the sixteenth century when Reuchlin, on the question of whether it was right for Christians to burn Jewish writings, defended the Jews as against Pfefferkorn and the Dominicans, the Franciscans supported Reuchlin.[1] Fra de Genova was evidently esteemed as a capable scholar for he appears along with the Bishop of Barcelona, de Pennaforte, Arnold of Segura,[2] Fra Paulo and Raymond Martin on the commission appointed by Jayme I in 1264 at the instance of the Pope to expunge from the Talmud passages that were inimical to Christianity.

---

[1] Danby, op. cit., p. 51.

[2] The edict calling the commission is given in Vol. XV, p. 17, *Revue des Études Juives* (1887) and gives the name as *Segarra*. Cf. note 34 on text below.

IV

In the disputation the subjects of debate are whether the Messiah has already come, as the Christians claim, or is yet to come, as the Jews believe; and whether the Messiah is divine or human. Although it was agreed to discuss whether the Jews or the Christians possessed the true Law, this topic did not come up for discussion.

It is not proposed here to describe what the translation (see below) of Nachman's account itself makes clear, but there are certain points which emerge in the course of the debate and certain facts, not mentioned in the debate, which nevertheless illumine it, and these should be treated of in introduction to what is, as represented by Steinschneider's edition of the Hebrew text, an important piece of polemic literature and a religious and historical document of much value.

The literature upon which Fra Paulo relies, to support his arguments, is *Haggadic,* that is, it may be roughly described as homiletic, illustrative, sermonic. The line of argument therefore which Nachman takes is to define the sources from which his opponent must take his proofs, if these proofs may claim to be drawn from what Judaism regards as writings authoritative for belief. The Bible, Nachman says, is authoritative and what it says has to be accepted and believed; and the Talmud, so far as it gives an exposition of the divine commandments, is authoritative. But the writings which are described as *Midrash* (expository—see note 16 on test) and *Haggadah* (narrative—see note 13 below on text) are intended for edification and have only the value or authority for conscience and belief which sermons may have, or fail to have, for those who hear or read them, but are not standard sources for the religion of Judaism. This is expressed at an early stage of the debate by Nachman who says that Paulo knows a little of the Haggadic exegesis of scripture but nothing of the legal decisions that have been deduced from the Law. Paulo, Nachman thus says, knows nothing of *Halakah* (see note 13 on text).

Nachman certainly seems to score a debating point in narrowing the field of discussion and in seeking to deprive Paulo of what the latter regarded as a quarry full of useful material for building his constructions. But we must not be too impressed with the point which Nachman made and regard Paulo as having made a gross error in not leaving the Haggadic literature severely alone.[1] The Haggadah, if used critically, is of great religious-historical value. The modern commentary of Strack and Billerbeck has for its purpose (see Vol. I, p. vi) the use of the Talmud and Midrashic writings to cast light upon the New Testament by an objective description 'of the belief, the views and the life of the Jews in the time of Jesus and of early Christianity'. There is a vast difference between this task which the Commentary fulfils very successfully and the task, for example, of shewing that certain passages in the Talmud testify to the truth of Christianity, a belief held firmly by Raymond Martin (see Graetz, VII, p. 136; Williams, op. cit., p. 248). But in regard to Jewish ideas concerning the Messiah, about whom the substance of the debate was, Fra Paulo was justified in exploring the Haggadic-Midrashic writings with a view to establishing what the history of Jewish thought and belief on the matter revealed. We are not here concerned with the question of what success Paulo had with the passages which he quoted from this literature but solely with the stricture passed by Nachman on its use.

In the thirteenth century it was certainly not the universal opinion in Judaism that Haggadah was theologically valueless and could not be resorted to in debate. One of Nachman's own friends, Solomon ben Abraham of Montpellier, whom Nachman supported in the attack upon Maimonides' writings, in the so-called anti-Maimunist movement for which Solomon (c. 1232) was mainly responsible, had no hesitation in employing Haggadah in defence of Judaism. Graetz (VII, p. 38) says of him: 'For Solomon not only the religious-legalistic decisions of the Talmud but also the Haggadic utterances in their naked revolting literalness were incontrovertible verities to which to make any objection was a heresy.' Solomon who represented the orthodox popular anthropomorphic religious views about God, and for whom the existence of evil spirits was a sort of article of faith resting upon Talmudic Haggadah, was 'an important Talmudic authority' (Graetz) and was the vital centre of the dust storm of the anti-Maimunist controversy for a decade or more. That he represented in his high estimate of

[1] L. Williams (op. cit.) would seem to take this view. Cf. his Epilogue, p. 417.

Haggadah a small minority or even a minority is not likely.

In the fifteenth century the Christian argumentation with Jews is seen to take account of the objection which has been brought against the use of Haggadah. Geronimo de Santa Fe (1414), a converted Spanish Jew, in disputation with members of his former faith might even be thought to be making an allusion to two arguments which Nachman urged a century and a half before at Barcelona, namely: The Haggadic literature has no binding authority for faith; and, if the authorities who speak in the Talmud testify to Jesus being the Messiah, then why did they and their children remain Jews? Thus Geronimo in his treatise called 'To prove the perfidy of the Jews' asserts: 'I have proved my case. . . . Yet someone will say, If the Talmud, etc., thus testify of the Messiah, why do the Jewish scholars "and in particular those who labour night and day in the study of this Talmud" refuse to listen to its teaching about Christ? There are two reasons. First, this doctrine about the Messiah is chiefly to be found in the part of the Talmud called *Haggadoth* ("narrationes") or *Midrassoth* ("sermocinationes") which, however, are intermingled with the rest, and the Jews, in their study, do not pay much attention to Haggadah "saying that it bears no fruit". . . . Secondly, perhaps on their reading they do note one or two, or even three, of these passages, and yet are not impressed. For they ought to consider many of these. . . .'[1] Geronimo therefore, fully aware of the type of counter-argument that would be raised against him in debate, does not consider that all Haggadic passages are irrelevant to an enquiry into Jewish Messianic conceptions. He practically takes up the position in this matter which Schechter takes in '*Some Aspects of Rabbinic Theology*' (1909).[2] There Schechter refers to the vast literature called Haggadah scattered over a multitude of Talmudical and Midrashic works, the earliest of which were compiled even before the time of the Mishnah (c. A.D. 200) and include many ancient elements of Rabbinic thought. Among the subjects of which this literature treats Schechter specifies 'Messianic aspirations' and cognate subjects 'no less interesting to the theologian than to the philosopher'.

An interesting phase of Nachman's thought is revealed with much critical insight by Graetz (VII, p. 48). Nachman could

[1] Cf. Williams, op. cit., p. 265.   [2] Some Aspects, etc., p. 3.

not follow the example of the northern French communities and accept the Haggadic passages in their literal sense. 'But (says Graetz) in this point he stood in contradiction with himself for he was not able to reject these passages since he was too much dominated by his belief in authority and by his admiration for the bearers of Talmudic tradition. Also when, compelled by circumstances, he occasionally declared certain Haggadic sentences were only rhetorical metaphors, sermonic in character, on which it was not a religious duty to believe, this was not his whole mind (*so war es nicht sein ganzer Ernst*).' Graetz then goes on to say that Nachman being unable to discard the Haggadic elements altogether, and fearing to interpret them in Maimunistic fashion, gave them a place in the mystical thought of Kabbalism with which he had come into contact in his youth and of the profundity and heavenly wisdom of which he was convinced.

To the lighter incidents of the debate belongs Fra Paulo's citation of the last section—called the Book of Judges—of Maimonides' work, the 'Mishneh Torah'. A passage occurs here, Paulo affirmed, which shews that Maimonides did not think of the Messiah as not being subject to death. On calling for the manuscript of the work in order to read the passage out, Paulo cannot locate the reference. Nothing is more calculated to impress an audience unfavourably than to be seen turning page after page in vain. Paulo appears to have thus turned the tables upon himself. The signal proof he was so confident that he could bring is not forthcoming. But the friar's claim that Maimonides (1135-1205) 'the like of whom', he says, 'has not been in Jewry for the last four hundred years'[1] was on his side would,

---

[1] Isidore Loeb in *Revue des Études Juives*, XV, 1887, pp. 1-18: 'La Controverse de 1263 à Barcelone' says (p. 10, note 1): 'De son côté, Pablo (p. 16 de la Relation) place Maimonide, qui était à peine mort depuis 60 ans, à 400 ans en arrière.' But M. Loeb misunderstands the Hebrew text here. Paulo was no fool, but a very competent person, and is not likely to have thought that the Maimunist disputes were about a person who had died 400 years ago. The Hebrew (in Steinschneider's edit. which M. Loeb also uses) is אֲנִי אָבִיא רְאָיָה מֵחָכָם גָּדוֹל שֶׁלָּהֶם לֹא הָיָה לָהֶם כְּמוֹתוֹ הַיּוֹם דּוּ מֵאוֹת שָׁנָה . . . which means literally: 'I shall bring a proof from a great scholar who belongs to them [i.e. to the Jews]. There has not been to them his like since 400 years.' M. Loeb's error would appear to arise from thinking that כְּמוֹתוֹ (=*his like*) has to do with the word for *death*. When Paulo speaks of Jewry not having had a man like Maimonides for the last 400 years, he is probably thinking of Saadia born 892 in Egypt as the last great figure in Jewry before Maimonides. Saadia was acquainted with Arabic philosophy, wrote in Arabic, sought to reconcile Scripture with reason, translated the Bible and was the author of the work *Beliefs and Dogmas*.

in the circumstances, have more behind it than the mere strength of the passage which, had he found it, would have supported his case.[1] Nachman, though he is said to have professed (see *Jewish Ency.*, IX, p. 87) great respect for Maimonides, was, in his ultra-conservatism, opposed to the liberal and philosophic thought of that great thinker. He had, though not allying himself with the anti-Maimunist party, supported Solomon of Montpellier, a leader of that party who in 1232, had with others, issued a ban against the Maimunists. The struggle between the two parties was keenly waged not only in Europe but in Asia in the Jewish communities. It is not to be supposed that the theological antagonism of Moses ben Nacham and Maimonides would be unknown to any of the Jews who attended the disputation or fail to be recalled by the mention of the latter's name.[2] The abortive attempt of Nachman to effect a reconciliation between the two parties by proposing that the 'Mishneh Torah' be not condemned but that the 'Guide of the Perplexed' should be banned shewed only too plainly that the tension between himself and Maimonides could not be removed. But in the discussion with Paulo we observe in Nachman a mind too well disciplined to let the heat of the Maimunist controversy enter into the present debate or let the praise of the great scholar Maimonides arouse the emotion of jealousy into which the emulation of scholarship is prone to turn. Possibly Paulo's praise of Maimonides had the intention of appealing to the Jewish portion of the audience and, by reminding them of the issues of the Maimunist quarrels, to divide their loyalties and sympathies.

Besides shewing the difference in emphasis and content of thought in regard to the Messiah which distinguishes Christianity and Judaism,[3] the disputation also touches upon (cf.

---

[1] That Paulo could not find the passage he thought to find in the MS. handed to him may be taken into relationship with the fact that two quotations made in a treatise of Nicolas de Lyra (1270-1349) from the same Book of Judges as Paulo cites are, as described by Dr Williams, *uncertain*. One of them Dr Williams regards as a summary of Maimonides' words, the other as a variant reading contained in the MS. of Maimonides used by de Lyra. Cf. Williams, op. cit., p. 410 f.

[2] Nachman's contemporaries, says Graetz, VII, p. 143, resented and blamed him because in his Commentary he made attacks upon Maimonides and still more violent ones on Ibn Ezra.

[3] *Jewish Ency.*, IX, p. 87, says that Nachman's argument that 'the question of the Messiah is of less dogmatic importance to the Jews than Christians imagine' is a 'bold statement' in which Nachman was certainly sincere.

M

notes 26 and 27 on text below) the Christian theological concept of original sin. This doctrine that 'a moral corruption or
deprivation passed down from Adam to his descendants' (Ste-
vens, *The Theology of the New Testament*, p. 354) was, as we have
seen, attacked in one of its aspects by the author of the Zikron
two centuries later than Nachman. The latter's attitude to the
idea of an inherited guilt falling upon the human race is also
one of rejection and of assurance that 'the righteous suffer no
penalty of Gehenna imposed on account of the sin of Adam'.
In a brief exegesis of Gen. III he shews that the consequences
of Adam's fall, so far as mankind is concerned, attach to man's
physical life only. As to the soul of a man it has, he says, as
much connection with the soul of Pharaoh as it has with Adam's
soul and it 'cannot be that on account of Pharaoh my soul will
enter Gehenna'. Here Nachman expresses the general view of
Judaism on the question of what the effects of Adam's disobedience are.

V

The discussion between Nachman and Fra Paulo in 1263 in
Barcelona had been preceded by a similar dispute in Paris, also
in the presence of royalty, in 1240, between the converted Jew
Nicholaus Donin of La Rochelle and Rabbi Jechiel of Paris
supported by three other rabbis. These disputations, in their
general character, differed in two respects. Jechiel, in the
earlier debate which was concerned mainly with the Talmud,
asserted that the Talmud did not refer to Jesus of Nazareth at
all, that the Jesus of the Talmud was the son of a certain
Pandera and had lived long before the Christian Jesus (cf. note
2 on text below). On the other hand, in the Barcelona conference Nachman affirms that it is the Jesus of Nazareth of
whom the Talmud reports and, basing upon the Talmud report,
he adopts a chronology which places Jesus much before the
beginning of the Christian era. The Talmudic evidence and
tradition in this respect are accepted by him absolutely. Even
the Haggadic passage from the Talmud with which he begins
the disputation apparently represents in his view good historical
data since the purpose of its citation is to justify his presence in
the debate for the purpose of answering the Christian arguments. The second general difference between the Paris and

the Barcelona disputes was that the disputation in the latter place ran smoother than in Paris. Graetz compares Jechiel and Nicholaus to two rough boxers. In Barcelona the proper spirit of discussion was on the whole well preserved.

It remains to recount briefly what befell Nachman after the disputation was over. Naturally enough both sides, the Dominicans and the Jews, claimed 'the victory'. In relatively recent times (1887) O. P. Denifle, a Dominican, has published, for the purpose of establishing some facts in the favour of Paulo, a version of the disputation that has been extant in Latin.[1] That this Latin account is signed by King Jayme and had probably been drawn up and approved by the Dominicans before the king signed it need not constitute anything to its prejudice. It is very brief. M. Isidore Loeb describes it as a sort of *procès-verbal* (op. cit., p. 4). But this Latin document is not Paulo's own personal account of the controversy. On the other hand the Hebrew account is Nachman's own description of what occurred and in particular of his own answers. It is the only version which comes from a participant in the dispute.

The two protagonists, Paulo and Nachman, do not seem to have been allotted each an equal length of time to set forth their views on the specific subjects agreed upon for discussion, but Paulo appears rather to be represented as petitioner—that is the person who had petitioned the Crown to call a conference for disputation—and as the one whose duty it was to formulate the questions to be asked. Nachman's part is that of defendant and answerer. The latter even complains of having occupied this role the whole time. The part allotted to each of them may explain why Paulo does not appear to speak so long as Nachman, for as a rule the answering of questions is a longer process than the asking of them. Nevertheless it is obvious that all of what Paulo said is not given by Nachman. The latter in one place speaks of Paulo as having made a speech in which there was no substance and then selects from it a statement which

---

[1] Denifle, 'Quellen zur Disputation Pablos Christiani mit Mose Nachmani zu Barcelona 1263' which appeared in the *Historisches Jahrbuch im Auftrage der Görres-Gesellschaft*, 1887, pp. 225-244. Isidore Loeb in the *Revue des Études Juives*, Vol. XV, 1887, criticizes Denifle's work (pp. 1-18). See also F. D. Swift (*James the First of Aragon*, p. 250, note 2) who appears to accept the report of 'the official version' that Nachman was handled so severely by his adversary so as to be obliged to leave the town secretly before the end of the debate.

Paulo had made about Maimonides. Naturally Nachman was concerned mainly with putting his own case forward and has had to judge of what in his opponent's pronouncements or views required to be refuted. Had each of the disputants written his own account there can, however, be no doubt that there would have been a great contrast between the two versions. John Knox's account of his interview with the young Queen Mary of Scots on the subject of her intended marriage to the king of Spain is a very graphic piece of writing.[1] It is as descriptive of Knox as of the Queen. It is a document held by historians to be, as far as is humanly possible, perfectly truthful. But yet Queen Mary's version, had this been recorded in writing, would have manifested other facets of the truth than those which Knox revealed.

Shortly after the disputation had ended Nachman published his account. This he must have done before 12th April 1265 for an official document of that date reports that Nachman had appeared before a special commission for having reviled Christ and the Catholic Faith in a book a transcript of which he had given to the bishop of Gerona (*librum fecerat de quo transcriptum dederat episcopo Gerunde*).[2] Nachman pleaded that at the disputation he had received, both from the king and from Raymond de Pennaforte, permission to exercise full freedom of speech. The court admitted that this was so. The gravamen of the charge seems to have lain, however, not upon Nachman having spoken things that were contrary to the Christian faith at the time of the controversy but upon the fact that he had published and broadcast the same in writing. The penalty pronounced was that Nachman be banished for two years and his pamphlet be burned. The penalty was a light one and probably was imposed by the king in the hope that the outcry against the accused would die down if the latter were absent for a couple of years from the scene of his labours. This sentence however appeared to be too lenient in the eyes of the Dominicans (*quam quidem sententiam dicti fratres predicatores admittere nullomodo*

---

[1] John Knox, *The History of the Reformation of Religion in Scotland* (with notes, etc., by W. McGavin) Glasgow, 1831, p. 290. Also in the more recent edition by Guthrie, pp. 328 f.

[2] See Graetz, op. cit., Vol. VII, 2nd edit., p. 418, note 2, where the whole document is given: also Denifle (op. cit.), document no. viii. Cf. Loeb (op. cit.), p. 17, who describes it as *Lettre-patente de Jayme Ier*.

voluerunt). Moreover the accused was granted the privilege that no further accusation could be preferred against him except only in the presence of the king. From what this document says of Nachman's pamphlet or account we cannot tell whether he first wrote the account in Hebrew and then, on the bishop asking for an account of the debate, gave the bishop a Spanish (or Latin) translation or whether the bishop, who possibly may have known Hebrew, received a Hebrew copy. On the other hand the words of this document of 12th April 1265 might be taken to imply that Nachman's pamphlet had been written in the first instance because the bishop had asked him for an account of the disputation (*maxime cum praedictum librum quem tradidit dicto episcopo Gerunde scripsisset ad preces ipsius*). In this case was the pamphlet first written in Spanish (or Latin)? The Commission which Jayme appointed to investigate the above-mentioned charges owed its origin to complaint having been made to him in regard to the content of Nachman's pamphlet by Raymond de Pennaforte, Arnold de Sigarra and Fra Paulo. The king probably thought that such a commission would be fairer to the accused than a Dominican tribunal would be. Graetz and the *Jewish Encyclopedia* (IX, op. cit.) assume that Nachman wrote his account because the Dominicans had been spreading reports of their 'victory' at Barcelona and he thought it advisable that his fellow Jews should know what his defence of Judaism in the disputation had been. But at the meeting of the Commission the appearance of the pamphlet is only associated with the request of the bishop of Gerona.

A second document,[1] a Papal Bull of Clement IV of date 1266 or 1267, impresses on King Jayme the need of restraining Jewish blasphemers in their attacks on the Christian Faith and especially of punishing the Jew who had spread abroad his errors in various regions after his controversy with Fra Paulo. It must have been on account of this communication from the Pope that Nachman's sentence was altered to that of perpetual banishment. In 1267 he emigrated to Palestine. In Acre he was active in spreading Jewish learning, but felt his exile greatly. He was buried at Haifa near the grave of another defender of the faith of Judaism, Jechiel of Paris.

---

[1] Loeb (op. cit.), p. 17, document no. ix.

VI

The text of Nachman's account. The translation which follows is made from Steinschneider's edition of the Hebrew text, which is held to be the most trustworthy (see Schiller-Szinessy, art. *Ramban* in *Ency. Brit.*, 9th ed.; and Williams, op. cit., p. 245, note 3). This edition, which also contains Nachman's exposition in Hebrew of Isaiah chapter 53, bears the Hebrew title: Wikkuach ha-Ramban b'inyan ha-emunah liphne melek w'sarim u-beur ha-Ramban 'al hinneh jaskil 'abdi (i.e. a discussion of Ramban on the subject of the Faith held in the presence of the king and the nobility. Also an exposition of the portion in Isaiah beginning: Behold my servant shall deal wisely) and the Latin title: Nachmanidis Disputatio publica pro fide Judaica (a. 1263) e Codd. MSS recognita, addita ejusdem expositione in Jesaiam LIII edidit M. Steinschneider, Berolini, 1860.

The first printed edition of the disputation of Nachman appeared in Wagenseil's *Tela* (1681) together with a Latin translation. The Hebrew text which Wagenseil gives is fragmentary and corrupt and the Latin translation is even more misleading than the Hebrew (see Steinschneider's Hebrew preface to his edition above mentioned). Wagenseil tells us in his introduction to the disputation that in the Strasburg Codex—in Codice Argentoratensi—where he found the Hebrew text of Nachman's account which he presents in his *Tela*, the two disputes, namely, Jechiel's with Nicholaus (1240) and Nachman's with Paulo (1263) had been combined together so as to represent one disputation, the whole composition forming, as it were, a web (πλοκή) or mixed drink (cinnus). The separation of what should never have been joined together and so intermingled was done, Wagenseil explains, with much conjecture and uncertainty. To the damage which the mingler of the disputes had done to the text more damage was added. This explains to a very large extent the mutilated and corrupted condition of the Hebrew text as the *Tela* presents it. The Wagenseil text invariably introduces any words of Fra Paulo with the remark 'then Paul the wicked one said' or 'the ass then opened his mouth' or 'Paul, may his name be blotted out, answered' or 'the heretic (min) replied'. This vituperative quality was probably added to the text by some copyist before the mingler had begun his operations. Steinschneider's text does not have it, nor does the vituperative element correspond with Nachman's general character, although twice he refers to Paulo as *'otho ha-ish* (that man). A better text of the Hebrew than Wagenseil presents is given in the Constantinople edition of 1710 but it too is not accurate (see Steinschneider's preface). Graetz used this edition, and, as may be seen on page 134 of the second German edition, Vol. VII, of his *History of the Jews* his description of the meeting in the synagogue on the last day of the disputation differs in matters of fact from Steinschneider's text.

THE DISPUTATION

OF

RABBI MOSES BEN NACHMAN (RAMBAN)

WITH

FRA PAULO CHRISTIANI

On the subject of the Jewish Faith

AND

HELD IN PUBLIC

BEFORE

KING JAYME I OF ARAGON

In July anno 1263

Translated from the text edited by Moses Steinschneider

CHAPTER X

TRANSLATION OF THE DEBATE

W E learn from the Talmud tractate Sanhedrin (43a) that our teachers taught that Jesus had five disciples: Mathai, Naqai, Neçer, Bunni and Thoda. When Mathai was brought before his judges he said to them: How can I, Mathai be put to death since it is said (in Ps. 42.2): 'When [Heb. =*mathai*] shall I come and appear before God?' They answered him: Mathai indeed shall be put to death, for Scripture states (Ps. 41.5): 'When [*mathai*] shall he die and his name perish?' When Naqai was brought before his judges, he said to them: How can you put me, Naqai, to death, since it is said (in Exod. 23.7): 'The innocent [*naqi*] and righteous slay thou not.' They answered him: Naqai indeed shall be put to death, for Scripture states (Ps. 10.8): 'in the covert places doth murder (1) *naqi*.' When Neçer was brought before his judges, he said: How can you put me, Neçer, to death, since it is said (in Isa. 11.1): 'a branch [*neçer*] out of his roots shall bear fruit.' They answered him: Neçer indeed shall be put to death, for Scripture states (Isa. 14.19): 'But thou art cast forth away from thy sepulchre like an abominable branch [*neçer*].' When Bunni was brought before them, he said: How can you put Bunni to death, since it is said (in Exod. 4.22): 'Israel is my son [*beni*], my first-born.' They answered him: Bunni indeed shall be put to death, for Scripture states (Exod. 4.23): 'I will slay thy son [*bin-kha*] thy firstborn.' When Thoda was brought before them he said: How can you put Thoda to death, since it is said (Ps. 100.1): 'A psalm of thanksgiving [*toda*].' They answered him: Thoda indeed shall be put to death, for Scripture states (Ps. 50.23): 'Whoso offereth the sacrifice of thanksgiving [*toda*] glorifieth me' (2).

As one of our teachers (3) has written, they (viz. the disciples of Jesus) were in close relation [cf. Sanh. 43a] to the government and it was necessary to answer all the vain and empty arguments which they brought. And so I also am writing down the remarks which I made in answer to the errors of Fra Paulo (4) who disgraced publicly his education (5) before our lord the king (6), his schoolmen and counsellors: may the king's majesty be extolled and his kingdom exalted!

Our lord the king had commanded me to debate with Fra Paulo in his majesty's palace, in the presence of himself and his council, in Barcelona. To this command I replied that I would accede if I were granted freedom of speech, whereby I craved both the permission of the king and of Fra Raymond (7) of Pennaforte and his associates who were present. Fra Raymond of Pennaforte replied that this I could have so long as I did not speak disrespectfully. Whereupon I rejoined: 'It is not my desire to be at variance with your rule on procedure of this matter but that I should speak as I wish on the subject of debate, as you on your part may speak entirely as you wish. For I know how to speak with self-control, as you insist, on a subject under dispute, but what to say must be within my own discretion.' So all of them gave their consent to my speaking freely. Thereupon I made the statement that disputation between Gentiles and Jews on many points arose out of customs of the Law upon which the substance of the Faith did not depend, but that I did not wish to argue in this honourable court except upon matters upon which religion as a whole depended. To this all present responded: 'You have well spoken.'

And so we agreed to discuss first of all the subject of the Messiah—whether he had come already as the Christian belief affirms or whether he is yet to come as the Jews believe. Later the topic would be whether the Messiah was really divine or if he was entirely human, born of man and woman. And after this the question whether the Jews maintained the true law or whether the Christians practised it would be debated.

Then Fra Paulo began by saying that he would prove from our Talmud that the Messiah of whom the prophets had witnessed had already come. I replied to that, that before we argued on that, I would like him to shew and tell me how this could possibly be true. For since the time that the king had been in the province (7a), and in many places I had heard that he, Fra Paulo, had made this statement to many Jews and I was most astonished at him. 'Let him answer me,' I said, 'on

this point: Did he wish to say that the scholars who appear in
the Talmud believed concerning Jesus, that he was the Messiah
and that they believed that he was completely man and truly
God in accordance with the Christian conceptions of him? Was
it not indeed a known fact that Jesus existed in the days of the
second temple, being born and put to death before the destruction of that temple? But the scholars of the Talmud were later
than this destruction, for example Rabbi Aqiba (8) and his
associates. And those who taught the Mishna, Rabbi Jehudah
(8) ha-Nasi and Rabbi Nathan, lived at a time that was many
years after the destruction; and much more remote from that
event was R. Ashi who composed the Talmud and reduced it
to writing, for he belonged to a period of about four centuries
later. Now, if these scholars had believed in the Messiahship of
Jesus and that he was genuine and his religious belief true; and
if they wrote those things which Fra Paulo affirms he is going
to prove that they wrote; then how was it that they continued
to hold by the Jewish faith and their original religious usage?
For they were Jews and continued to abide in the religion of
the Jews all their days. They died as Jews, they and their
children, and their disciples who heard all the words they
uttered. Why did they not apostatize and turn to the religion
of Jesus as has done Fra Paulo who understands from their
sayings that the Christian faith is the true faith? Far be it so!
But he has gone and apostatized on the ground of their words,
while they and their disciples who received the law from their
lips lived and died Jews as we today are! Moreover these were
they who taught us the Mosaic law and Jewish custom. For all
our religious practices today are in accordance with what the
Talmud teaches and with what we have observed of the scholars
of the Talmud who have followed and performed its teaching
from the time it was composed up to the present. For the whole
Talmud has no other end in view than to teach us the practice
of Law and Precept. Just as in this regard when the sanctuary
stood our forefathers were guided by the authority of the prophets and of Moses our teacher, on whom be blessing. So if
the scholars who appear in the Talmud had believed in Jesus
and his religion, how is it that they did not act as Fra Paulo
has acted, who understands their words better than they themselves did?'

Fra Paulo replied: 'These statements of yours are lengthy pronouncements designed to make the debate fruitless. But at any rate you will hear what I have to say; and I say to those who are here that of a surety I have complete and clear evidence that there is absolutely nothing in the statements which this man makes. Indeed the attention I pay to them is given solely because such is the wish of our lord the king.' Fra Paulo then began: 'This is what we have in scripture, in Genesis 49.10: "The sceptre shall not depart from Judah . . . until Shiloh come." It is the Messiah who is here meant, and the prophet asserts that Judah will always possess power until the Messiah who proceeds from him shall come. That being so, today when you Jews have no longer any sceptre or ruler's staff [or law-giver] (9), it follows that the Messiah, who is of the seed of Judah and whose is the rulership, has already come.'

My answer to him was: 'The prophet's intention was not to declare that the government of Judah should not at all be suspended at any time but he states that it *shall not depart* or cease entirely from Judah. For his view was that whenever sovereign power should fall to the lot of Israelites it was appropriate that it should reside in Judah. And if their kingdom should be interrupted because of sin, to Judah it would return. But the proof of my words is that already for a long time before Jesus lived the kingdom had lapsed from Judah, though not from Israel, and for long had lapsed both from Israel and from Judah. For you must note that during the seventy years of the captivity in Babylon there was no kingdom at all either in Judah or Israel. At the time of the second temple there was no king of Judah—only Zerubbabel and his sons were governors for a short period. And so thereafter for three hundred and eighty years the position remained unchanged until the laying waste of the temple when the Hasmonean (10) priestly dynasty with their satellites became kings. And so much the more now when the people are in exile does the principle apply that if there be no people there can be no king.'

Fra Paulo then said: 'Although throughout all those times the Jews had no kings, they nevertheless possessed ruling powers. For the explanation in the Talmud of the words "the sceptre shall not depart from Judah" is that this refers to the chiefs of the exile in Babylon who ruled the people with the· sceptre.

Further it is there explained that "the ruler's staff [or lawgiver] from between his feet" refers to the descendants of Hillel who were public teachers of the Law [cf. Sanh. 5a]. But at the present time you Jews have no longer the Ordination of scholars (11) [cf. Sanh. 14a] which was known to the Talmud. So even that ruling power has now come to an end. And today there is no one among you fit to be called *Rabbi* (12). And whatever you yourself may be called now-a-days, to designate you as *Master* [lit. Maestro = teacher] is misleading and it is dishonest of you to make use of that title.'

To this I replied with some irony: 'This point which you have just raised does not belong to the question we are debating. But even so you are not speaking the truth. For it is not *Rabbi* but *Rab* which is the equivalent of *Master* [Maestro] and in the Talmud the title *Rab* is bestowed without ordination having taken place. But I confess I am neither a master nor a good pupil.' This last remark I made by way of correcting him, then, returning to the subject of discussion, observed: 'Were it not that you have no understanding of Law and the legal decisions that have been deduced from it [viz. Halakah] (13) but are only versed a little in the homiletic exegesis of scripture [viz. Haggadah] (13) with which you have made yourself acquainted, I might convince you that our teachers of blessed memory had no intention of expounding the verse Genesis 49.10 in any other way than as referring to kingdom properly so called. And this view which the scholars have recorded is to the following effect, namely: The Law in its strict interpretation lays down that no man can hold court as a single judge [cf. Ab. IV.8] (14) and exempt anyone from the payment of a penalty unless authority to do so be received from the prince who is the factual king. Further, they stated that at the time of the captivity, whenever anyone of royal blood appeared to whom some rulership might be committed by the Gentile monarchs, as was the case with the Chiefs of the exile in Babylon and princes in Palestine, there was a (special) bestowal of authority together with ordination. And this was the customary procedure (namely the bestowal of authority through ordination) among the scholars of the Talmud for more than four centuries after the time of Jesus. For it was not the opinion of the scholars who appear in the Talmud that there must (always) be one of Judah's lineage (exercising ruling power)—a sceptre and ruler's staff [or Lawgiver] which is Judah's—but on the other hand the prophet who speaks in Genesis 49 did make the promise to Judah that the kingdom of Israel will be his and that promise was made in regard to real kingdom. But nevertheless that sovereignty has been suspended for a long time now as I have remarked. For during the period of the Babylonian captivity there was no sceptre or ruler's staff at all in Judah's hands. When the kingdom in the time of the second temple fell to the lot of the priests and their officials, no rulership pertained to the tribe of Judah (15). There was then no Chief of the exile, no prince. For the offices of prince and chief belonged to the priest-kings, to their administrators of Justice, to their officers and to whomsoever they deemed proper.'

Fra Peire de Genova then spoke: 'The fact is,' he said, 'that the Scriptures go no further than expressing that the rulership of Judah would not entirely cease but that there might possibly be a pause in its exercise, or, as a current term of Latin origin has it, a *vacation*.' Here I observed to the king: 'You will notice that Fra Peire confirms what I have said.' Fra Peire however said: 'I make no such confirmatory judgment, since the seventy years in Babylon was a short time, and, when it had passed, there were many who yet remembered the first temple as the Book of Ezra (3.12) reports, and this period of exile might be called a suspension of rulership, that is, a vacation. But now that you Jews have remained in this state of vacation for a millennium and more, a complete alienation of your rulership has taken place.'

I then said to him in reply: 'You are now the recipient of our consolation and comfort, because there can be no alienation of a thing that reverts again to its owner, nor is there any discrimination in what the prophet says between periods long and brief. Further, because the periods to which I referred were long periods. And still further because Jacob our father, on whom be blessing, did not promise Judah that his sceptre and ruler's staff [or Lawgiver] would rule over his own tribe only but that the kingdom of all Israel was to be given to him. For Scripture says (Gen. 49.8): "Judah thee shall thy brethren praise", and (1 Chron. 5.2): "For Judah prevailed above his brethren, and of him came the prince." But now, as you see, the kingdom over all the tribes of Israel has fallen away from

Judah in abeyance since the death of Solomon, as we learn (from 1 Kings 12.20): "There was none that followed the house of David but the tribe of Judah only." Under these circumstances it is clear that the prophet (in Gen. 49) asserted no more than that the rulership would not depart altogether from Judah; and this was the truth, for at the time of the exile this was not described either as an alienation or as a complete suspension of rulership, since the exile was the concern not (only) of Judah but of the people as a whole. For the prophet did not promise Judah that the children of Israel would never go into captivity, and this for the reason that he, Judah, might become ruler [lit. king] over them at any time.'

Here Fra Paulo again took up the debate and claimed that in the Talmud (cf. Jer. Ber. II.5a: Lam. R to I.16) it was stated that the Messiah had already come. He brought forward that Haggadic story, contained in the Midrash (16) [i.e. commentary] to the Book of Lamentations, about the man who was ploughing when his cow began lowing. An Arab was passing by and said to the man: O Jew, O Jew, untie your cow, untie your plough, untie your coulter, for the temple has been destroyed. The man untied his cow, his plough and his coulter. The cow lowed a second time. The Arab said to the man: Tie your cow, tie your plough, tie your coulter, for your Messiah has been born.'

To this I answered: 'I do not give any credence at all to this Haggadah but it provides proof of my argument.' At this the fellow (17) shouted: 'See how the writings of his fellow-Jews are denied by him!' I replied: 'I certainly do not believe that the Messiah was born on the day of the destruction of the temple and as for this Haggadah, either it is not true or it has another interpretation of the sort called the mystical explanations of the wise. But I shall accept the story's plain literal statement, which you have put forward, since it furnishes me with support. Observe then that the story says that at the time of the destruction of the temple, after it had been destroyed, on that very day, the Messiah was born. If this be so, then Jesus is not the Messiah as you affirm that he is. For he was born and was put to death before the destruction of the temple took place, his birth being nearly two hundred years (18) before that event according to the true chronology and seventy-three years previous to that event according to your reckonings.' At these words of mine my opponent [lit. the man] was reduced to silence.

Master Gilles (19), who was the king's justiciary, then replied to me with the remark: 'At the present moment we are not discussing about Jesus, but the question rather is: whether the Messiah has come or not? You say that he has not come, but this Jewish book says that he has come.' To this I said: 'You are, as is the practice of those of your profession, taking refuge in a subtlety of retort and argument. But nevertheless I shall answer you on this point. The scholars have not stated that the Messiah has come, but they have said that he has been born. For, for example, on the day when Moses our teacher, on whom be blessing, was born he had not come, nor was he a redeemer, but when he came to Pharaoh by the commandment of the Holy One and said to Pharaoh (Exod. 8.1): "Thus saith the Lord, Let my people go", then he had come. And likewise the Messiah when he shall come to the Pope and shall say to him by the commandment of God: "Let my people go", then he shall have come. But until that day comes, he shall not have come, nor (till then) will there be any Messiah at all. For David the king, on the day when he was born, was not a king nor was he a Messiah, but when Samuel anointed him he was a Messiah. And when Elijah shall anoint one to be a Messiah by the commandment of the deity he (the anointed one) shall be called Messiah and when, afterwards, the Messiah shall come to the Pope to redeem us, then it shall be announced that a redeemer has come.'

Hereupon my opponent (20) Fra Paulo urged that the biblical section Isaiah 52.13 beginning with the words 'Behold, my servant shall deal wisely' [so R.V. R.Vm. my servant shall prosper] treats of the subject of the death of the Messiah, of his coming into the power of his enemies and that they set him among the wicked as happened also in the case of Jesus. 'You do believe,' asked Fra Paulo, 'that this section is speaking of the Messiah?' I answered him: 'According to the real meaning of the passage the section speaks only of the community of Israel the people (21). For thus the prophets address them constantly, as in Isaiah 41.8: "Thou Israel my servant" and as in Isaiah 44.1: "O Jacob my servant".' Fra Paulo then rejoined: 'But I can shew you from the statements of the scholars that in their view the biblical section is speaking of the Messiah.' I replied

N

to this as follows: 'It is true that our teachers, of blessed memory, in the Haggadic books do interpret the *servant*, in the biblical section referred to, as indicating the Messiah. But they never assert that he was slain by his enemies. For you will never find in any of the writings of the Israelite people, neither in the Talmud nor in the Haggadic works, that the Messiah the son of David will be slain or that he will ever be delivered into the hands of his foes or buried among them that are wicked. Moreover, even the Messiah whom you have constituted for yourselves was not buried (22). But I shall give you, if you wish, a sound and clear exposition of the section in question and you will see that there is nothing in it at all about the servant being slain as was the case with your Messiah.' But they did not wish to listen.

My opponent, Fra Paulo, returned again to the point discussed, with the assertion that in the Talmud it was distinctly stated that Rabbi Jehoshua ben Levi had asked Elijah when the Messiah would come and Elijah had given him the reply: Ask the Messiah himself [cf. Sanh. 98a]. Jehoshua then asked: And where is he? Elijah said: At the gates of Rome among the sick. Jehoshua went there and found him and put a question to him, etc. 'Now,' said Fra Paulo, 'if what the Talmud here says be so, then the Messiah has already come and has been in Rome—but it was Jesus who was the ruler in Rome.' I said to him in reply to this: 'And is it not plain from this very passage you cite that the Messiah has not come? For you will observe that Jehoshua asked Elijah when the Messiah would come. Likewise also the latter himself was asked by Jehoshua: when will the Master come? Thus he had not yet come. Yet, according to the literal sense of these Haggadic narratives, the Messiah has been born; but such is not my own belief.'[1]

---

[1] The Talmud passage (Sanh. 98a) to which reference is made runs as follows (cf. Goldschmidt' *Der Babylonische Talmud*, Bd. IX): 'Rabbi Jehoshuah ben Levi once met Elijah who stood at the entrance of Simeon ben Jochai's cave. He said to him [i.e. to Elijah]: Shall I be permitted entrance into the future world? Elijah answered: When the Lord here [i.e. God] permits it. . . . Then R. Jehoshuah asked further: When will the Messiah come? Elijah answered: Go and ask him himself. Where is he? asked R. Jehoshuah. At the gate of Rome. How is he to be recognized? He sits among the poor folk that are smitten with disease. . . . After this R. Jehoshuah went to him [i.e. the Messiah] and said: Peace be to thee, O Lord and Master! The Master answered: Peace be to thee, Son of Levi. The latter asked: When will the Master come? He replied: To-day. Thereupon R. Jehoshuah returned to Elijah who asked him: What did he say to you? . . . R. Jehoshuah answered: He did not speak the truth to me for he said to me that he

At this point our lord the king interposed with the question that if the Messiah had been born on the day of the destruction of the temple, which was more than a thousand years ago, and had not yet come, how could he come now, seeing that it was not in the nature of man to live a thousand years? My answer to him was: 'Already the conditions of discussion have been laid down which preclude me from disputing with you and you from interposing in this debate—but among those who have been in former times, Adam and Methuselah were well nigh a thousand years old, and Elijah and Enoch more than this since these are they who (yet) are alive with God.' The king then put the question: 'Where then is the Messiah at present?' To this I replied: 'That question does not serve the purposes of this discussion and I shall not give an answer to it but perchance you will find him, whom you ask about, at the gates of Toledo if you send thither one of your couriers.' This last remark I made to the king in irony. The assembly then stood adjourned, the king appointing the time for the resumption of the debate to be the day after next.

On the day appointed, the king came to a convent that was within the city bounds, where was assembled all the male population, both Gentiles and Jews. There were present the bishop, all the priests, the scholars of the Minorites [i.e. the Franciscans] and the Preaching Friars [i.e. the Dominicans]. Fra Paulo, my opponent, stood up to speak, when I, intervening, requested our lord the king that I should now be heard. The king replied that Fra Paulo should speak first because he was the petitioner. But I urged that I should now be allowed to express my opinion on the subject of the Messiah and then afterwards he, Fra Paulo, could reply on the question of accuracy.

I then rose and calling upon all the people to attend said: 'Fra Paulo has asked me if the Messiah of whom the prophets have spoken has already come and I have asserted that he has not come. Also a Haggadic work, in which someone states that on the very day on which the temple was destroyed the Messiah was born, was brought by Fra Paulo as evidence on his behalf.

would come to-day, but he has not come. Elijah said: His answer to you had the following meaning (as in Ps. 95.7): "To-day, O that ye would hear his voice".' In the same Talmud tractate 99a we have the view of R. Hillel: 'R. Hillel said: The Israelites have no longer a Messiah for they have already enjoyed him in the days of Hezekiah.'

I then stated that I gave no credence to this pronouncement of the Haggadah but that it lent support to my contention. And now I am going to explain to you why I said that I do not believe it. I would have you know that we Jews have three kinds of writings—first, the *Bible* in which we all believe with perfect faith. The second kind is that which is called *Talmud* which provides a commentary to the commandments of the Law, for in the Law there are six hundred and thirteen commandments and there is not a single one of them which is not expounded in the Talmud and we believe in it in regard to the exposition of the commandments. Further, there is a third kind of writing, which we have, called *Midrash* (23), that is to say sermonic literature [*sermones*] of the sort that would be produced if the bishop here should stand up and deliver a sermon which some-one in the audience who liked it should write down. To a document of this sort, should any of us extend belief, then well and good, but if he refuses to do so no one will do him any harm. For we have scholars who in their writings say that the Messiah will not be born until the approach of the End-time when he will come to deliver us from exile. For this reason I do not believe in this book (which Fra Paulo cites) when it makes the assertion that the Messiah was born on the day of the destruction of the temple.'

'Furthermore, this (third kind of) literature is given by us the title *Haggadah* (24) which is the equivalent of *razionamiento* in the current speech, that is to say that it is purely conversational in character. Nevertheless, as you wish, I shall accept in its literal sense that Haggadic narrative which Fra Paulo has quoted, because, as I have already remarked to you, it supplies manifest proof that your Jesus is not Messiah, in as much as he was not born on the day mentioned, the day of the destruction of the temple. In fact his whole career was already over long before. But you, our lord the king, more fittingly than the others put a question to me raising the objection that it was not customary for man to live a thousand years. And now I shall give you a plain answer to your question. You will observe that the first man lived for a thousand years all but seventy and it is made clear in the Scripture that it was through his transgression that he died and, had he not sinned, he would have lived much longer or even for ever. Also, Gentiles and Jews alike all confess that the sin and punishment of the first man will be rendered ineffective in the days of the Messiah. If this be so, then, after the Messiah shall come, transgression and its penalty will cease in all of us, but (especially) in the Messiah himself will they be entirely absent. Consequently it is appropriate that he who is the Messiah should live for thousands of years or for ever, as is said in Psalm 21.4 (5): "He asked life of thee, thou gavest it him; even length of days for ever and ever." That point then has been explained. But our lord the king further has raised the question: Where then does the Messiah (meanwhile) reside? It is manifest from Scripture that the abode of the first man was in the garden of Eden which is upon earth; and after he had sinned, as is said in Genesis 3.23, "the Lord God sent him forth from the garden of Eden." That being the case, the Messiah, he who is exempt from the penalty incurred by Adam, has his abode in the garden of Eden, and so affirmed the scholars in the Haggadic writings to which I have referred.'

Hereupon the king remarked: 'But in that Haggadic book have not you Jews asserted that the Messiah was in Rome?' I replied to him that I had not asserted that the Messiah's abode was in Rome but that he had appeared there on a certain day, for Elijah had told the scholar Jehoshua ben Levi that the latter would find the Messiah there on that day and there he did appear. Moreover the reason for the Messiah being seen in Rome was recorded in the Haggagic traditions but I was unwilling to communicate it before so many people as those here assembled—the matter of which I did not wish to speak to the people was that which is spoken of in the Haggadah, namely, that the Messiah will remain [or abide, lit. stand] in Rome until he has destroyed the city. Just as in the case of Moses our teacher, upon whom be blessing, we find that he grew up in the palace of Pharaoh until he, Moses, had called Pharaoh to account and had drowned all Pharaoh's people in the sea. As also is said of Hiram king of Tyre (in Ezek. 28.18): 'Therefore have I [the Lord] brought forth a fire from the midst of thee; it hath devoured thee'; and in Isaiah 27.10: 'There shall the calf feed and there shall he lie down and consume the branches thereof.' And as is said in the chapters of the Hekaloth Rabbathi (V 21) (25): 'When a man shall say to his neighbour: Here you are, here you are! Rome and all that is in it for a farthing (Perutah)! And his neighbours shall reply: It is not going to be bid for by me.' All this I said to the king in private.

Continuing the discussion, I asked the question: 'You will agree, would you not, with my statement that in the Messianic age the sin of Adam is made of no effect?' Our lord the king and also Fra Paulo answered: 'Yes, we agree upon that but think otherwise than you upon the manner of its happening, for the fact is that, in virtue of that penalty which the sin of Adam incurred, all mankind had to enter Gehenna, but in the days of Jesus the Messiah this penalty was brought to nought, for he led them forth from that place.' My reply to this claim was: 'In our home-land we Jews have a saying that he who intends to tell a falsehood must get rid of the witnesses who testify against him. And, in Genesis chapter 3, many are the penalties which Scripture records as falling upon Adam and Eve, such as: "Cursed is the ground for thy sake . . . thorns also and thistles shall it bring forth to thee . . . in the sweat of thy face shalt thou eat bread . . . for dust thou art." And so also upon the woman does punishment fall: "in sorrow thou shalt bring forth children." Now, all these conditions endure even up to the present day and nothing of what is seen and experienced of them was cancelled by expiatory action in the time of your Messiah. But of the penalty of Gehenna (26), of which the scripture says nothing, you affirm that this has been thus cancelled. In order then that no one may be able to contradict you on this point send one of your number to Gehenna that he may come back and report to you! But far be it from God that He should do as you say! For the righteous suffer no penalty of Gehenna imposed on account of the sin of Adam their first parent. For my soul is related to the soul of my father (Adam) in as equal a degree as it is related to the soul of Pharaoh and it cannot be that on account of Pharaoh's sin my soul will enter Gehenna. But the penalties of sin are inflicted *on the body*, because my body is derived from my father (Adam) and my mother (Eve) and when judgment was made upon both of them (in the Garden of Eden) and they became subject to death, their descendants also for ever became by nature subject to death (27).'

My opponent now stood up and said: 'I shall bring further evidence that the Messianic age has already been.' But I craved

my lord the king to be allowed to speak a little longer and spoke
as follows: 'Religion and truth, and justice which for us Jews is
the substance of religion, does not depend upon a Messiah. For
you, our lord the king, are, in my view, more profitable than a
Messiah. You are a king and he is a king, you a Gentile, and
he (to be) king of Israel—for a Messiah is but a human monarch
as you are. And when I, in exile and in affliction and servitude,
under the reproach of the peoples who reproach us continually,
can yet worship my Creator with your permission, my gain is
great. For now I make of my body a whole-burnt offering to
God and thus become more and more worthy of the life of the
world to come. But when there shall be a king of Israel of my
own religion ruling over all peoples then I would be forced to
abide in the law of the Jews, and my gain would not be so much
increased. But the core of the contention and the disagreement
between Jews and Christians lies in what you Christians assert
in regard to the chief topic of faith, namely the deity, for here
you make an assertion that is exceedingly distasteful. And you,
our lord the king, are a Christian born of a Christian [man and
of a Christian woman] (28) and all your days you have listened
to priests [and Minorites and Preaching Friars talking of the
nativity of Jesus] (28) and they have filled your brain and the
marrow of your bones with this doctrine and I would set you
free again from that realm of habit and custom. Of a certainty
the doctrine which you believe and which is a dogma of your
faith cannot be accepted by reason. Nature does not admit of
it. The prophets have never said anything that would support
it. Also the miracle itself cannot be made intelligible by the
doctrine in question as I shall make clear with ample proofs at
the proper time and place. That the Creator of heaven and
earth and all that in them is should withdraw into and pass
through the womb of a certain Jewess and should grow there
for seven months and be born a small child and after this grow
up to be handed over to his enemies who condemn him to death
and kill him, after which, you say, he came to life and returned
to his former abode—neither the mind of Jew nor of any man
will sustain this. Hence vain and fruitless is your arguing with
us, for here lies the root of our disagreement. However, as it is
your wish, let us further discuss the question of the Messiah.'

Fra Paulo then said to me: 'Then you do believe that the

Messiah has come?' I replied: 'No, but I believe and am convinced that he has not come and there never has been anyone (29) who has said concerning himself that he was Messiah—nor will there ever be such who will say so [viz. concerning themselves]—except Jesus. And it is impossible for me to believe in the Messiahship of Jesus, because the prophet says of the Messiah (in Ps. 72.8) that "he shall have dominion from sea to sea and from the River until the ends of the earth". Jesus, on the other hand, never had dominion, but in his lifetime he was pursued by his enemies and hid himself from them, falling finally into their power whence he was not able to liberate himself. How then could he save all Israel? Moreover, after his death dominion was not his. For in regard to the Empire of Rome, he had no part in the growth of that. Since, before men believed in him the city of Rome ruled over most of the world and after faith in him had spread, Rome lost many lands over which it once held sovereign power. And now the followers of Muhammad possess a larger empire than Rome has. In like manner the prophet Jeremiah (31.34) says that in the Messianic age "they shall teach no more every man his neighbour, and every man his brother, saying, Know the Lord: for they shall all know me", while in Isaiah (11.9) it is written, that "the earth shall be full of the knowledge of the Lord, as the waters cover the sea". Moreover the latter prophet states (2.4) that, in this time, "they shall beat their swords into ploughshares . . . nation shall not lift up sword against nation, neither shall they learn war any more". But since the days of Jesus up to the present the whole world has been full of violence and rapine, the Christians more than other peoples being shedders of blood and revealers likewise of indecencies. And how hard it would be for you, my lord the king, and for those knights of yours, if they should learn war no more! And yet another oracle of the prophet Isaiah (11.4) is to this effect: "He shall smite the earth with the rod of his mouth." In the Haggadic work in the hands of Fra Paulo [see above] this verse receives the following commentary: "It was reported to the king Messiah that a certain province had rebelled against him. The king Messiah commanded the locusts to come and destroy the province. He was told that such and such an eparchy had rebelled against him. He commanded a swarm of insects to come and consume it."

But it was not thus in the case of Jesus. And you his servants deem to be better for your purposes horses that are clad in armour; and sometimes even all this proves to be of no avail for you. But I would yet submit for your attention many other arguments drawn from what the prophets have said.' At this juncture my opponent called out: 'Such is always his method —to make a long speech when I have a question to put to him.' The king thereupon told me to cease speaking on the ground that he, Fra Paulo, was asking a question (30). So I was silent.

Fra Paulo said: 'The Jewish scholars say of the Messiah that he is to be more honoured than the angels. This cannot apply to any but Jesus who in his one person was both the Messiah and God.' Then he adduced the Haggadic interpretation of the words 'my servant shall be exalted and lifted up and shall be very high' (Isa. 52.13), namely, that the Messiah is exalted above Abraham, lifted up above Moses and higher than the ministering angels. My answer to him on this point was: 'Our scholars constantly speak in this manner of all the eminently righteous, saying that they are more righteous than the ministering angels (31). Our teacher Moses said to an angel: "In the place where I have my dwelling, you have not authority to stand." And, in general, Israel avers that Israel is more beloved of God than are the angelic ministrants. But what the author of this Haggadic passage on the Messiah proposes to say is that Abraham, our father, on whom be blessing, wrought the conversion of Gentiles, explained to the peoples his faith in the Holy One, and in debate opposed Nimrod without fear. Yet, Moses did more than he. For Moses in his meekness stood before the great and wicked king Pharaoh and did not spare him in the mighty plagues with which he smote him, and brought Israel out beyond the range of Pharaoh's power. But exceedingly zealous were the ministering angels in the task of redemption. As is written in the Book of Daniel (10.21): "And now will I return to fight with the prince of Persia." Yet more than these all will the Messiah do. For his courage will be high in the performance of the purposes of the Lord. For he will come and command the Pope and all the kings of the nations in the name of God, saying: "Let my people go that they may serve me." And he will do among them many mighty signs and wonders and in no wise will he be afraid of them. He will make his abode (will stand) in their city of Rome until he has destroyed it (31a).' Having spoken thus, I said to Fra Paulo that I would give an exposition of the whole of the Haggadic passage if he cared to have it; but he did not so desire.

Fra Paulo now submitted another Haggadic passage where it is said about the Messiah that he prays for Israel that the Holy One may pardon their iniquities and undertakes to endure sufferings in behalf of others. In his prayer he says to God: 'I undertake to endure sufferings on condition that the resurrection of the dead be in my days, and I undertake this not only on account of the dead of my generation but for all the dead who have died from the days of the first men up to the present, and not only those who died [and whom the earth received] but even those who were cast into the sea and drowned or who were devoured by wolves and wild beasts.' 'Now,' claimed Fra Paulo, 'the suffering which the Messiah took upon himself to endure refers to the death of Jesus which Jesus willingly bore.'

To that argument I replied: 'Woe be to him who is shameless! All that is spoken of in the prayer of the Messiah was not performed by Jesus. Jesus has not raised to life those who have died from the time of Adam up till now, nor has he done anything at all of this sort. Furthermore that a prayer is spoken of in the passage shews that he, the Messiah, is human and not divine and that he has not power to raise from the dead. Moreover those so-named sufferings of the Messiah signify nothing other than the grief he endures because his advent is exceeding long delayed and he sees his people in exile and he has not power (to deliver them). Also he beholds brought to honour above his own people them that worship that which is not God and who have denied him and make for themselves a Messiah other than himself.'

Fra Paulo, in his reply to this, cited the Book of Daniel (9.24) where it is said: 'Seventy weeks are decreed upon thy people and upon thy holy city, to finish transgression, and to make an end of sins, and to make reconciliation for iniquity, and to bring in everlasting righteousness, and to seal up vision and prophecy, and to anoint the most holy.' 'The *seventy weeks*,' said Fra Paulo, 'signify years, namely the four hundred and twenty years when the second temple stood plus the seventy years of the exile in Babylon; and *the most holy* is Jesus.'

My answer was: 'Was not Jesus before this time (viz. the destruction of the second temple)? According to our reckoning he was more than thirty *weeks* (two hundred and ten years) before (2). And that this reckoning is the correct one is shown by the fact that Jesus' contemporaries, who were acquainted with him or knew him by sight witness in its behalf. And even according to your own chronology Jesus was more than *ten weeks* (seventy years) before.' Fra Paulo said that this was so, but that in the same scriptural passage (namely Dan. 9.25) where it is written: 'Know therefore and discern, that from the going forth of the commandment to restore and to build Jerusalem unto a Messiah (E.V. the anointed one) a prince . . . ' he who is here *a Messiah* is *a prince* and that is what Jesus was.

To this I replied: 'This statement which you make is likewise obviously wrong. For the Daniel passage divides the seventy weeks there mentioned, counting (from their beginning) up to the appearing of a Messiah prince, seven weeks; then after that, to the building of street and moat sixty-two weeks; then after that, one week [and half a week] when "he shall make a firm covenant with many" (9.27). And so the seventy weeks are completed. But Jesus whom you call Messiah prince did not come at the conclusion of the seven weeks, but after sixty weeks and more according to your reckoning. Give me an explanation of the whole Daniel section according to your own scheme and let me reply! For you could not with any sense in the world give an explanation of it. Nevertheless you are not ashamed to speak of what you know nothing about. But I may inform you that *a Messiah, a prince* (of Dan. 9.25) is Zerubbabel who came at the end of the seven weeks, for so is it made plain in the scriptures.'

On the remark of Fra Paulo: 'How can he, Zerubbabel, be called *Messiah?*' I commented: 'Even Cyrus is called Messiah (Isa. 45.1), and of Abraham, Isaac and Jacob it is said (Ps. 105.15; 1 Chron. 16.22): "Touch not my Messiahs (E.V. mine anointed ones)." Besides Zerubbabel is also entitled *prince* for though his government was not respected yet he himself was honoured and respected among his own people. And as Psalm 47.10 (9) says: "The princes of the people are gathered together even the people of the God of Abraham" (so A.V. cf. R.V.) (32). But now, if you and these associates of yours desire to learn or if there is in you a mind to understand, I shall make, in a clear exposition, the whole Daniel passage (ch. 9) intelligible to you. In the presence of our lord the king and before all peoples I assert that neither in this passage nor in what elsewhere is said in Daniel, except at the very end of the book, is the end-time which is preparatory to the coming of the Messiah mentioned. Nevertheless it is clearly evident from the text of scripture which reports all that is said to Daniel in this section (ch. 9) and in the other sections of the book that Daniel was constant in prayer to know the end-time. And so at last he is told, in chap. 12.11, when the end-time will be. This verse reads: "And from the time when the daily burnt offering shall be removed in order to set up [So Kautzsch et al., cf. R.V.] the abomination that makes desolate, there shall be one thousand two hundred and ninety days." And now even though this verse may be difficult for the Jews that are here present I shall interpret it to Gentiles. The verse means that from the time when the daily burnt offering shall be removed *until there shall be set up* the one who makes desolate, namely the one who is the abomination that has removed the daily burnt offering—a reference to the Roman people who destroyed the temple—there shall be one thousand two hundred and ninety *years*. For in this particular text the *days* that are mentioned represent years, a usage which occurs, for example, in Leviticus 25.29: "for a full year [lit. for days] shall he have the right of redemption" and also in Exodus 13.10 and elsewhere: "from year to year" [lit. from days to days]; likewise in Genesis 24.55: "a full year or ten months" [lit. days or, etc. Cf. A.V.m] (33). After this verse (Dan. 12.11) the book then, in verse 12, declares: "Blessed is he that waiteth, and cometh to the thousand three hundred and five and thirty days." Here there is an addition made of forty-five years (to the number that is given in the preceding verse). And the reason for this is that when the Messiah shall first come, then the abomination, which worships that which is not God, the one that makes desolate, shall be delivered up and exterminated from the world. After this the Messiah will gather together the dispersed of Israel to "the wilderness of the peoples" (Ezek. 20.35) as is written in Hosea (2.14): "I will bring her into the wilderness and speak comfortably unto her." And he will bring Israel to their own land, thus performing a like task to that which was performed by the first redeemer, namely Moses our teacher on whom be blessing. Thus will be fulfilled the forty-five years. From that time onwards Israel shall rest upon their own land and shall be glad in "the Lord their God and in David their king" (Jer. 30.9; Hos. 3.5); and "blessed is he that waiteth and cometh" to those good days. Now you will observe that up to the present day [the debate was held anno 1263] from the time of the destruction of the temple, 1,195 years have passed. In which case 95 years are yet awanting from the number of years (viz. 1,290 years) announced by the Book of Daniel (12.11) and we Jews expect that the redeemer will come at the time when those years that are lacking are fulfilled. For this interpretation which I have given of the Daniel passages is a well founded, fitting and probable explanation.'

Fra Paulo then made reply as follows: 'In the Haggadic interpretations scholars have asked what those days signified which (in Dan. 12.12) are additional to those of Daniel 12.11? These days, they said, are the forty-five days when the redeemer is concealed. Just as Moses the first redeemer appeared and was then concealed, so also the redeemer who is to come afterwards will reveal himself and then be hidden from men. But whenever these scholars mention the word *day*, actual days are intended and not years.' My answer to this was: 'The scriptural exposition [the Midrash] deals with the language of the text and notes that in this passage the forty-five days signify that number of years. It thus follows the instructions of our teachers to "pay close attention to [lit. to hold on to] the language of a biblical verse".' Fra Paulo addressing those present said: 'Except this man here who changes the meaning of words according to his own good pleasure there is no Jew in all the world who won't acknowledge that the Hebrew word *yom* means an actual *day*.' He then called upon the king to give his consent and a certain Jew, the first whom they found, was brought before the assembly and the question was put to him: 'The word *yom* in your language, what does it mean?' He answered: 'day.' My rejoinder was: 'My lord the king, this Jew is more fitted to be a judge on this matter than is Fra Paulo but is not more fitted to judge than I. For, in scripture, the word *yom* is used to signify the time when an event occurs, as for example (Num. 3.13, 8.17): "On the day that [=when] I smote all the firstborn." Moreover in the collective sense the plural of the word *yom* may signify years [see above]; and here in the Daniel passage the reference is to years. Furthermore, this meaning, years, is here required because the Book of Daniel seeks to draw a veil over the subject (of the end-time) since the angel has twice (viz. 8.26, 12.4; cf. 12.9) commanded him to do so, saying (12.4): "Shut up the words, and seal the book, even to the time of the end: many shall run to and fro, and knowledge shall be increased." But here am I giving utterance to words of wisdom to a man who has neither knowledge nor understanding and for whom it is entirely appropriate that fools should arbitrate in his behalf!'

Fra Arnol of Segura (34) observed: 'You will notice that when Jerome comments on the plural of *yom* in the Daniel passage of which we here speak, he interprets the word as meaning *days* in the sense in which that term (35) is popularly used.' I rejoiced to hear him say so and I said to them: 'You are now able to perceive from what I have already said that the word *days* in the text under dispute is not to be taken in the literal sense in which it occurs elsewhere. Wherefore one must needs find an interpretation of the word, and in my opinion it is the expression *days* in the popular usage which conveys the meaning of *years*. People, for instance, say: "It is many days since such and such a thing happened." By this they mean many years.'

My opponent Fra Paulo again took up the discussion with the statement: 'Jewish scholars have asserted that the Messiah has entered into the Garden of Eden, and there in the Haggadah the Messiah explains why, namely because he saw his fathers engaged in idolatry and dissociating himself from their practices he worshipped the Holy One, Blessed be He, who hid him in the Garden of Eden.' I laughed at him and said: 'This that you have quoted is for me an argument that the Messiah is a descendant of idolaters and entirely human and when he had dissociated himself from the practices of his fathers and did not worship idolatrously as they had done, the Holy One reckoned this to him as merit. But would this (that is here said about the Messiah) be said about absolute Deity?' Then I took up the book which Fra Paulo had with him and read out to those present the Haggadah passage from its beginning. The passage says that there have been fourteen persons who have entered the Garden of Eden without first having died and it numbers among these Serah the daughter of Asher and Bithiah the daughter of Pharaoh (36). 'Now,' I said, 'had the Messiah of this passage been Jesus, and he the Deity as you think he was, then he would not have been the companion of women in the Garden of Eden for assuredly God's throne is in heaven and the earth is his footstool. God forbid that what you suppose should be true! But what I have stated is that the Messiah has his abode in the Garden of Eden which was the place where the first man dwelt before he sinned. For this is the view of the scholars in the Haggadic books as has been explained.' Then our lord the king rose and the assembly dispersed.

Our lord the king had arranged that on the next Thurdsay the debate should be held in his palace and had commanded that it be in private. So we had our session in the fore-hall of the palace, Fra Paulo beginning with an airy speech in which there was no substance at all. After this he declared: 'I bring the testimony of a great Jewish scholar named Master Moses of Egypt [i.e. Moses Maimonides, 1135-1205] (37) the like of whom has not been in Jewry for the last four hundred years. This scholar says that the Messiah will die and his son and son's son rule in succession. Thus he does not say, as you have said, that the Messiah is not mortal like other men are.' Then Fra Paulo asked for the Book of Judges to be brought to him. Whereupon I said to my audience: 'In that book there appears nothing of that sort but I admit that some of our scholars think as has been described. As I mentioned at the beginning, the view of Haggadic authors is that the Messiah was born on the day of the destruction of the temple and lives for ever, while the view of those who study the literal sense of scripture is that the Messiah will be born when the end-time, the period of redemption, is at hand, and will live for many years and will die in honour bequeathing his crown to his son. And I have already stated that this latter is the opinion I hold. "For between this world and the days of the Messiah there is no difference except the delivery from servitude to the secular government" [cf. R. Samuel in Sanh. 99a] (38).'

The book which Fra Paulo had asked for was now brought, and he sought for what he wanted in it and could not find it. So I received the book from his hands, and, calling for attention to the statements of the work which he had introduced into the discussion, read aloud from the beginning of the chapter where it is said that the king Messiah is in the future to be designated for Israel and that he will build the temple and gather together Israel's dispersed. At these words of Maimonides, Fra Arnol of Segura exclaimed: 'He is speaking lies.' To which I replied: 'Up till now he has been a "great scholar" that has "none like him" and now he is a liar!' But the king rebuked Fra Arnol, observing that it was not seemly to offer insults to the learned. Addressing my remarks to the king I now continued: 'The author of this book is not speaking falsehood for I could prove from the Law and the prophets that what he says is true. For upon the Messiah rests the duty of gathering the dispersed of Israel, the scattered ones of Judah, the whole twelve tribes. But your Messiah Jesus did not gather a single individual of them, nor was he living at the time of the Exile. Further, to the Messiah belongs the task of building the Sanctuary in Jerusalem. But Jesus had nothing to do with that, neither with building it nor with its destruction. Also the Messiah will rule over all peoples. But Jesus did not rule even over himself.' Then I read to all present the Scripture-portion (Deut. 30.1 f): 'And it shall come to pass when all these things are come upon thee, the blessing and the curse which I have set before thee etc. etc., the Lord thy God will put these curses upon thine enemies and on them that hate thee, which persecuted thee.' I explained to them that in this portion the words 'thine enemies' referred to the Christians and 'them that hate thee' to the Moslems, the two peoples who have persecuted us. No reply was given to this and the assembly rose.

On the morrow on the Friday they marshalled their array in the palace, the king sitting as usual on his chair by the place where was situated the recess with his throne, and with him were the bishop and many nobles, Gilles of Sarnon (?), Peire Braga, numerous knights, all the people of the suburbs as well as of the poorer folk. Addressing the king I told him that I did not wish to continue the debate and he enquired my reason for this. I said: 'There is a large body of people here who have all sought to bring pressure upon me and to make me amenable to taking this step, for they are very apprehensive of those persons, the preaching friars, who are casting the world into a panic. Moreover the highest and most honoured of the priesthood have sent to me to say that I should proceed no further in this discussion. Also many knights of your own household, my lord the king, have informed me that I am doing an evil deed in speaking in their presence contrary to their faith. Likewise Fra Peire of Genoa, the Minorite scholar, has told me that this is not proper. Besides people from the suburbs have said to certain of the Jewish community that I should desist.' Indeed such was the case. But when those concerned saw what was the king's wish in the matter, with hesitation they all urged that I should continue. So after much talk between us on the matter I at length said that I would debate on the condition that the court would allow me a day for putting questions, when Fra Paulo would answer me, since for three days he had been the questioner and I had answered. The king (consenting) said: 'At any rate answer him (now).' So I thanked him.

Fra Paulo then stood up and put the question: 'The Messiah of whom the prophets spoke, do you believe that he was to be both completely man and very God?' I replied: 'From the beginning of this debate we agreed that we should first discuss whether the Messiah had come, as you Christians say he has, and then afterwards address ourselves to the question of whether he was absolute Deity. But you have not proven that he has come; because I have dissolved all the flimsy arguments which you brought. And thus far I have won my case, for the *onus* has been upon you to bring proof, for so you took upon yourselves to do. Yet, if you will not acknowledge that I have won this case, I take it upon myself to bring valid arguments on the subject under dispute if you will listen to me. But it having been made clear that your Jesus was not the Messiah, it is not for you to argue in regard to the Messiah who in future is going to come to us as to whether he will be a real man or what he will be.' The learned lawyers who were present confirmed that the right lay with me on this point. The king, however, said that in any case I should answer the question that had been asked.

I therefore answered thus: 'Surely when the Messiah shall come he shall be truly man, born, as I am, of a man and woman who had been married. And he will be of the line and seed of David, as is written in Isaiah 11.1: "And there shall come forth a shoot out of the stock of Jesse" and as is said in Genesis 49.10: "Until Shiloh come"—Shiloh here meaning *his son* and deriving

o

from the word *shilyah* which signifies *afterbirth* (39). For the
Messiah is to be born as are all members of the human race in
connection with the *afterbirth* (that is with the membrane en-
veloping the foetus in the womb). And were it the Spirit of God
(through whom) as you say (the Messiah should be conceived)
then he would not be of the stock of Jesse, even had the Spirit
lodged in the womb of a woman who was of Jesse's seed. Nor
in such case would he be the heir of David's kingdom, for by the
Law the daughters and their progeny do not inherit so long as
direct male issue exists. And, in regard to David, in all ages
there have been male children of his line.'

Here Fra Paulo interposed and said: 'There is, however, the
110th Psalm which begins with the statement "A psalm of
David—the Lord said to my lord, Sit thou at my right hand".
Now who is this to whom David the king refers as "my lord"
except it be deity? For how should a man sit at the right hand
of God?' Upon this, Fra Paulo's question, the king observed:
'That is a good point which the questioner has made, for if the
Messiah were merely a man of the seed of David and nothing
else, David would not refer to him as "my lord". And had I a
son or grandson, even though he should rule over the whole
world I would not refer to him as "my lord", but I should desire
that he should say to me "my lord" and that he should kiss
my hand.'

Turning to Fra Paulo I remarked: 'Are you the learned Jew
who discovered this new interpretation and on the strength of
it became an apostate? Are you the one who asked the king to
assemble the Jewish scholars for you that you might debate
with them about the new interpretations that you have found?
And is it the case that up till now we have never heard of this
matter you mention? And yet is there any priest or child who
has not cast up to the Jews this very objection which you raise,
this extremely ancient question which you ask?'

On the king intervening to say that I should nevertheless
answer the question that had been asked, I craved the attention
of the audience and explained as follows: 'King David was the
singer who composed the psalms through the inspiration of the
Holy Spirit. He composed them for the service of praise which
took place before the altar of God. But he himself did not sing
them (there) and was not entitled to do so, this being forbidden

him by the enactment of the Law. He, however, gave the psalms to the Levites to sing, as appears clearly from 1 Chronicles 15.2. Well then, this being the case, the composer of this psalm (110) had necessarily to compose it in language which was appropriate to a Levite reciting it. For had the Levite recited "the Lord said to me" he would not have been speaking truthfully; but it was appropriate that the Levite when he recited in the sanctuary should say "the Lord said to my lord —namely to David—Sit thou at my right hand". The meaning of the expression *sitting* (at the right hand of God) is that the Holy One, Blessed be He, would protect David all his days and deliver him and make him prevail over his foes. As happened when one (of David's mighty men, cf. 1 Chron. 11.11; 2 Sam. 23.8) lifting up his spear against eight hundred men slew them at one time. Is there any one among these knights who are in attendance upon you, who in his valour could do likewise? And this is also what *the right hand* of God signifies in Psalm 110. Even as it is written by David in Psalm 18.35: "Thy right hand supports me" [R.V. hath holden me up] and in Psalm 118.15 f: "The right hand of the Lord does valiantly. The right hand of the Lord is exalted." Similarly it is written of Moses, our teacher, on whom be blessing, in Isaiah 63.12: "(God) that causeth his glorious arm to go at the right hand of Moses"; and it is said of the downfall of Pharaoh in Exodous 15.6: "Thy right hand, O Lord, dasheth in pieces the enemy." Moreover it is apparent that the Scriptures in several places speak in the same manner [as in Psalm 110 where David does not speak of himself directly in the first person]. For example in the Book of Samuel (1 Sam. 12.11) the author speaks of "Jephthah and Samuel". In Genesis (4.23) Lamech says to his wives: "ye wives of Lamech." And a similar mode of speech occurs in the Pentateuch in regard to all the words of Moses our teacher. But of course here in Psalm 110 the author was under a necessity of speaking so as you have observed. But, furthermore, I would bring to your notice that the psalms were composed through the inspiration of the Holy Spirit, and are spoken concerning David's son who is to sit upon his throne—the latter being the Messiah. Therefore according as the content of the Psalms had *in part* a reference to David, this will be fulfilled in the Messiah David's son *in its entirety*. Is it that (cf. Ps. 18.35 f) the right

hand of the Holy one supports David so that he prevails over
his enemies round about him, so will the Holy One help the
Messiah to make all the peoples his footstool. For they all are
his enemies. They have subjected his people to servitude and
have denied his coming and his kingdom. And some of them
have constituted another as Messiah. . . . Hence it was proper
to sing this Psalm 110 in the sanctuary in the days of David, and
will be so in the days of the Messiah his son; for this psalm refers
to the throne of David and to his kingdom.'

The reply of Fra Paulo to this exegesis of mine was: 'How
can the explanation which you have given possibly be right,
since your own Jewish scholars assert that the Psalm (in the
words "said to my lord, etc.") speaks of the Messiah? For
the words in their plain sense mean that he sits on the right
hand of God.' Fra Paulo then submitted a passage from
the Haggadah which says that in the future the Holy One
will let the Messiah sit at his right hand and Abraham at
his left.

I replied: 'Also this passage accords with what I already have
said, as the view which I then expressed set aside all reference
to David and in the main was wholly concerned with the Messiah
himself.' I then asked to see the book with the passage Fra
Paulo had mentioned and on receiving it I declared: 'Mark you
and observe that Fra Paulo here has been concealing the facts
of the case. For what this Haggadic passage says is that in the
future the Holy One will let the Messiah sit at his right hand
and Abraham at his left. And the face of Abraham will turn
pale and he will say: "the son of my son will sit on the right
hand of the Holy One and I on his left" and the Holy One will
console him, etc. Now note that in this text that has been cited
it is manifest that the Messiah is not divine and that in no way
is Jesus regarded as the Messiah. For had the Messiah been
divine, Abraham would not be abashed if deity were given
more honour than he. Nor in that case would his face turn pale
or blanch at all. Accordingly Abraham says "the son of my
son". He does not say "the son of my daughter". And according to your own statements Jesus was not a son of the son of
Abraham in any case. Hence whether it be the Messiah sitting
at the right hand of God, or Abraham sitting at the left hand,
both of these persons are entirely human. Likewise it necessarily

follows that Jesus is not the Messiah from the point of view of the passage, for this speaks of the future and the scholars who speak as described in the passage lived about five centuries after Jesus' time.'

But Fra Paulo, demolished utterly in debate, without being ashamed, brought yet another argument, namely from a Midrash where the verse 'I will walk among you' (Lev. 26.12) is treated of as follows: 'We have a parable by way of illustration to the effect that once upon a time a king went out to take a walk in his park in the company of one of his tenant-farmers. The latter sought to hide himself away from the king, and the king said to him: "What ails you that you seek to hide yourself? Lo! I am like unto you." So the Holy One, Blessed be He, is ready to walk in the company of the righteous in the hereafter in the garden of Eden but the righteous will see him and tremble before him. And the Holy One will say to them: "What ails you that you tremble before me? Lo! I am like unto you. Perchance you have no reverence for me".' 'But, thanks be to God,' said Fra Paulo, 'the verse (Lev. 26.12) affirms: "And I will be your God and ye shall be my people." Whenever God said "Lo! I am like unto you", he had become, in that circumstance, *man* even as they were men to whom he spoke.'

My reply to this was: 'All that Fra Paulo brings as proof he brings as against himself—if he could only comprehend this fact —for this event, of which the Midrash speaks, is to occur in the future and will take place in the Garden of Eden. Now Jesus did not walk in the company of the righteous in the Garden of Eden when he was a man, but all his days he was a fugitive before his enemies and persecutors. This Midrash passage is, however, a parable and accordingly begins with the words: "we have a parable by way of illustration." And its meaning is that the righteous are not able in this world to attain to the true nature of prophecy and are unable to look upon the *Splendour* which is called *The Glory*. As is said in Numbers 12.6: "I the Lord will make myself known unto him in a vision." For even Moses our teacher in the beginning of his prophesying trembled —as scripture (Exod. 3.6) records: "And Moses hid his face; for he was afraid to look upon God." But in the hereafter the souls of the righteous will be free from all sin and from all blemish. And they will have permission to contemplate (the

Deity) through *The Shining Mirror*,[1] even as Moses, our teacher, on whom be blessing, had permission, and of whom it is said (Exod. 33.11): "And the Lord spake unto Moses face to face, as a man speaketh unto his friend." So the words: "Lo! I am like unto you" are said by way of parable to teach that the righteous should not tremble or be afraid before God: just as they are not afraid of one another. And that too is what scripture means when it says: "As a man speaketh unto his friend." For God did not actually become a man when he was speaking with Moses. But the intention of the scholars who write in the Midrashic commentaries is to assert, as they have asserted in the *Midrash Yelamedenu* (40), that God says to man: "If thou wilt do my commandments, behold thou shalt be like unto me." Thus it is in this sense that we have to understand such scriptural utterances as Genesis 3.5: "And ye shall be as God, knowing good and evil"; Genesis 3.22: "God said, Behold the man is become as one of us"; Zechariah 12.8: "And he that is feeble among them at that day shall be as David; and the house of David shall be as God." For such sentences do not mean that God and man would be the same in appearance.'

My opponent in reply adduced as an objection to what I had said the fact that in the Midrash Bereshith Rabbah the verse Genesis 1.2 'And the spirit of God moved upon the face of the waters' is said to refer to the spirit of the Messiah and that, if this be accepted, the Messiah is not a man but the spirit of God. I answered: 'Alas for him who knows nothing, but imagines that he is a scholar and an expert! For, you may notice, in that Midrash the words "The spirit of God moved" are explained yet again, and this time as referring to the spirit of the first man, Adam. And would you say therefore that the Midrash really affirms thereby that the first man was divine?

---

[1] Heb. = *haispaklaria ham' irah*. These words and the idea appear in the Talmud (Succ. 45b). Jastrow (Talm. Dictionary) translates: 'who contemplate (Deity) through a *lucid speculum*.' The lucid speculum is a metaphor for *prophetic vision*. Of this vision the above-named tractate asks: 'Are then those who see the shining radiance (Goldschmidt, *den leuchtenden Glanz*) so very few? Abajje said that the world has not less than thirty-six righteous persons who daily receive the vision of the Deity.' The Mirror as symbol of the prophetic faculty appears also in Kabbalism. See p. 389 of the Zohar, Vol. I, translated by Sperling and Simon. Jehuda ha-Levi (*The Kusari*, IV.15, Cassel's ed., p. 337) writes: 'The activity of the "Eternal" is not to be comprehended through speculation but through prophetic insight, the possession of which distinguishes man from man and brings man nearer to the angels.'

'Truly he who will not observe what comes first and what follows later in the books he reads will turn upside down the very oracles of the living God. Now, the expositor [viz. Rabbi Simeon ben Lakish] who in the Midrash Bereshith Rabbah explains the words "the spirit of God" as referring to the spirit of the Messiah had (already) interpreted the Bible-verse Genesis 1.2 as referring to the kingdoms of the world and according to him the scriptures here allude to events that were to happen in the future. This is what he says: The words "And the earth was waste" signify Babylon, because it is written in Jeremiah 4.23: "I beheld the earth, and lo, it was waste." "And void" signify the kingdom of Media, since in the Book of Esther we read (6.14): "They hasted to bring Haman." "And darkness" points to Greece which had darkened the eyes of Israel by (tyrannical) decrees. While the words "upon the face of the deep" indicate the wicked kingdom and "and the spirit of God" means the spirit of the Messiah. The Midrash then asks the question: "To effect what benefit did the spirit of God move upon the face of the waters?" and answers: "To effect the benefit of repentance which is compared with water" [cf. Lam. 2.19]. From this we see that the Midrash in explaining the verse lets pass before our eyes four kingdoms, the fourth kingdom being Rome, and then following this introduces "the spirit of God" which it says is the spirit of the Messiah, that is, a being who is entirely human, full of wisdom, full of the spirit of God as was Bezalel of whom it is said in Exodus 31.3: "And I [the Lord] have filled him with the spirit of God, etc." Also of Joshua it is said [Deut. 34.9]: "And Joshua the son of Nun was full of the spirit of wisdom." Hence it is clear that the Midrash is speaking about the Messiah who is to come after the fourth kingdom has been. But I have not been able to explain to Fra Paulo the character of the Midrashic exposition, namely that it contains (allegoric) allusions (41) whose expounding requires the assistance of the knowledge of the language. It has not to be considered that the essential meaning of the scripture text will be dealt with in this Midrashic literature and, similarly, this is true in regard to many passages of the Midrash Bereshith Rabbah, as for example what is there said in explanation of the biblical-section Genesis 28.10 f: "And Jacob went out, etc. (42)."' I made these last remarks in order to shew to all who were present that Fra Paulo was not competent to read from the book which he had brought as evidence, as he could not without blundering read the language in which it was written. The king now rose and the assembly took its departure.

This is a full account of the discussions. To my knowledge I have made no alteration in the recording of them. Afterwards on the same day (as the discussion in the palace ended) I had audience of the king who remarked: 'The debate still remains to be concluded. For I have never seen anyone who was in the wrong argue so well as you have (42a).' Then I heard in the palace-court that it was the will of the king and of the Preaching Friars (the Dominicans) to visit the synagogue on the Sabbath. So I tarried in the city for eight days.

When they came to the synagogue on the following Sabbath I addressed our lord the king in words that were worthy of the occasion and of his office. When he expounded earnestly to the effect that Jesus was the Messiah, I rose up and said: 'The words of our lord the king in my eyes are noble words, exalted and to be held in honour since they proceed from the mouth of a nobleman highly esteemed and honoured, the like of whom is not in our time, but I do not appraise them as the truth in as much as I have proofs and arguments clear as sunlight that the truth does not correspond with his words. Though it be not seemly to have controversy with the king, one thing I would like to say, namely that I am very astonished at him, for the arguments we have heard from him persuading us to believe in Jesus that he is the Messiah, Jesus himself employed to persuade our fathers, and himself endeavoured to propound this doctrine to them. And to his face they refuted it with a complete and valid refutation. Now, since in your opinion Jesus was divine, he was better equipped with knowledge and ability to establish his own claims than is the king, and if our fathers who saw him and were acquainted with him did not listen to him, how then shall we believe and listen to the king who has no knowledge of him in actual experience but only through a remote report which he has heard from men who did not know Jesus and were not Jesus' countrymen as were our fathers who knew him and were witnesses [that they had seen one who was human as they were] (43).'

After I had spoken thus Fra Raymond of Pennaforte rose up

and gave a discourse on the subject of the Trinity and asserted that the Trinity was wisdom and will and power. 'And had not also the Master,' he said, 'in a synagogue in Gerona assented to what Fra Paulo had said on this point?' At this I got to my feet and spoke as follows: 'I ask both Jews and Gentiles to give me their attention on this matter. When Fra Paulo asked me in Gerona if I believed in the Trinity, I replied: "What is the Trinity? Do you mean that three material bodies, of the sort that men have, constitute the Godhead?" He said: "No." Then I asked: "Do you mean that the Trinity consists of three subtle substances such as souls or that it is three angels?" He said: "No." "Or do you mean," I enquired, "that the Trinity is one substance which is a compound of three substances such as are those bodies which are compounded of the four elements?" He said: "No." "If that is the case" said I "then what is the Trinity?" He answered: "Wisdom and will and power." To which I replied that I acknowledged that the deity was wise and not foolish, and will without passibility (44), and powerful and not weak, but that the expression *Trinity* was entirely misleading. For wisdom in the Creator is not an unessential quality (44) but He and His wisdom are one and He and His will are one and He and His power are one—and, if this be so, the wisdom and the will and the power are one whole. And even if these were unessential qualities of God, the thing which is the Godhead is not three but is one, bearing three unessential qualities.'

Our lord the king here spoke, drawing an analogy which they who err (45) had taught him. He said that in wine there are three things, colour and taste and fragrance, and that these constitute one thing. . . . But this is entirely erroneous, since the redness and the taste and the fragrance in wine are three distinct things each of which might be present without the others. For there are red and white and other colours of wine. The same holds true in regard to taste and fragrance. Moreover the redness is not the wine, nor is the taste the wine, nor is the fragrance the wine. But the essence of the wine is the thing which fills the whole, and is a body which bears three distinct accidents; a body in which there is no unity. And if (in regard to the deity) we should proceed on this false analogy to calculate as has been done we would be compelled to affirm a quaternity.

For the thing which constitutes deity together with his wisdom and his will and his power when counted up is four. Further, you could have a fivefold deity, since God is a living being and just as wisdom is in Him so is life; in which case his definition would be: a living being, wise, willing, powerful and having the essence of Godhead. All which comes to five. But this whole mode of thought is manifestly wrong.

Then Fra Paulo stood up and said that he believed in the perfect unity of the Deity but that nevertheless there was in that unity a Trinity, and this was a doctrine very profound for neither the angels nor the princes of the upper regions could comprehend it. My answer to this was: 'It is clear that no person believes what he does not know. Hence it is that the angels do not believe in a Trinity.' The associates of Fra Paulo made him remain silent. Our lord the king rose up and he and those with him descended from the place where the prayer-desk was, each going their several ways. On the morrow I had audience of our lord the king whose words to me were: 'Return to your city in safety and in peace.' Then he gave me three hundred *dinars* (46) and I took my leave of him with much affection. May God make him worthy of the life of the world to come. Amen.

NOTES ON THE LETTERS

(1) *of absolute and genuine sincerity.* lit. 'and the truth was contained under their clothing.' Cf. Prov. 31.25: 'strength and dignity are her clothing.' Possibly the literal translation should be 'and the truth was altogether *instead of* (i.e. for Heb. taḥath) their clothing.'

Vestments. The good works which man performs cause a reflection or part of the supreme light of heaven to descend upon him. This reflection (Abglanz) serves the man as a vestment or garment when he enters the world to come. The soul has a different garment for this world and for the other world. (Zohar II.229b. See Bischoff, First Part, *Die Elemente der Kabbalah*, p. 113.) Thus 'the truth was instead of their garments' would mean served as the vestments of the great commentators.

(2) *p. 53 col. 2.* Wagenseil adds: 'of the greater Pentateuch edition' (*majoris Pentateuchi editione*). This may refer to the Ḥumash 'im Targum = Pentateuch with Targum (Onkelos) which in 1587 Genebrard (in Reland's *Analecta*, p. 202) mentions in his *Index Librorum Rabbinicorum editorum qui ad meam notitiam pervenerunt.* He also mentions the 'Twenty-Four (i.e. O.T. of twenty-four books) in large', *Viginti quatuor (libri scripturae) magni*, with commentaries of Rashi, Ibn Ezra, the Targums, and the greater and lesser Massora. Also the 'Twenty-Four in small', i.e. *Biblia minora*, which is without these commentaries.

(3) *The Targum* (Onkelos). Targums were Aramaic translations of the Hebrew text which were rendered necessary, when Hebrew was no longer a living language, for explaining the scriptures in the Synagogue. The Targums have a large admixture of paraphrase and midrashic (homiletic, narrative) elements. The two most important Targums are (1) the so-called Babylonian (in which the Pentateuch (Torah) is ascribed to Onkelos and the prophets to Jonathan), and (2) the Jerusalem Targum to the Pentateuch (Jerushalmi I) wrongly ascribed also to Jonathan and called sometimes Pseudo-Jonathan. Both these Targums are of Palestinian origin, the former redacted in Babylonia in fifth century A.D. and belonging to the second century, the latter belonging to a later date, although large portions of their text must go back into pre-Christian times.

Another Targum to the Pentateuch, called Jerushalmi II or the Fragment-Targum, is not complete. (See Eissfeldt, *Einleitung*, p. 710; Sellin, *Intro. to O.T.*, p. 21.) For translations into English see Etheridge, *The Targums of the Pentateuch*.

(4) *Ibn Ezra.* Abraham ben Meïr ibn Ezra (1093-1168), born in Toledo, was a man of many interests, a constant traveller, poet, mathematician and above all biblical exegete. Karpeles (*Gesch. d. jüd. Literatur*, Vol. 1, p. 424) describes his temperament as to-day piously orthodox, to-morrow a free-thinking critic, now earnest, even downcast, now humorous and satiric. In his introduction to the Pentateuch he speaks of the method of his exegesis: 'At first every word is examined from the point of view of grammar and then explained, without troubling about massoretic (traditional) data, where the views that are set out are arbitrary and fit only for children, and without paying attention to the alleged later emendations made by the scribes. But regard is taken of the Targums which indeed often vary from the simple interpretation, for which divergence they no doubt have their reasons. So far as the juristic portion of scripture is concerned however, that explanation which agrees with the view of tradition deserves the unconditional preference, since it is true.' In other words Ibn Ezra knows how to sail his ship into the open sea, but appreciates the safety of the calm harbour. He does point out the difficulties of the text and few escape him. He is rationalist and traditionalist and combines clear exegesis with symbolizing mysticism. Karpeles calls him the first witty Jewish writer and Spinoza described him as *liberioris ingenii vir et non mediocris eruditionis*. David Daiches, in *The King James Version of the English Bible*, says that the translators of A.V. made much use of Kimchi's commentary (p. 91), that Rashi, the most popular exegete among Jews, was rarely used by non-Jews, while Ibn Ezra was employed more rarely still (op. cit., p. 159). Daiches explains the use of Kimchi by Christians as owing to his writing an easy Hebrew. But there is no doubt that it was Kimchi's keeping to the literal sense of scripture that made him acceptable to the men of the Reformation. Bartolocci says (Reland, op. cit., 'Lives of famous Rabbis') that Kimchi 'was more accurate and faithful in explaining the text than were all the other expositors of sacred writ.' On the other hand there was much more than a sense for the accurate rendering of the literal meaning of scripture in Ibn Ezra and much to explain why he was neglected by those who eschewed a *manifold* sense in scripture. Ibn Ezra was a man of correspondingly manifold gifts—*philosophus, astronomus, medicus, poeta, grammaticus, Cabalista et sacrae scripturae famosus interpres* (Bartol., op. cit.). That he was a Kabbalist would make him acceptable to Rittangel.

(5) *Rashi*, i.e. Rabbi Solomon ben Isaac (1040-1105), born in Troyes, sometimes called Salomon Isaacides (Jizhaki) sometimes Jarchi. He and Maimonides are the most influential and notable figures in the Jewish learned world of the Middle Ages. Nicholas de Lyra (1270-1340), a Christian who may have been of Jewish origin, born at Lyre in Normandy, and who wrote commentaries on the Bible and thus influenced Martin Luther in his Bible-translation by his emphasis on the importance of the plain sense of scripture, had evidently (cf. Karpeles, op. cit., Vol. 1, p. 457; and Daiches, op. cit., p. 123) made good use of Rashi's Bible-commentary. *Si Lyra non lyrasset | Lutherus non saltasset*, a popular couplet, recognized the link between Lyra and Luther. Neither Lyra nor Rashi abandoned the idea of a manifold sense of scripture current in the mediaeval Church but both prepared the way for the appreciation of the 'natural' meaning of the sacred text. For Rashi on the Pentateuch, see Pentateuch with Targum Onkelos, Haphtaroth . . . and Rashi's commentary, translated into English and annotated by Rev. M. Rosenbaum and Dr A. M. Silbermann, London, 1929. A good example of Rashi's exegesis is given in the passage here cited from his commentary where he explains Gen. 49.10.

(6) *For this refers to the Chiefs of the exile*, etc. The authority for this is Talmud Sanh. 5a (cf. Hor. 11b): '*The ruler's staff will not pass from Judah*—that is a reference to the Chiefs of the exile in Babylonia, who bring the people into subjection by the staff: *nor a Lawgiver from between his feet*—this refers to the descendants of Hillel who are public teachers of the law.' Pesaḥim 66a speaks of the authority given to Hillel: 'Then they set him [i.e. Hillel] on high and made him Prince.' The purpose of Sanh, 5a and Rashi is to shew that the power of Judah did not pass away with the destruction in 586 B.C. of the kingdom of Judah but was continued in the rule of the Exilarchs or Chiefs of the Exile who were appointed by the Babylonian government, and in Palestine by Hillel and his descendants who were heads of schools though they had no political power.

(7) *gathering*. So Rashi interprets the word, deriving it from קוה (qavah) = collect, gather. Cf. Gen. 1.9 (gathering of waters): Jer. 3.17 (of nations).

(8) For מגילות which is corrupt, read perhaps מגלה אות = revealing or *shewing a sign* (of your own fingers or handwriting). Possibly the original text was מעשה א״ = the work (of your fingers), cf. Ps. 8.4, which phrase occurs several times in the correspondence. In which case the translation is 'a reply, the work of your (own) fingers.'

(9) *to explore its depth*. lit. to come 'into a path (or pass) of depth' or 'enter in a profound way'.

(10) *with a metal pen* (or stylus). Cf. Kelim XI 3, where קְצוּצָה =
cut metal, wire; cf. Jast. Dictionary and *Kelim* XII. 8 where metal
pens are mentioned. Wagenseil translates *calamo quasso* (*quassus*, from
quatio, meaning shaken, broken, split) which would mean a shaking,
trembling or damaged pen. But as the Heb. word for pen קוֹלְמוֹס =
calamus is masculine and קְצוּצָה is feminine, the latter is not an adjective at all. In view of the question (which arises later) of the
manner in which this letter is written, it might seem appropriate
that Rittangel excuses himself on the score of a damaged pen or
quill, but he does not do so.

(11) *your epistles.* If the plural is to be understood literally this
would mean that Rittangel had written to the Jew another letter
besides his letter called No. 1 (above). Previous to writing letter
No. 1 Rittangel knew the Jew's views on Gen. 49.10 for there he
wrote (p. 1): 'I have taken note of your arguments.' As the Jew did
not know Rittangel, the latter must have come to the knowledge of
the Jew's interpretations of the scripture-passage through others,
probably through those who suggested to Rittangel that he should
debate with the Jew on the disputed text. The Jew's views as expressed in this letter (see below) presuppose that on some occasion
he had announced them before, though briefly, in writing (cf. p. 110,
line 25; p. 111, line 9) namely in the letter he later speaks of (p. 111,
line 40).

(12) *true intention* of scripture—the text here varies slightly from
that given in Rittangel's letter.

(13) *whose names are cited.* Lit. who are expressed by name (cf.
Num. 1.17).

(14) *Midrash Aggadah.* This refers to Rashi's words: 'A Midrashic
interpretation, etc.," quoted by Rittangel (p. 109, line 15 f). Aggadah (Haggadah) is a tale or story and refers especially to that class
of Rabbinic literature which explains the Bible homiletically. Aggadah is to be contrasted with Halakah or legal interpretation. There
are Midrashim (commentaries on scripture of a discursive sort)
which are of Aggadic and others of Halakic character.

(15) *after the analogy of chastisement and suffering* (or affliction). The
word rendered *analogy* here, *gezera*, is a term. tech. of logic = *category*.
The second of the thirteen exegetical principles by which the Law is
expounded, as laid down by Rabbi Ishmael (see Singer's Prayer
Book, 13th edit., p. 13) reads: *u-mi-gezera shavah* = *the inference from a
similarity of phrases*, lit. *from an equal or identic category*, i.e. an analogy
on the basis of verbal congruities in the text (see Jast. Dictionary).
The first interpretation which the Jew offers of the word *shebet* is that
rod or *staff* is a symbol or instrument of suffering or affliction, and that
if this sense be given to the word in Gen. 49.10 it can claim the

analogy of other congruous biblical passages or usages (where rod signifies punishment, correction and suffering) in its support. His argument would be that Gen. 49.10 means that chastisement and affliction will not pass from Judah until [if he gives '*ad ki* this sense here] Shilo (the Messiah) comes. To this argument corresponds the Jew's view that while some explanations are better than others, yet even the others, if they be well-intentioned efforts, have a contribution to make. There are many facets of divine truth (cf. below).

(16) *for ever* (*Aramaic* = '*ad 'alma*). Cf. Targum text and translation, p. 211 above. In Onkelos' paraphrase the words '*ad 'alma* = *for ever* are an explanatory addition to the words that precede them. They do not translate the words '*ad ki* of Gen. 49 which are translated by *until* in '*until* the Messiah come' ('*ad d* jethe Meshiḥa). It is obvious however that both the Targum Onkelos and Rashi (p. 109 above) are conscious of the fact that other interpretations have been offered and are rebutting explanations as given by Christians. That the sovereignty or power of Judah will ever cease or has ever ceased is what both Targum and Rashi are at pains to deny.

(17) *when* the Messiah will come. I.e. the Jew separates the '*ad* of Gen. 49.10 from the *ki*, though these words cannot, without violence, be separated.

(18) *Rabbi Bechai*, i.e. *Bachja ben Asher* (1291) of Saragossa, was writer of a commentary on the Pentateuch, employing a fourfold scheme of exegesis: the philosophic, the kabbalistic, the plain sense and haggadic. He was a contemporary of Nachman (Ramban) and followed his teaching. But he appears to have had rather 'a short way with dissenters' for he taught that only Israelites had a part in the Resurrection and Paradise. His commentary seems to have gained great popularity and the most popular of narrative commentaries on the Pentateuch, viz. that called *Ẓe'ena u-Re'ena* ('Come and See') in Yiddish by Jakob ben Isaac of Janow in Poland and published in Basel 1590 and 1622, quotes copiously from Bechai. The *Ẓe'ena u-Re'ena* which was specially intended for the womenfolk 'Zu Ehren Weiber und Maiden' still fulfils its role in Poland to-day as family reading-book. Hershon has published Ze'ena u-Re'ena on Genesis in English. See Karpeles, op. cit., Vol. II, pp. 66, 328. A copy of Bechai's *Be'ur al ha-Tora* (*Exposition of the Torah*), Amsterdam, 1726, is in the Guildhall Library, London. Cf. Catalogue of Hebraica of Corporation of London, 1891, p. 12.

(19) *expositors*. I.e. reading ha-mephareshim. Pi.ptc.pl.

(20) *in previous exposition* (or what I have said expressly before) refers to the letter or writing which preceded this letter (cf. p. 111, line 40).

(21) *exegesis*—peshat (lit. *literal sense*, but apparently here used more generally).

(22) *readily allows.* Lit. be pleased, willing, German einwilligen—ho'il here is a verb, and not = ho'il we = for (as Wagenseil regards it). See *Oxf. Heb. Dic.*, j'al.

(23) *Genesis 41.49. until he (Joseph) left numbering.* To reconcile the two notions of the external sovereignty of Judah and of a limit of time apparently fixed for that sovereignty by the advent of Shilo (until Shilo come), the Jew quotes Gen. 41.49: 'And Joseph laid up corn as the sand of the sea, very much, until he left numbering, for it was without number.' In this text he sees the combination of both ideas—the grain that Joseph gathers is limitless, without number, and the laying of it up would therefore constitute an eternal, infinite process of gathering while at the same time there is a limit set, viz. 'until (*ad ki*) he left numbering.' The Jew though he denies that *ad ki* means *until* in his second explanation of the verse must retain this sense for the *ad ki* of his first explanation where *shebet* is interpreted as meaning chastisement, for there must be a limit to this chastisement, for this, unlike Judah's sovereignty, cannot be conceived of as going on *for ever*, without any cessation whatsoever.

(24) *sanctuary* (or *palace*). (*May your palace* (sanctuary) etc.) In one of the most mysterious portions of heaven there is a palace called the 'palace of (divine) love'. All the souls that are acceptable to God the heavenly king are there (Zohar II.97a; Bischoff, op. cit., p. 114). The word *Hekal* = mansion, temple or palace. These mansions were said to be seven or nine in number (see Waite, op. cit., p. 175). 'Within each of the seven regions of the Paradise, there is a Palace. The aim of the Heavenly Palaces is to preserve the *Shekina* for the world, and it is done by keeping the contact between upper worlds and this world of ours' (Bension, op. cit., p. 197). Corresponding to each of the celestial palaces there is a palace of Hell. The fourth palace is the Palace of Merit. In the sixth Palace are 'the Lovers of God'. The Palaces are described by the Zohar as 'Thoughts-seen-through-curtains. Take away the thought and the Palace becomes nothing that the mind can grasp' (Bension, p. 220).

(25) *riches and honour*, etc. Cf. Prov. 3.16.

(26) *inconsistencies.* I.e. reading ha-se'iphim lit. fissures, breaks [instead of he-se'uphim; W. *montes (absurditatum)*]. Perhaps the original text was seippim = hesitating ideas.

(27) *banner* (or standard) with signs and signals (mophethim = signs, portents, proofs). Cf. Num. 1.52, 2.1 f and Intro. p. 6.

(28) *as before* = Heb. b^e'eno, lit. *in his (its) eye*, but idiom for *in original state.* Cf. Jastrow; and Silbermann (im ursprünglichen Zustande).

(29) This is Targum Jerushalmi II or the Fragment-Targum. Cf. Etheridge, p. 336, and above, note 3.

(30) Targum of Jonathan ben Uzziel of Jerushalmi I called by Etheridge (cf. pp. 157, 331) the Targum of Palestine.

(31) *Tractate Sanhedrin 5a.* Text gives ch. 1, p. 8, column a, where ה = 8 is error for ה = 5. Cf. note 6 above for translation of this passage from Goldschmidt's Talmud and note on Pes. 66a.

(32) *Tosaphoth* are the collections of oral laws (Mishnahs) outside of the regular Mishnah. In Talmudic literature, Tosaphoth are the annotations to the Talmud mostly by French scholars (Tosaphists). Cf. Jast. Dictionary.

(33) *Hazzekuni.* This would appear to be Hezekiah ben Manoah who wrote under the name of Hazzekuni (1240) a Kabbalistic work on the Pentateuch and whom the *Jewish Ency.* describes as a French exegete of the thirteenth century. His name also has the forms Chazkuni and Chizkuni. Cf. Catalogue of Hebraica and Judaica in Library of Corporation of City of London, 1891 (pp. 18 and 30) by Rev. A. Löwy.

(34) *Joshua ibn Schuaib*—a preacher and Kabbalist who flourished about 1328, was an author of homilies on the Pentateuch which he entitled 'derashoth 'al ha-Torah'.

(35) the book Rabboth (*Sepher Rabboth*) = Sepher Midrash Rabboth also called Midrash Rabbah.

(36) *Kebod ha-Ḥakamim* (Honour of the Ḥakamim). Cf. p. 46, line 2. The title of a work written by David ben Jehuda, Messer Leon (1490) the son of Jehuda ben Jehiel who was called Messer Leon (1475). The book was published in Berlin in 1898, edited by S. Bernfeld. See Karpeles Vol. II, p. 193, who however does not mention the *Kebod ha-Ḥakamim*.

(37) *Rabbi Moses ben Nachman* called Ramban or Nachmanides was born before 1200 at Gerona where he was Rabbi and physician, and died between 1268 and 1270 in Palestine. His controversy with the convert to Christianity, Pablo Christiani, the teacher of Raymundus Martini, was waged in the presence of Jayme I, king of Aragon. This debate is contained in Nachman's Wikkuah ha-RAMBAN (The disputation of Ramban) and was held in the year 1263. See 'Catalogue of Hebraica' of the City of London, 1891, p. 114, on the Wikkuah, edited by M. Steinschneider, Berlin, 1860. Cf. also Schiller-Szinessy on Ramban (Nachman) in *Ency. Brit.*, 9th-10th ed.

(38) *'Aqedath Jiçhaq* (Binding of Issac), Religious philosophy adapted to the weekly portions of the Law, was the last great exegetical work written in Spain before the expulsion of Jews from that country. Its author was Isaac ben Moses Arama of Zamora (1494).

P

The book won a great popularity. See Karpeles (*Gesch.*, Vol. II, p. 179).

(39) *words or mouth*—since there is no word עֵד meaning exactly *words* or *mouth*, the reference must be to *ēd* i.e. עֵד = witness whose root meaning, see Jastrow, is *confirmation.* Cf. Bekh. 36a עֵד מִפִּי עֵד 'a witness testifying to what he has heard from a witness', lit. a witness *from the mouth* of a witness. Without the vowel-points there is no distinction in form between עַד = until, booty, for ever, and עֵד = witness.

(40) *worn or ragged cloths.* The word עַד here has also the form עֵד (ēd) when it is supplied with a vowel.

(41) *until the King Messiah.* Rittangel makes a slight mistake here in form, though not in substance, since what Onkelos says is: 'until the Messiah come, whose is the kingdom.'

(42) *malka* = King. Cf. note above.

(43) *expansions.* See note 16 above on words *for ever* = 'ad 'alma.

(44) *flavour and fragrance.* i.e. the whole sense of the passage would be adversely affected and the style of the oracle destroyed, if the words 'Shilo (will) come' were cut off from what went before and formed a new sentence by themselves.

(45) *Be'er Moshe* (The Well of Moses) by Moses ben Issachar Saertels (or Schaertels) 1604 and his work *Lekach Tob* (good doctrine) treated of the Pentateuch and the Prophets. See Karpeles, Vol. II, p. 329.

(46) *tangled skein* lit. *knot.* What Rittangel wishes to say is that it is obvious that in Gen. 24.33 the words *until I have spoken my words* are exactly parallel to *until Shiloh come* so far as syntax is concerned, only in the former case *until* is expressed by 'ad 'im (lit. till if) while in the latter *until* is 'ad ki (lit. till if, or till when). Rashi on Gen. 24.33 says that *ki* has four meanings and one of these is if. Rittangel argues from Rashi's comment, that, as in Gen. 24 both particles 'ad and 'im go together to form one expression = *until*, so also in Gen. 49 both 'ad and ki go together; and secondly that since ki is = 'im = if, the Jew, in not applying the conditional sense (viz. if Shiloh come) to the latter part of Gen. 49.10, has lost an opportunity of giving another explanation no less complicated and absurd than the one he has given in his second interpretation. There is no doubt that in referring to Gen. 24.33 Rittangel is exercising a certain amount of humour and has his tongue in his cheek.

(47) *allusion to the captivity.* This must allude to the contents of the first letter or narrative of his views on Gen. 49.10 which the Jew wrote in Dutch (see below) before he wrote his first letter in Hebrew belonging to this correspondence. See note 11 above.

(48) *Book of Formation* (Hebrew: *Sepher Jeçira*), in its original form

probably belongs to the ninth century. At the end of the book mention is made of 'Abraham our father' and this led early to the belief that Abraham had written the book. Its earliest commentator Saadjah (892-942) traced its teaching to Abraham although he made clear that he did not mean that the Patriarch had composed the work but only that he had known the doctrine. Rittangel accepted, apparently without any scruple, that Abraham was the author, just as he shared with Rosenroth (1636-1689) the view that Simeon ben Jochai (c. A.D. 150) was the author of the Zohar.

(49) *seven twofold expressions . . . seven letters . . . seven conditions of existence.* Rittangel (p. 203 of his translation of the *Sepher Jeçira*) translates the Heb. *sheba' kephuloth* as *septem duplices.* E. Bischoff (*Die Elemente der Kabbalah*, Berlin, 1920, where on p. 63 f, Part I, there is a translation of the *Sepher Jeçira*) renders the phrase as *sieben doppelte (Buchstaben)* i.e. *seven double (consonants)*, but *twofold expressions* seems a better rendering, since the hard and the soft forms of the *seven letters* of the Heb. alphabet which are mentioned—the so-called B^eG^aDK^eP^a(R)Th letters—stand in relationship to each other as complements of each other. They are pairs not doubles. As one shoe to the other they complement each other. In respect too of the *conditions of existence* that are mentioned, death is not a double of life nor is poverty the double of riches, but each is a counterpart of the other. Together the various pairs form, each with its counterpart, twofold expressions. That in Heb. the soft form of *b*, *g*, etc. may be so represented or by *bh*, *gh*, etc. and the hard form by *bb*, *gg*, etc. (where the letters appear as doubled) is irrelevant to the thought of the *Jeçira* passage here cited.

(50) *Moses Botarel* (1409), a Spaniard, wrote a commentary on the *Sepher Jeçira*, in which among others such as Saadja and Meir of Rothenburg he cites *Aaron of Babylon*. Botarel, whom Wagenseil here in his translation and Rittangel in his commentary to his translation of the *Sepher Jeçira* call Botril, has been accused of citing, as authorities, persons and books that never existed, in order to enhance both the antiquity and the authority of Kabbalah (see Karpeles, Vol. II, p. 144). Rittangel in his commentary to *Sepher Jeçira*—Liber IEZIRAH Amsterdam, 1642, p. 37—refers to Aaron in much the same language in Heb. and Latin as he does here—*R. Aharon magnificus ille et eminentissimus Cabilista, caput et singulare ornamentum totius Babylonicae Synagogae.* The commentary of R. Aaron the Great, according to A. E. Waite 'The Holy Kabbalah', p. 111, was called *The Book of the Points.*

(51) *ancillary*—lit. serve or are applicable to or attend upon.

(52) In *bb*, *gg*, etc. See note 49 above on the *seven letters*.

(53) *We* (Christians) . . . *you* (Jews). The words in brackets do

not appear in the text. It is characteristic of the correspondence that even when it is clear that *Christians* are intended there is a reluctance to use the word *Christian* (or *Jew*). This explains why the Jew would prefer to debate with Rittangel, a man of his own race, by word of mouth, rather than by writing. Conversation is freer; in writing the Jew feels he is dealing not plainly but 'in riddles' so far as the root of the discussion is concerned. (See above p. 112.)

(54) '*in the letter.*' Here Rittangel bases upon Epistle to the Romans 2.27-29. Cf. Delitzsch's translation ad loc. into Heb.—*welo' kephi ha-kethab.*

(55) '*the Shells*' (Qeliphin) *that is, the Law which is in the letter.* The contrast which St. Paul draws in Rom. 2.27-29, between the *letter and the spirit,* gives Rittangel a chance of plunging more deeply than hitherto into Kabbalistic ideas. The Pauline and the Johannine conceptions certainly offered an opportunity of contact between Jewish Kabbalists and Christian mystics and Rittangel here gives an example of Kabbalistic thought applied to scripture and Christian teaching. When Rittangel speaks of the King Messiah breaking 'the *shells*', namely the Law which is 'in the letter', he is referring to the Kabbalistic *Qelippoth* = envelopes, shells, cortices. What these are is explained by the following passage from the Zohar III.132a: 'In truth there is hidden in every word of the Torah (the Law) a deep mystery. . . . For all that comes down from above, must, in order to be made available for us, receive an earthly covering. Just as the Angels of God when they were sent to the earth, had to clothe themselves in human guise, so the Holy Torah, which is intended for our use, could not be comprehended by us unless it had a vestment. So it obtained one. The narratives which it contains are the clothing of the (higher, hidden) teaching. . . . The moral elements that are deduced from the narratives are the body. The hidden mystical meaning is, lastly, the soul of the Torah. The foolish think that the narratives are the body of the Torah. . . . The rational man looks only for what the clothing covers (that is, the moral substance of the narratives). The truly wise pay attention alone to the soul of the Torah. They alone (therefore) are destined in the future world to behold the soul of the soul (namely God) which breathes in the Torah.' (From Dr E. Bischoff's *Die Elemente,* Part I, p. 88.) In later Kabbalism, these shells or cortices signified demons (cf. Waite, op. cit., p. 256). Christian Kabbalism, we see, contained within it the tendency and danger of reverting to the *manifold sense* of scripture which the Reformation discarded. Cf. Intro. above. After mentioning 'the shells' Rittangel now launches out upon a long mystical passage currently believed then to be from the teaching of the chief exponent of Jewish mysticism, Simeon ben Jochai.

(56) *Simeon ben Jochai . . . Supplements of the Zohar.* See for notes on and explanation of this citation the chapter on 'The Zoharic passage in the letters'.

(57) *Targum of Jerusalem,* i.e. Jerushalmi II. Cf. note 3 above and Etheridge (op. cit.), Vol. I, p. 166.

(58) *Hakamim* = wise men, sages. But later the word appears as an official title of teachers of the Law, or authorities on scripture.

(59) *Ancient Wisdom* (Hokmah) *which for the righteous man* (for the *Zaddik*) *is the chief thing* (lit. is head). This seems to be the meaning of the words so translated, the word *Zaddik* being understood in the sense of the righteous or pious person. See the chapter on 'The Zoharic passage in the letters'. Rittangel's correspondent is called upon to listen to the voice of divine and eternal Wisdom who (Prov. 8-9) calls upon the sons of men to pay heed to her teaching. On the other hand, beyond this practical sense there may be a reference to the Kabbalistic teaching concerning the second *Sephirah* (or mode of the divine manifestation) called 'Wisdom' through which the world exists and upon which all other mysteries depend (cf. Waite, *The Holy Kabbalah,* p. 204). If this be so and if we take *the Zaddik* as referring to the ninth Sephirah which is named '*The Righteous One, the Foundation of the World*', we may understand the sentence as follows: 'They . . . will bring you under the shadow of the *Ancient Wisdom which is Head* (or source) *for the Righteous One* (the Foundation of the world) *and indwells it with power.*' Understood in this sense, the following passage from the Zohar (I.229a; Sperling, Vol. II, p. 334) provides a commentary on the words. There Rabbi Judah says about prayer that 'prayer offered with true devotion is directed on high to the supernal recess from whence issue all blessings and all freedom, to support the universe. It is attached above to the mystery of the supreme Wisdom. . . . When the blessings issue from the supernal recess . . . they flow down until they come to the place called the "Righteous One the foundation of the world".' See diagram of the Sephiroth p. 154. The Zohar passage, portion only of which has been cited, speaks of the descent of the blessings which prayer is granted as proceeding from Hokmah (Wisdom, the second Sephirah) through the sixth Sephirah (the grade Heaven or Tiphereth) right down to the ninth Sephirah (the Righteous One called Foundation or Jesod) where they are ready to descend and 'to support the universe'. In Rittangel's letter the blessings spoken of are the possession of the hidden mysteries of salvation and the spiritual blessings which are conducive of eternal welfare for the soul. The Kabbalistic interpretation of *Head* and *Zaddik* seems on the whole to be the more suitable.

(60) *With the bread of Mighty Ones* ('*Abirim*) *and with the spiritual*

Leviathan. The *'Abirim* (see Sperling, *Zohar*, Vol. III, p. 192) are the *celestial princes*, i.e. angelic beings. As the manna eaten by the Israelites in the wilderness became the type of symbol of the spiritual food or bread which the saints enjoy in this world or in the world to come, so also does the flesh of the Leviathan which in Ps. 74.14 was given by God 'to be meat for the people inhabiting the wilderness' become the emblem of Spiritual nourishment. In the Talmud (Baba Bathra 74b) it is said that God created at the beginning a male and a female Leviathan but lest these great sea-monsters should have offspring and so the work of creation might be jeopardised, God 'castrated the male and killed the female and pickled it for the righteous in the future world' that is, in the Messianic Kingdom. In Kabbalistic thought Leviathan is the symbol of the visible creation; cf. Zohar I.35b and Isaac Myer, *The Qabbala. The Philosophy of Ibn Gabirol*, p. 234. See chapter (below) on 'The Zoharic passage in the Letters'.

(61) *to judge the high mountains . . . in behalf of the sons of the Shekinah.*
For the metaphors here employed cf. Isa. 41.15; Jer. 51.25; especially Obad. v. 21: 'And saviours shall come up on mount Zion to judge the mount of Esau: and the kingdom shall be the Lord's.'
Sons of the Shekinah—Shekinah (= Divine Presence) in this passage appears to indicate the Shekinah as representing the Community of Israel (cf. Sperling, *Zohar*, Vol. III, p. 189, and Glossary of Technical Terms). Rittangel is thinking of the Community of Israel in the spiritual sense.

(62) *that you do not . . . reject the Corner-stone of your salvation.* The reference is in the first place to Christ who (Matt. 21.42) quotes Ps. 118.22: 'The stone which the builders rejected is become the head of the corner' (cf. Mark 12.10; Luke 20.17; Acts 4.11; Eph. 2.20; 1 Pet. 2.6f). In the New Testament a mystical sense has already attached to the *Corner-stone*. The Corner-stone of Psalm 118 (see Waite, op. cit., p. 228 f, and Müller, op. cit., p. 72 f) was according to legend and Kabbalistic symbolism the Shetija or Foundation-stone which, at the beginning of Creation, God cast into the abyss of chaos to serve as a firm and sure basis for the creation of the world. The stone was at first a jewel in the Throne of God. Then it became the Foundation-stone of the world which emerges as the projecting rock on the site of the temple of Jerusalem (the Dome of the Rock) and is designated 'the navel of the earth'. The character of this mystical stone as without comparison or dimension is apparent from its history for in addition to what has been said of it, it was the stone which served as Jacob's pillow which he set up as an altar and was later held in the hands of David. It is said also 'to be destined for the salvation of the world'.

(63) *'In the covert of the steep place'* (R.V. Songs 2.14) or (cf. Cohen,

The Five Magilloth, p. 9, ad loc.) 'in the covert of the cliff'. This refers at least to the privacy in which Rittangel kept himself. As he preferred written correspondence to any other (see below), he probably kept on purpose out of the Jew's way. Whether 'steep place' or 'cliff' corresponded to any feature of Rittangel's residence in Amsterdam or of the city itself we cannot tell. The Hebrew word *madregah* = steep place or cliff is the word used to translate the Aramaic word *darga* used in the Zohar for *grade* or *degree*. In Kabbalist thought, God descends to man and man ascends to God through grades or degrees. Rosenberg in his Hebrew translation of the Zohar (*Sepher Zohar Torah*, New York, 1927; cf. p. 69, Vol. I) translates *dargin* (the plural of Aramaic *darga*) by *madregoth* (Heb. plural of *madregah*) where it is said: 'Abraham sought to know all those grades'. Possibly the Jew of Amsterdam by his biblical quotation is not only rallying Rittangel on his stay-in-doors habits but on his exalted Kabbalist studies, and suggesting to him that he should 'come off his perch'.

(64) *full of strong reasons*. The Heb. word here translated *strong reasons* as it appears in the text which is without vowels is *'çmuth*. Wagenseil translates *plena ossium* as = *full of bones*, i.e. regarding the Heb. word when supplied with the necessary vowels as being *a'çamoth*. It is not clear what is meant by a letter being 'full of bones' unless it be intended to say that Rittangel's letter was dry and uninteresting. But that bones are dry bones is not always true. Rittangel (see below p. 69) himself challenges the word *'çmuth* but does not say what he thought the Jew intended by it. The word *'çmuth* appears (with vowels) as *a'çumoth* in Isa. 41.21 = *strong reasons* (R.V.): *Bring forth your strong reasons, saith the King of Jacob*, the strong reasons being the specious arguments or defences which the heathen deities are summoned to bring forth at a tribunal set up by Jehovah. The word for *strong reasons* is with suffix in Isa. 41.21 and is a hapaxlegomenon in the Old Testament. There can be little doubt that this is the word the Jew had in mind. For him Rittangel's arguments were specious reasonings urged ultimately in the interest of a 'strange' religion.

(65) *the voice of your letter*. Cf. Eccles. 5.3; Heb. 5.2 = the voice of a fool. R.V. 5.3 a fool's voice.

(66) *which do not affect*, etc., lit. *do not benefit and do not lower*. The phrase in the text seems to be a reminiscence or even a corruption of the current phrase *l'o ma'aleh wel'o morid* = neither raises nor lowers, i.e. has no effect or influence. See Jastrow under ירד.

(67) *my judgment of this your attitude*. Heb. = upon (or concerning) this.

(68) *Don't imagine you can drive me off with a bruised reed*. Bruised reed

(cf. Isa. 42.3. Vulg. calamum quassatum). *To drive or push off with a reed* is a phrase which occurs in the Midrashic literature = *to give an insuffici·it answer or proof*. E.g. in the Midrash on Genesis (Bereshith Rabbah Par. viii, Cap. 1, v. 26): 'When the heretics departed, his disciples said to Rabbi Simlai: Rabbi, you have driven (or pushed off) these with a reed, but what answer do you give to us?' See Theodor, *Bereshith Rabba*, p. 63.

(69) *relevant substance.* Heb. = *Toref* = that which is essential in a legal document, e.g. name, date, sums of money involved, etc. But see note 93 below for another possible rendering. Rittangel in reply to this letter understands the word differently as if the Jew had meant 'I shall reply in brevity and in order to the *rigmarole* of your words.' But it is not obvious that the Jew uses the word in this sense here.

(70) In Gen. 49.10 the word '*ad* (עד) has under it *the accent* < called Jethib. Cf. Ungnad's Hebräische Grammatik, p. 17.

(71) The argument appears to be that if it be granted that *Onkelos* paraphrases '*ad* of Gen. 49.10 by '*ad* '*alma* = for ever, it cannot be held that while he has erred here yet he is right in his interpretation of the verse as a whole, for this would mean that Onkelos was both right and wrong at the same time in respect of the same verse. In which case, what about Rittangel's dictum about two contraries not being able to be predicated of one and the same subject?!

(72) See p. 128 above for Onkelos' paraphrase. In his paraphrase the '*ad* '*alma* = *for ever* is attached to the words preceding, while the word '*ad* does again appear and is attached to *djethe meshiha* which follows. It is clear that in Onkelos '*ad* '*alma* is an addition by way of explanation and does not translate or paraphrase the '*ad ki* of the verse.

(73) *complete dominion,* etc., or to the effect that dominion shall not altogether depart from Judah, so that, etc.

(74) *faithfulness.* Here = true religion or faith; but the word *faithfulness* is retained on account of the scripture passages which follow.

(75) *disposition.* reading *jeçer* instead of *çir*. The latter word could mean *messenger* or *distress*. Other instances of displacement of consonants appear in the text.

(76) Job 41.2—in reference to the Leviathan.

(77) *perpetuating* or substantiating.

(78) *in Aggadoth.* Halakah (from halak = to walk, to proceed) denotes a precept for the practice of a Jewish observance in conformity with the accepted ruling of an ancient authority or authorities. Most parts of the Mishnah are made up of Halakic propositions. Maimonides in his Introduction to the Mishnah reckons that there are 23 such precepts as given to Moses on Sinai. (See Strack, *Einleitung in den Talmud*, p. 8.) Freedom of interpretation was, on the other

hand, accorded where Haggadic (or Aggadic), i.e. homiletic or non-Halakic matter was concerned. It was of some polemic value to shew that only Halakah is binding for Judaism. Nachman in his controversy with Paulus Christiani makes use of this point.

(79) *kisses.* There are many instances in the Zohar of the practice of kissing those who give a new, fitting, relevant or pleasing interpretation of scripture. E.g. Zohar I.6a: 'Rabbi Eleazar and R. Abba came up to the stranger and kissed him. They said: "With all this profound knowledge thou hast displayed, is it meet thou shouldest journey behind us? Who art thou?" '

(80) *the lips of my father of blessed memory murmur in the grave.* Cf. Jab. 97a: 'R. Jochanan said in the name of Rabbi Simeon ben Jochai: When a doctrine is given in this world in the name of a (deceased) scholar, then his lips murmur in the grave [cf. Cant. 7.10].... As the heated mass of grapes drips so soon as you apply your finger ... so do the lips of scholars murmur in the grave when their names are cited.' See Goldschmidt, *Bab. Talmud,* ad loc. and Jastrow, Talmud Dictionary, on the word דבב.

(81) *Salutation.* This refers particularly to the concluding words of the preceding letter where the Jew speaks of God's favour towards Israel and His plan for Israel and the Gentiles. Rittangel replies that this question concerning the future, God alone can answer.

(82) *The Eagle.* Cf. Hag. 13b. The *dove* however lowly is a bird at least able to communicate with the eagle, the head of the bird-kingdom. Rittangel infers that his correspondent professes to know the mind of God and to be the recipient of special revelation. *A dove covered with silver* (Ps. 68.13 (14)). Delitzsch comments on this verse: 'Israel is God's turtle-dove (Ps. 74.19) and accordingly the new prosperity is compared to the play of colour on the wings of the dove basking in the sunshine.'

(83) *I (who) am but a wisp of straw, a grain of dust.* This sentence is in Aramaic and possibly is culled from the Supplements of the Zohar. The text is corrupt. The words rendered *a wisp, a grain* are uncertain but follow so far as possible Wagenseil's translation *ego straminis festuca sum et terrae glebula* which may have been made before the corruptions in the text appeared and seems to have read מקיסמא = of a chip (or מקיסומא = of rakings) and מטחינה = of a grinding. Dr Lazarus Goldschmidt kindly suggested to me that the original text may have been: 'I am but a *spreading* (משטיחא = layer) of straw, a *vessel* (משיכלא) of dust' (i.e. as indicating the human body, an earthen vessel).

(84) *term* (lit. terms). Heb. = Qeçavoth = terms of a syllogism (see Reland, *Analecta,* p. 186): in the translation the word is regarded as referring to the logical points or parts of an argument. Rittangel

speaks of *terms and points*, the former being the single parts of a logical whole and being contrasted with the latter word denoting the vowel-points put to the Hebrew consonants.

(85) *signals*. See note 27 above.

(86) *correctly*. For 'al 'ophanav = in its (proper) way. See Jastrow ('ophan).

(87) *aṣmuth = essence, substance*. Cf. note 64 above.

(88) *conclusions* = Heb. Toledoth (lit. *births, histories*). In logical terminology (see Genebrard's Rabbinical Tables, p. 187, in Reland's *Analecta*) *Toledah = conclusio, consequentia, id quod e principio manat*.

(89) *by* scholars. late use of prep. 'al (see B.D.B. *Heb. Dict.*, p. 758, col. 1) sometimes used by writers of the silver age with the force of a dative, e.g. 'if it seems good *to you*' ('alekem) 1 Chr. 13.2.

(90) *cursive.*—Heb. metushtash (Pilpel partc. pass. of ṭush). Lit. smeared, blurred.

(91) *a successful liar*, etc. Heb. = the liar (shakran) needs to be a remembrancer (Zakran) i.e. to have a good memory.

(92) *From John to John*, etc. This is on the model of the saying about Moses Maimonides the Codifier of the Law: 'From Moses to Moses there is no one like Moses'. The words 'from John (Jochanan) to John (Jochanan)', Wagenseil regards as relating to John the Baptist, but it is hardly likely that Rittangel's Jewish friends were thinking of John the Baptist or of anything that Rittangel had in common with John the Baptist. More probable is that Rittangel's Jewish friends were thinking of Jochanan ben Zakkai the famous schoolman or teacher who during the war with Rome which culminated in the destruction of Jerusalem in A.D. 70 transferred his college to Jamnia. Many of his disciples became famous teachers. The Mishnah tractate Sota IX.15 (Danby p. 306) says that 'When Rabban Johanan ben Zakkai died the splendour of wisdom ceased.' John Rittangel as teacher in Königsberg would be proud of the testimonial to his rank as scholar and teacher. Another famous Jewish Jochanan was Jochanan Aleman who was a mystic and initiated Pico della Miran-dola (1642-1694) into the wisdom and mysteries of the Kabbalah. (Cf. Daiches, *The King James Version of the English Bible*, p. 127.) Pico was 'one of the first to interest himself in cabalistic literature' (Daiches, op. cit., p. 126).

(93) *a rigmarole of words*. Cf. note 69 above. Heb. = *toref debarim*. *Toref* = (1) that which makes a debt collectable from real estate, a mortgage, (2) the passage in a document that makes it binding. See Jastrow, Talmud Dictionary. Silbermann in his 'Menorah'—Wörter-buch gives under *Toref* the meanings (1) shame, disgrace (Scham), and (2) the relevant substance of a document (e.g. signature, sums of money involved, etc., date). Wagenseil who renders *toref* by *male-*

dicta evidently regards *toref* as = shame (of your words); cf. Jastrow under *torephah* = filth, decay, obscenity. Jac. Klatzkin in his *Thesaurus Philosophicus linguae Hebraicae*, Berlin, 1935, gives the following significances of *toref*: (1) Text or content e.g. this is the toref (text, or content) of his words. *Toref* = 'ikaro shel dabar i.e. *toref* = the root of a matter (or substance as opposed to form merely). (2) Form or impression. (3) Formulary, i.e. prescribed form. It seems clear that the Jew (on p. 127 above) uses *toref* in the sense of *relevant substance* or *content* (of your words). But Rittangel evidently misunderstands the words *toref debareka* as used by the Jew and in replying to the Jew speaks of 'statements which you term a *toref* of words'. What Rittangel says in his letter after this shews that he understands by *toref* something that implies reiteration and repetition. Thus he takes *toref* in the sense of *formulary*, that is a mere *rigmarole* or prescribed form.

(94) The citation is in Dutch, from the letter which the Jew had written previous to the Hebrew correspondence here collected.

NOTES ON THE TEXT OF THE DISPUTATION OF NACHMAN

(1) Naqi is here taken as the subject of the verb *murder*, i.e. he is a murderer and must be put to death.

(2) This passage from Talmud Sanhedrin 43a is an example of Midrashic exegesis. Lazarus Goldschmidt (Talmud, ad loc., in a note) mentions that as the information of Sanh. 43a on Jesus and his disciples does not appear to apply to the founder of Christianity, some Jewish and Christian apologists have supposed that the Talmud had some other person called Jesus in view. Since in Sotah 47a Jesus is represented as having been a pupil of R. Joshua ben Perachja (*c.* 100 B.C.) this supposition finds support. But Goldschmidt rightly says that the probable explanation of those Talmudic data is not that there was another Jesus than that of the Christian Confession but that legends were current about the latter which had no historical value. But that which is of much interest is that in his disputation in Barcelona Nachman, the Talmud scholar, holds to the Talmud chronology and regards the Christian calculations about the time when Jesus lived as being entirely wrong. According to Nachman Jesus lived about two centuries before the destruction of the Temple which took place in the year 70 of our era. Another Jewish scholar Solomon Zewi of Offenhausen (1615) came in his book *Jüdische Theriac* to other conclusions. Zewi, who went very thoroughly over the Talmud references to Jesus, brings 'ten faithful witnesses' or proofs to shew that the Jesus of the Talmud is not the Jesus of the Gospels. One of these witnesses is the passage Sotah 47a with its reference to Perachja. The latter is placed by Zewi in the fourth generation of teachers mentioned in the first chapter of the 'Sayings of the Fathers' and his date is given as 207 years before the destruction of the second temple. The Jesus who was Perachja's pupil would therefore have been at least 130 years old when Pilate condemned the Jesus of the Christians. For Zewi's conclusions, which al;o, apart from this question, are of considerable interest, see Wagenseil, *Sota. Hoc est Liber Mischnicus de uxore adulterii suspecta*, Altdorf, 1674, p. 1054.

(3) In Sanh. 43a it is R. Ula who says that Jesus had close rela-

tions with the government and therefore had to have a trial in which his defences had to receive a hearing.

(4) *Fra Paulo*—Friar (Latin *frater* through the French *frère*: Italian *frate* or *fra*: Spanish is *frayle* or *fray* as in our Heb. text) is a name given to any member of a mendicant order in the Church of Rome. The Dominican or Black Friars were sometimes called Preaching Friars. The Franciscans were called Minors or Grey Friars. Fra Paulo was a Dominican. In the edict of King Jayme of Aragon giving Fra Paulo permission to visit the Jewish synagogues and houses for the purpose of the conversion of the Jews—29th August 1263—Fra Paulo is styled *dilectus filius noster Fr. Paulus Christiani de Ordine Fratrum Praedicatorum*, i.e. of the Order of the Preaching Friars. See Wagenseil's Introductory notes on Ramban's disputation.

(5) *disgraced his education* (or up-bringing). The verb here used is in the Hiphil = cause burning, spoil a dish and, in a transferred sense, to misapply learning, disgrace one's education. Cf. Ber. 17b, Sanh. 103a.

(6) Jayme I (1213-1276) of Aragon, called 'the Conqueror'.

(7) Fra Raymond of Pennaforte—Pope Gregory IX had commissioned this Raymond, his chaplain and formerly a professor of Canon Law in Bologna University (and since canonised), to digest into a code the decretals passed since the time of Gratian. The work was completed in four years and promulgated in 1234. In Wagenseil's introduction (op. cit.) Bishop Bosquet is cited as saying of Raymond that he was a man of wonderful sanctity, skilled in divine matters and in Ecclesiastical law. He is there referred to as 'Ex-magister Generalis Ordinis Praedicatorum'. He founded an institute of biblical studies where were taught Arabic, Hebrew and Aramaic. Pennaforte is near Barcelona.

(7a) Steinschneider's text here is: כי מאד שהמלך בפרבינצה =
For since (the time that) the king had been in the province. The meaning of the last word would appear to be the *province of Aragon.* Cf. Bosquet's letter to Joseph de Voison (*Tela*, p. 2 of Introduction to the Disputation of Nachman) where Jayme I is styled king of the Province of Aragon—*Jacobo Tarraconensis Provinciae Regi.* Graetz, cf. note on p. 131 Vol. VII, reads acc. to the Constantinople (1710) edition of the text: ומקומות רבים כי מאד שהמלך בפרובינסה and understands this to mean that Paulo had made a missionary tour in *Provence* and elsewhere (dass Pablo vor der Disputation Bekehrungsreisen in der Provence und anderswo gemacht). J.E. which in its article on Nachman is largely dependent on Graetz follows him and the Constantinople edit. here in respect of Provence.

(8) Rabbi Aqiba died A.D. 135. Rabbi Jehuda *ha-Nasi* (i.e. *the prince* or president or patriarch of the Council or Sanhedrin which

administered and interpreted the religious law) called simply 'Rabbi' in the Mishnah was the editor of the Mishnah *c.* A.D. 200. Nathan the Babylonian was a teacher of Rabbi Jehuda. The Mishnah (derived from a word meaning *to repeat* or to learn) is the content of the traditional law as developed up to near the end of the second century, that is, it is the substance of the Oral Law. It is divided into six main sections. See Strack's *Einleitung in den Talmud*, p. 2 f, and *The Mishnah* (Danby, p. xx f). The Talmud consists of the Mishnah and the Gemara, the latter being the collection of discussions upon the Mishnah. R. Ashi, the president of the Academy of Sura (fifth century) is generally accepted as the redactor of the Gemara.

(9) Ruler's staff = Heb. mehoqeq—so Gressmann (S.A.T.) Moffatt, R.V., Oesterley, etc.: A.V. and others translate *Lawgiver*.

(10) *Maccabaeus* was the name given to the priest Judas who became the military leader of Judaism against Antiochus Epiphanes and his successors (167 B.C.). This period of history thus begun with Judas' revolt is generally called Maccabean. In Palestine the family to which Judas belonged and which gradually gained in power was called *Hasmonean* from an ancestor Hasmonai. The Hasmonean Aristobulus I who was high priest also adopted the title of king in the year 105. His brother Alexander Jannaeus was priest-king from 104-78. The son of the Idumean Antipater, namely Herod (the Great), succeeded to the Hasmonean dynasty in 37 B.C. Antipater had assisted Jannaeus' son Hyrkanus against the latter's brother.

(11) Cf. Sanh. 13b. R. Aha the son of Raha asked R. Ashi: 'Is the Ordination bestowed through the actual [laying on] of hands?' The latter answered: 'Authorization is given through the title. The person ordained is called Rabbi.' Cf. 14a: R. Joshua ben Levi said: 'Outside the land [i.e. of Palestine] there is no ordination.' See Schürer, *Geschichte d. jüd. Volkes*, Vol. II, p. 251, where it is said: 'The rite [of laying on of hands in ordination] is thus comparatively ancient. According to Deut. 34.9 the laying on of hands conveys the holy Spirit from one person to other persons, while in Num. 27.18 f it is clearly the bestowal of dignity of office. This was certainly the ruling notion in the Rabbinic practice of the rite. In the Talmudic period the rite of laying on of hands at ordination was no longer practised. Possibly the reason for this rite being given up was that meanwhile it had been adopted by the Christian Church.' The Synagogue appears to have used this rite of Ordination since the time of Hillel. Fra Paulo's point is that it cannot be contended that power or rule has never ceased from Judah, that this has resided in the teachers or authorized Rabbis since the time of Hillel, for the Ordination of scholars no longer exists and the Rabbinic succession

has been broken. Ramban himself has no right, Fra Paulo contends, to be called Rabbi Moses or *magister* (maestro). Further, see Strack and Billerbeck, Vol. II, p. 648 f, on Ordination.

(12) See article on Rab, Rabbi, etc., in *Ency. Brit.*, 9th ed., by Schiller-Szinessy. 'Rabbi = "my teacher" is a title of a teacher fully ordained in Palestine.' 'Rab = "lord", "master" or "teacher" is the title prefixed to the name of such a Babylonian teacher of the Law or expounder of the Mishnah as, though authorized to "judge" and to decide other religious questions, has not been ordained or fully ordained in Palestine.' The title Rab when not affixed to a name signifies Abba Arekha, the most eminent of the teachers of Law and Mishnah in Babylonia. *Jewish Ency.* on Jerome says that Jerome (comm. on Isa. 22.15) speaks of traditions originating with the *magistri* (i.e. the Rabbis).

(13) *Halakah* is 'an accepted decision in Rabbinic law, usually, but not necessarily, derivable from scripture' (Danby, *Mishnah*, p. 794). The term signifies also the parts of the Talmud concerned with legal questions.

Haggadah. Lit. 'narration' has to do with the interpretation of Scripture and aims at edification. (Op. cit., p. 793.)

(14) 'Sayings of the Fathers', IV.8: 'Do not hold court as a single judge.'

(15) The Hasmonean dynasty springing from Mattathias the father of Judas Maccabaeus was of priestly, that is of Levitic, origin.

(16) *Midrash.* (Cf. Danby, op. cit., p. 795.) Lit. 'exposition', is originally the deducing of an idea or rule from Scripture in the manner either of Haggadah (see above) or Halakah. Midrash comes to mean the verse by verse commentary on Scripture.

(17) *The fellow.* Lit. 'that man'. This phrase occurs several times as applied to Fra Paulo and has been rendered by the expression 'my opponent' in the other passages where it appears, as being on the whole more adequate. In the Talmud, more often than by his own name, Jesus is referred to as 'that man', a term which was devised to evade the attention of mediaeval censorship.

(18) *Two hundred years.* See note 2 above on chronology.

(19) *Master Gilles*—The name is either *Gillaume* or *Gilles*. See Steinschneider's note on the Heb. text. The king's justiciary, the *justiciar*, was, next to the king, the most important office-holder in Aragon. See Swift, op. cit., p. 171 (cf. pp. 155-158). He presided over the *Cortes* to whom alone he was responsible. By the fourteenth century he had become almost the supreme arbiter in constitutional questions and his office was a safeguard against despotism. The political constitution of Aragon previous to the reign of Ferdinand and Isabella is said to have been, thanks to the office of the *justiciar*,

the most liberal in Europe. See *Ency. Brit.*, 9th ed., Vol. XXII (art. *Spain*) and Vol. II (*Aragon*).

(20) *my opponent.* Cf. note 17.

(21) On the interpretation of Isa. 53 in the older Jewish literature see Strack and Billerbeck's *Kommentar zum neuen Testament aus Talmud und Midrasch*, Vol. I, p. 481, where the history of the exposition of Isa. 53 is described thus: The Messianic interpretation first appears in the parables [105-64 B.C. according to Charles' Apoc.] of the Book of Enoch (cf. 38.2, 47.1, 4 with Isa. 53.11, 46.4, 62.5 f with 52.13 f). 'In the Rabbinic literature that has been preserved, the interpretation of Isa. 53 as concerning the Messiah appears first in the third century A.D. and this is represented particularly in the Targum to the prophets. Side by side with the Messianic exegesis is that which interprets the passage as referring to righteous persons.—Comparatively late a third point of view arises, namely that which understands "the servant of Jahve" to mean the people of Israel. This interpretation now dominant in Judaism had indeed, in the time of Origen, its adherents (cf. Contra Celsum I.55) but so far as the sources are concerned only appears since the time of Rashi (1105). In the Midrashic literature it occurs in the Midrash Rabba on Numbers which is hardly older than the twelfth century.' Ramban's exposition on Isa. 53 was published by Steinschneider (Berlin, 1860).

(22) *was not buried.* This may be an allusion to the Christian doctrine of the resurrection of Jesus, which Christians claimed was alluded to in Ps. 16; or Nachman may here be basing on Jewish tradition (cf. 'The Letter of Amulo': L. Williams, *Adv. Judaeos*, p. 362) 'that Jesus was taken down quickly from the tree, and thrown into a tomb in a certain garden full of vegetables, for fear lest their land should be polluted.'

(23) *Midrash.* See note 16 above.

(24) *Haggadah.* See note 13 above.

(25) *Hekaloth Rabbathi* (the great Halls) is a theosophic Midrash. Cf. Karpeles, *Gesch. d. jüd. Lit.*, Vol. I, p. 285. A *Perutah* is a small amount ($\frac{1}{8}$ of an *as*). The Messiah will not come 'until the money is gone out from the bag'. (Sanh. 97a.)

(26) *Gehenna.* See Charles' *Apocrypha and Pseudepigrapha*, Vol. II, p. 593. According to the school of Shammai the truly pious passed at once after death to bliss. The very wicked went at once to Gehenna, while the intermediate class (the majority) were only assigned to Gehenna for a time and were released later, ultimately to inherit eternal life.

(27) This accords also with what Edersheim (*Life and Times of Jesus the Messiah*, 1894, I.52) has to say on 'the doctrine of hereditary

guilt and sin through the fall of Adam' being 'unknown to Rabbinical Judaism'.

(28) The square brackets enclose words which Steinschneider regards as glosses.

(29) Sanh. 93b. 'Bar Kochba, who ruled for two and a half years, said to the wise (i.e. the scholars) that he was the Messiah. They said to him: Of the Messiah it is written (Isa. 11.3): "He will scent out" [A.V. and shall make him of quick understanding]. . . . When they saw that he could not scent out and judge, they killed him.'

(30) Lit. *the asker*. The debate owed its origin to the request of Fra Paulo to King James to order Moses ben Nachman to take part in a public disputation. See J.E. on Moses ben Nachman Gerondi. Fra Paulo appears to have had the part of questioner and Nachman the part of answerer.

(31) Sanh. 93a. 'R. Johanan said: The righteous are more eminent than the ministering angels for it is said in Dan. 3.25: " . . . Lo, I see four men loose, walking in the midst of the fire and they have no hurt; and the aspect of the fourth is like a son of the gods." '

(31a) Already in IV Ezra (c. A.D. 120) the destruction of the power of Rome appears as one of the principal tasks of the Messiah. Cf. Chs. XI-XII (the Eagle vision and its interpretation).

(32) The application of the Psalm would appear to be either (a) that Z. though a prince of Persia was honoured by his own people and so in reality was an Israelite prince, or (b) that when the peoples of the world in the future become the people of the God of Abraham (the father of a multitude of nations, Gen. 17.4) Z. the Israelite man but Persian prince will appear as a prince of Israel.

(33) Gen. 24.55. A.V. = a few days or at least ten: A.V.m = a full year or ten months: R.V. = a few days, at the least ten.

(34) Segura—south of Huesca in Aragon may be the place intended. Another Segura is near the Sierra de Segura in Murcia. Graetz (*Gesch. d. Juden*, VII, p. 136) gives the name of the town as Sigarra (Arnoldus de Sigarra) i.e. acc. to the Constantinople 1710 text, cf. p. 131 op. cit.

(35) See Jerome—In *Danielis Prophetae Caput*, XII: Hos. 1290 dies, Porphyrius in tempore Antiochi, et in desolatione Templi dicit completos, quam et Josephus et Machabaeorum (ut diximus) liber tribus tantum annis fuisse commemorant.

(36) IV Ezra VI.26 mentions as partaking in the felicity of the Messianic age 'the men who have been taken up, who have not tasted death from their birth.' To this group belong Enoch and Elijah. The role of the latter is to anoint the Messiah. To the immortal companions of the Messiah in the Garden of Eden belong Ezra, Baruch and Jeremiah. See Charles' *Pseudep.*, Vol. II, on

IV Ezra VI.26; VII.28; 2 Bar. 76.2; 2. Macc. 2.1 f, 15.13 f. Serach (cf. Sotah 13a) was a legendary prophetess who survived all the Israelite immigrants to Egypt, living to the period of the Exodus. Bithiah, the daughter of Pharaoh, was Moses' foster-mother (1 Chron. 4.18).

(37) Joh. Drusius (in Reland's *Analecta*): 'Moses Cordubensis qui vulgo Aegyptius.' Albertus Magnus, who *c.* 1250 wrote his philosophical works, knows of Maimonides' 'Guide of the Perplexed' under the title of 'Dux Neutrorum of Rabbi Moyses Aegyptus'. (Cf. note 2 Graetz, *Gesch. d. Juden*, Vol. VII, p. 59.)

(38) It was commonly believed that the Messianic Days would be limited in number: 40 years (R. Eliezer); 400 years (R. Dosa; cf. also IV Ezra 7.26-30); 365 years (Rabbi); 7000 years (Abimi), etc. Cf. Sanh. 99a.

(39) So Targum Ps.-Jonathan on Gen. 49.10. Cf. Deut. 28.57. See Spurrell *Notes on the Text of Genesis*, 2nd ed., p. 380, and notes to Zikron, Stanza VIII, p. 65.

(40) The Midrash *Tanchuma* on the Pentateuch (called after a Rabbi Tanchuma *c.* A.D. 350) appears later in a fragmentary form called *Jelamedenu* (= he will teach us) a word which introduces certain of its chapters. See Karpeles, Vol. I, p. 264.

(41) *allusions.* Heb. *remizoth.* See p. 225 of Bischoff's *Elemente der Kabbalah.* The fourfold method of exegesis was designated as PaRDeS. (P = Peshat, i.e. literal; R = Remez or Remizah = allegoric; D = Derush = moral; S = Sod = mystical.)

(42) Gen. 28.10 f. (And Jacob went out.) The kind of allusion which this scripture-portion undergoes is mentioned in Ber. 26b e.g. Abraham ordained the morning prayer for it is said (Gen. 19.27) 'And A. rose early in the morning, etc.'; Isaac ordained the Vesper-prayer, for (Gen. 24.63) 'Isaac went towards evening to the field in order to reflect.' While Jacob ordained the Evening-prayer for it is said (Gen. 28.11) 'he lighted upon a certain place and tarried there all night.' Cf. Midrash Bereschith R. on this section.

(42a) Steinschneider's text is: עמדתי לפני אדובנו המלך ואמר
ישאר הויכוח· כי לא ראיתי אדם שאין הדין עמו שטען אותו
יפה כאשר עשיתי·

The variations in translation and in understanding of the text to be noticed. Graetz, VII, p. 134, says: 'Der König bemerkte . . .: Er habe noch nie eine so ungerechte Sache so geistvoll verteidigen gehört.' Loeb, *R.E.J.*, XV, 1887, p. 12: 'Le roi lui dit: Je n'ai jamais vu si bien défendre une plus mauvaise cause.' L. Williams, *Adversus Judaeos*, p. 247: 'The king said that he had never seen anyone who was in the wrong argue so well as he had.' The Hebrew text says: 'argue so well as *I had* (*or have*) *done.*' The rendering given in the translation emends and reads 'as you have', and retains the Hebrew (cf. above) '*I have never seen.*'

(43) Words in brackets Steinschneider thinks to be a gloss.

(44) Heb. *hargashah* = lit. feeling, emotion.

Heb. *Miqreh* = happening, chance. In a philosophic sense = *accident* i.e. unessential quality or property.

(45) *They who err*—a common expression in Talmud referring to the Minim (heretics). Cf. Jer. Ber. 55b, 56a.

(46) *dinars.* J. E. says that these were 300 *maravedis.*

INDEX

(1) AUTHORITIES, NAMES AND SUBJECTS

R

(2) SCRIPTURE REFERENCES

(3) JEWISH AUTHORITIES

(a) MIDRASHIM

(b) MISHNA

OTHER WORDS